Banana Republic

The failure of the Irish state and how to fix it

Banana Republic
The failure of the Irish state and how to fix it

338. 9417

Anthony Sweeney

Gill & Macmillan

Gill & Macmillan Ltd
Hume Avenue, Park West, Dublin 12
with associated companies throughout the world
www.gillmacmillan.ie

© Anthony Sweeney 2009
978 07171 4612 3

Type design by Make Communication
Print origination by Carrigboy Typesetting Services
Printed by ColourBooks Ltd, Dublin

This book is typeset in Linotype Minion and Neue Helvetica.

The paper used in this book comes from the wood pulp of
managed forests. For every tree felled, at least one tree is
planted, thereby renewing natural resources.

A CIP catalogue record for this book is available from the
British Library.

5 4 3 2 1

Contents

Introduction

In 2009 the Economic and Social Research Institute (ESRI) began its first quarterly report by stating that the contraction forecast for the Irish economy in 2009 was expected to be 'the biggest contraction in an industrialised country since the Great Depression'. Unemployment was estimated to rise to 17 per cent, while it was predicted that emigration figures would surge once again. The Celtic Tiger had come to a shuddering halt as banks failed, government and personal finances spiralled out of control and the populace's newfound confidence evaporated in a tide of recriminations and bitter regrets. Where, people wanted to know, had it all gone wrong?

The premise informing this book is simple: as a state, the Irish Republic has failed. It has failed in the sense that since its inception in 1922, successive generations of politicians have failed to provide the services a government should provide for its citizens. And why have they failed to do this? An analysis of the political life of the country over the last eight decades suggests the answer is often a photo-finish between incompetence and corruption. Ireland has staggered from economic famine to economic feast and back again, without ever laying down the basic foundations for *sustainable* economic growth. There is little doubt that what you read in this book will be considered controversial, but I would like to make it clear from the outset that I do not question the abilities or the dedication of the Irish people. What I want to question very closely, however, is the political class that has dominated Irish society since Independence.

The Republic of Ireland is less than a century old. Like every country, it has a foundation myth and an enabling myth and these are related to each other. The popular image of the country's past entails a heroic struggle, over centuries, against a powerful empire before final glorious liberation, sparked by the 1916 Rising. One

could argue that from 1922 to 1992 Ireland would have been richer
and enjoyed better infrastructure, better educational and transport
systems and better welfare provisions had it remained in the United
Kingdom. This is an untenable argument, however, because it is
historical supposition and because the UK had lost all political
legitimacy in nationalist Ireland by 1922. After 1916 there was a
strong desire for self-government, even though there had been little
real demand for a full constitutional break with the UK up to and
including the period following the 1916 Rising. In fact, a full
constitutional break with the UK may not have occurred unless
driven forward by Éamon de Valera, who was the overarching figure
in Irish politics until 1959. His total focus on a complete break with
the UK—in constitutional theory, if not in economic practice—
arguably contributed to a Civil War (1922–3) that proved even more
divisive than the War of Independence (1919–21).

Nevertheless, self-government was ultimately secured, but it came
at a very expensive price: bad government. The population of the
Republic declined from the 1920s until it was briefly interrupted in
the 1960s by an upswing, only to return to the doldrums again for a
generation in the 1980s. Throughout this time politicians continually stressed aspirational national and cultural issues, but proved
to be utterly inept at the important business of forming social and
economic policies. Instead of bread today, we had partition and the
Irish language advanced as the supreme ambitions of Irish public
life—two of life's great lost causes, about which the general
populace could hardly care less. Irish politicians were doing what
politicians do the world over: pandering to the national myth in
order to deflect attention from their daily shortcomings. De Valera's
cultural crowing in the 1950s—still dreaming of a Jeffersonian world
of devout, chaste, Irish-speaking subsistence farmers—was the low-
water mark of this philosophy. It distracted him from the economy
and led him to make three key mistakes that have been having an
impact on Ireland ever since.

First, de Valera pursued a broadly autarkist economic policy,
which attempted to achieve a form of national self-sufficiency
by coercing people, through tariffs and levies, to buy Irish products
rather than imports. The lure of such policies for newly independent countries is strong, but inevitably this approach fails

because of a simple economic theory that was proved almost 200 years ago by an economist called David Ricardo. His trade theory demonstrated that countries should focus on exporting the maximum amount of products in which they enjoy a competitive advantage. If Ireland had adopted this approach, as it did in more recent years, it could have added value to specific, exportable products and thereby enhanced its economic base.

The second mistake de Valera made was to pick economic/political fights he had little chance of winning. A classic example of this was his withholding of monies owed to Britain, which the Free State had agreed to pay under the 1921 Anglo-Irish Treaty. The UK government retaliated, quite predictably, by placing a tariff on Irish exports, sparking the so-called Economic War. This presented an acute difficulty for the Irish economy as 90 per cent of total exports went to the UK. The Irish government responded in kind and placed tariffs on incoming British goods, but considering the relative size of the two economies and the diversity of the UK economy, it was painfully obvious who was going to emerge with a bloody nose. The Irish economy was severely impacted until a 'truce' was reached.

The final, and most serious, mistake de Valera made was his failure to realise that his economic policies were failing. Mistakes can be forgiven, but not vanity, and to persist with policies that are patently unhelpful is a very damaging kind of vanity. By the 1950s Ireland was an economic and social backwater; in that decade alone 13 per cent of the population emigrated. This drain on human resources stunted, and in some cases killed, economic growth across the country, yet de Valera seemed not to recognise this blatant fact. Instead, he appeared to resent those who emigrated, as if aspirations for a better life were a distasteful trait that Irish people should not display.

After de Valera's long reign came to an end in 1959,[1] Seán Lemass succeeded him. Lemass is arguably the finest Taoiseach the country has ever seen, largely because he recognised de Valera's mistakes, learned from them and attempted to steer Ireland on a new course, both economically and socially. It was very unfortunate for the country that he lasted only seven years at the helm of Irish politics.

---

1   The year in which he left the office of Taoiseach.

Nonetheless, he made huge strides in the little time he had. Lemass was followed by a collection of the mediocre, the incompetent and the corrupt, leaders who deprived Ireland of a chance for slow and consistent growth. There was much to be done to bring the nation into the modern age, but there seemed little appetite to make the hard decisions and engage in a 'big picture' analysis. A number of factors contributed to this political and intellectual malaise, one of the most important being the nature of Irish democracy, which merits a slight digression for closer examination.

The territory that is now the Republic of Ireland withdrew from the United Kingdom because its overwhelmingly Catholic population could not find a comfortable home in the pan-Protestant UK. It is no accident that the part of the island with a local Protestant majority chose to remain within the larger state. Moreover, Ireland had a long history of cultural and linguistic distinctiveness, which complemented and was eventually subsumed by nationalism. That nationalism assumed a form unknown in the rest of the nineteenth-century world.

Daniel O'Connell's mass mobilisation of Irish Catholics was the first organised and disciplined populist movement in modern European history. It established a tradition of representative politics in which mass as well as elite interests were catered for, a process that accelerated with the progressive widening of the franchise throughout the nineteenth and twentieth century. Charles Stuart Parnell took matters a step further by imposing hitherto unknown levels of iron discipline on his parliamentary representatives, while ensuring strong community support through a *de facto* alliance with the all-powerful Catholic Church and influential community figures, such as local newspaper publishers and editors. The democratisation of Irish local government in 1898 established the present system of county councils and local district councils.

All this brought representation very close to the people. For a country with a small population, there were an awful lot of public representatives who were eager to please. The adoption of proportional representation (PR) compounded this effect by making competition within constituencies even more intense and putting a premium on populism and localism generally. The effect was the creation of a 'clientelist' political culture, fixated on local grievance and the brokering of influence within the state apparatus instead of being concerned with high parliamentary politics and policy. Just about every book ever written on Irish politics makes this observation sooner or later—usually sooner.

We therefore have a fatal conjunction: a populist political tradition, allied to a PR system of voting, produces messenger boys instead of bona fide public representatives. It makes governments—even the single-party governments that were the norm until 1989—reluctant to take hard decisions that might alienate powerful interest groups or the population at large. It places long-term strategic thinking at a discount. For this reason, T.K. Whitaker's famous Programme for Economic Expansion (1958) shines like a beacon through the dark abyss of Irish politics in the twentieth century. It is the one moment in the history of the Irish state when a lucid, tough-minded analysis was applied to society and politics and then acted upon, thanks to the fortuitous accession of Seán Lemass.

In the course of the last twenty years Ireland's standard of living has risen to levels similar to that of the Western world generally. To be fair, the political system helped this process by overcoming its own inertia and taking the crucial decisions required to pull the country out of the economic quagmire that was the miserable 1980s. It helped that the opposition stood aside (the famous Tallaght Strategy) and gave free reign. Thereafter, however, governments operated on cruise control, believing that all economic growth was good economic growth. This error of judgment meant that instead of controlling the unprecedented growth that was the 'Celtic Tiger', the government invested in and supported excessive economic growth on the basis that it was better than what we had before. Thus the country went from economic starvation to economic obesity, never realising that there was an enduring, healthy and long-lasting happy medium.

A cursory overview must therefore conclude that Ireland raced from one unsatisfactory economic situation to another, albeit in a very different guise, and in doing so failed to establish sustainable growth or to provide adequate public services. The never-ending chaos in the public health system, the lack of an integrated, fully modernised transport infrastructure, funding crises throughout the educational system, especially in the pure and applied sciences— these should not be the fruits of the biggest boom in Irish history. Yet, this is what we are now left with and these problems are the product of a system whose default position is to funk hard decisions in the hope that something will turn up to save the day. What's more, because that has been the default position for so long, the populace became accustomed to it and now regard it as perfectly normal; the levels of public denial and hysteria in the responses to the many budgetary retrenchments bear this out. For all their political ineptitude, the fiscal changes to date do represent an attempt to address some profoundly serious issues. The reckless insouciance of the public reaction to the recent budgetary moves, and the thinking that informed it, was born of a comfort culture in which hard decisions are habitually avoided. As a result of this national myopia, the country is facing a period of economic turmoil that will affect every person on this island, yet we are the victims of our own wrong-thinking. Now that the curse has fallen upon us, we are unprepared for the price that will be exacted from us in the wake of the 'boom' years.

The first section of this book demonstrates the latest episode of economic mismanagement by the Irish government, in the 1990s–2000s, and how it dovetails with the broader economic history of Ireland. It goes on to explain briefly some of the relevant economic principles that should inform and enlighten any discussion on the future of the economy. In the second section the key problems impacting on Irish society and the economy are identified, along with a discussion of how these can be solved. This is not, nor is it intended to be, an exercise in blame and criticism. While we must examine the problems and the causes of those problems in order to arrive at the best solutions, the point is that there are solutions. Ireland can develop into a world-class economy: we can have an excellent health service, we can have crime-free streets, low unemployment and affordable housing and a political class that serves us rather than rules us. There are no limits to what we can achieve. If we are managed and led with the same levels of competence we show as a workforce, then Ireland can become one of the most prosperous countries in the world, but this time, we could do it the right way.

Part One

Chapter 1

The History of the Boom

The de Valera ideal, which defined Irish politics for four decades, envisioned a self-sufficient Ireland with 'cosy homesteads'[1] peopled by Irish men and women who were amply 'satisfied with frugal comforts'. The net result of this blatantly unrealistic approach was the stunting of the country's economic growth in its formative years and mass emigration. Between 1921 and 1959[2] more than one million people left Ireland, 400,000 of those leaving in the 1950s alone. This exodus saw the population shrink to 2.8 million by 1961,[3] thus depriving the economy of its greatest resource: people. The irony is that those who might have ousted the dominant political party, Fianna Fáil, for this gross ineptitude were unable to do so because they had been forced to emigrate, in other words the government's incompetence was what kept it in power. Most of those who left during this period went to the UK and there contributed to the growth of that burgeoning economy. The level of their impact there is evident when one considers that in 2001 six million Britons could claim at

1 From a speech given by de Valera on 17 March 1943 in which he outlined his hopes for Ireland's future.
2 The date when de Valera left the office of Taoiseach for the last time; he subsequently served as President, but that office's influence on government policy is extremely limited.
3 Irish Central Statistics Office.

least one Irish grandparent.[4] Or, to put it in a more critical frame, there are more Irish, in the broad sense of the word, in the UK than in Ireland.

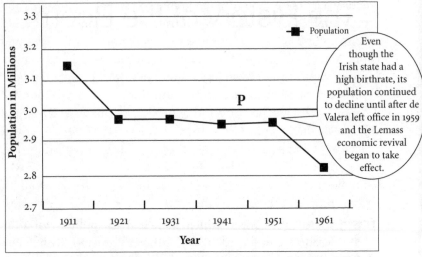

Fig. 1: Irish population figures, 1911–61. (Data source: Irish Central Statistics Office)

When de Valera's tenure finally came to an end in 1959, Ireland gained a capable and forward-thinking Taoiseach in Seán Lemass and the country boomed in the 1960s. The economy began to demonstrate just what it was capable of when in competent hands. Lemass' Cabinet, enlightened by the standards of the time, began the process of drawing back the social and economic shroud that had been wrapped tightly around Irish society by de Valera and the Catholic Church in the form of Archbishop of Dublin John Charles McQuaid.

It was not all good news, however. The Lemass era also created a small cabal of men, such as Charles Haughey, who became intoxicated by power. Without the requisite legal controls in place to police them, once these men obtained positions of power they tarnished the achievements of other politicians, often ignored the letter of the law, demeaned our democracy and brought the country to its knees financially. These men were guided mostly by opportunism, which meant that for two long decades much of the

4 *Manchester Guardian*, 13 September 2008.

country's infrastructure was shaped by greed, not civic-mindedness. Irish citizens are still affected by those decisions to this day: we have shopping centres where there should be social facilities, congested roads where there should be integrated transportation systems and cronyism in high places instead of rigorous efficiency. As a result, the 1970s and 1980s are a time most people prefer to forget, and hope never to see again. When that era came to an end, the country eagerly leapt forward to embrace a very new world.

Once released from incessant corruption in the early 1990s, the economy was launched on another productive phase, which would in time be dubbed 'the Celtic Tiger'. However, the Celtic Tiger was never what it appeared to be. Yes, there was an enormous improvement in the mid- to late 1990s and the economy was finally allowed to move towards reaching its potential, but our politicians cannot claim full credit for this, as they like to do. While they did most certainly contribute to bringing about this new state of affairs, to a large extent it was simply a case of them being less incompetent and less corrupt. It is like saying that politicians were responsible for improving the flow of traffic on the M50 by removing the toll barriers, without noting that it was they who erected the barriers in the first place. Where the government got it right was in attracting foreign business to the country with favourable tax incentives and by providing and promoting a highly skilled and flexible workforce. This influx of corporate funding reduced unemployment dramatically, resulting in a reversal of the flow of people as emigrants returned to good jobs at home. The economic success of the Irish workforce created a growing budgetary surplus for the government, which was used to initiate much-needed improvements in the national infrastructure. This was all to the good.

Where the government let the country down was in managing this growth incompetently, specifically the process of accession to the EMU. Consequently, it lost control of the economy and sparked an asset (and commensurate debt) bubble that was allowed to grow and that ultimately mesmerised the entire country in a breathtaking example of 'Emperor's New Clothes' syndrome. This fundamental error was compounded by disbursing generous tax-breaks that pushed demand still higher for properties that had no real market. As a result, productive growth ceased around 2001/2 and was

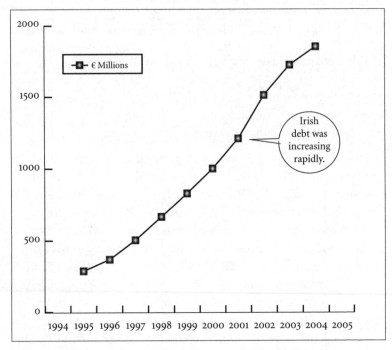

Fig. 2: Credit card debt levels, 1995–2004. (Data source: Irish Central Bank)

replaced by debt-fuelled pseudo-growth.[5] Whatever figures you look at from this period onwards, it is clear that this is when things began to go seriously wrong as a property-based asset bubble displaced real growth and the government squandered the money it was raising in taxes from activities related to this bubble. But whilst the debts were growing to startling levels, the Irish Financial Services Regulatory Authority assured the populace that the national debt levels were not out of line with the norm.[6] A debt-counselling service summed up the situation rather differently, however: 'consumer demand has been fuelled by an explosive growth in lending and the extension of credit.'[7] Furthermore, by 2005 the Central Bank was

5   There is little doubt that if the economy had been firmly controlled, then we could have engineered real change in the country, i.e. a reform of the public service, or at least not pursued the benevolent benchmarking process, and focused on developing the country's infrastructure, etc. with the surpluses the economy was generating.

6   See *Sunday Business Post*, 28 December 2003, 'European Average Irish Debt Not Above'.

7   Myvesta Ireland.

already issuing warnings due to the rapidly rising debt levels: 'This rapid accumulation of debt has increased the vulnerability of Irish households to fluctuations in income.' The long-term consequences of this debt mountain are being realised only now. To give just one example: in 2007 the price of a hectare of farm land in Ireland was the highest in the EU, at nearly €60,000.[8] This was twice the level of the runner-up: Luxembourg. This would have encouraged speculative sales and diverted resources away from farming.

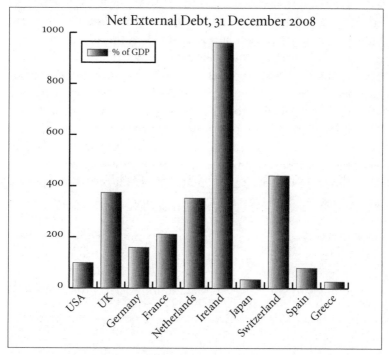

Fig. 3: Net external debt as a percentage of GDP. (Data source: www.cia.gov)

Whatever figures are examined, be it household debt, net external debt,[9] average mortgages or credit cards, they were all growing at an alarming rate (see Fig. 2 and Fig. 3). For example, outstanding

8   Savills Estate Agents, UK.
9   Controversy has emerged recently relating to this figure and its use—see *Sunday Tribune*, 3 May 2009—because it shows Ireland with the highest per capita debt in

mortgage debt went from €33 billion in 2000 to €100 billion in 2005.[10] The warning signs were clear, yet these tell-tale figures were continually explained away by financial commentators, who used the media to address the population and continually soothe any worries that what was occurring was abnormal. A sample of these comments reveals the extent of the misunderstanding. In 2004 NCB stockbrokers issued a report on the growth in credit called *Credit Growth In Ireland Sustainable 20% Pace: Underpinned by Demographics.* It acknowledged that: 'There have been concerns about the rapid growth of credit in Ireland for a number of years', but then proceeded to explain away much of this growth as being due to the housing boom, the number of credit cards issued, expected population growth, etc. Individually, the arguments often had merit, although the publication concluded by saying: 'Thus, the prospects for credit growth of 20%–25% per annum in the next four years appear good.' The report not only appeared to assuage any worries about a credit growth rate that was abnormal but in fact welcomed future growth that would double debt within four years!

In 2005 a newspaper commentator glibly suggested that people should just 'load up with debt' to buy houses, which were close to their peak prices, and not worry about it too much as house prices would keep rising.[11] Even as the economy imploded in 2008 there was still the view that credit growth was good and commentators were suggesting that ECB rate reductions 'should be positive for lending growth'.[12] Never was the long-term impact of such

the world as a percentage of GDP. The argument is that the figure includes debts held by institutions in the IFSC. Whilst true, this figure is a standard international comparator of the debt position of the country and the CSO calculates it regularly. It also displays the distorted nature of the banking in the IFSC compared to the rest of the economy. If the financial regulator could not regulate the indigenous banks, then it is highly unlikely that the regulator could have any knowledge of the activities or implications of debts held by the funds/banks in the IFSC. Furthermore, both the UK and Switzerland are also big financial centres and yet their net external debt is substantially lower than Ireland's. The IFSC's influence on the economy is worrying and may yet be the 'second shoe' to drop in the banking system.

10 CSO.
11 See, for example, 'Bubble intact despite high house prices', *The Irish Times*, 18 November 2005.
12 Alan McQuaid, Bloxham Stockbrokers.

borrowing questioned nor the impact it was having on the elements of the economy which had no long-term future.

Throughout the Celtic Tiger, as credit boomed, no one asked the obvious, simple question: what type of economic success story requires so many people to borrow so much money? The obvious answer is, of course, that economic success should not require people to borrow so much money. The argument put forward against this common-sense reply was that most of the borrowed money was being used to buy property, an argument that appeared rational only when property prices were rising. Debt is debt, it has to be repaid. If we wanted a warning of what was coming down the line, we need only have looked to Iceland. In 2006 that country's Central Bank reported on its own economy that 'one of the most important lessons to come out of the Asia crisis was that countries with seemingly sound public finances ignore private sector imbalances at their peril. Iceland's net external debt is higher than virtually any other Fitch-rated sovereign.'[13]

It is important to point out that many people did not rack up serious debts and that many people are debt-free, but the problem is that this does not immunise them from the effect of excessive debt. Many people's incomes, however carefully they might have managed them themselves, were based on debt because their salaries came from debt-related spending either through taxes or through spending that was artificially propped up by borrowing on behalf of customers. This is the insidious nature of pumping credit into an economy: many sensible people are dependent on debt, but don't realise it. In fact, the artificial expansion of smaller businesses could have left them high and dry when the bubble burst. In 2009 the call was often heard from SMEs for the banks to 'get lending going again'. The simple fact is that a successful business should only need cyclical credit or credit for justifiable capital expenditures that will produce long-term sustainable profits to repay that loan. Viable businesses should not need to constantly borrow money; they should generate money, not consume it. The simple fact is that much of the new Celtic Tiger economy is unsustainable. Car dealerships are a classic example. It is obvious to everyone that car

13 Sedlabanki.is.

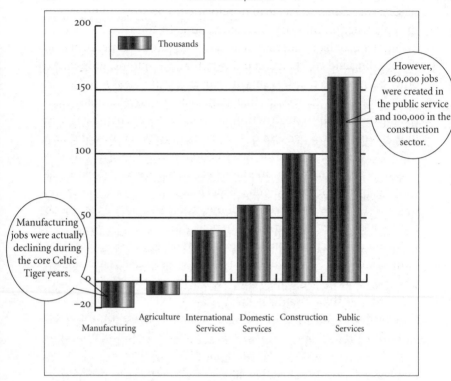

Fig. 4: Jobs growth in Ireland, 2003–6. (Data source: ESRI)

sales reached a fevered pitch during the boom. This number of cars will not be sold again for many years, even decades, to come. In the intervening period, many car dealers will fail and go out of business. This is a personal tragedy for many people, but the economic reality is that there is not enough business to support the number of retailers that have developed around a spin-off from the lending boom. Valuable resources that could have been pumped into vital infrastructure or public services were diverted to build new, or to expand existing, car dealerships. These resources have been wasted and can never be recovered. The sorry fact is that gleaming show-rooms were built to sell imported, over-taxed cars whilst many children are still being educated in what can only be described as prefabricated boxes.

At this juncture the government was taxing this borrowed money heavily as it flowed into and around the economy, and the public service was expanded instead of reformed. The size and impact of the construction industry was astonishing. In 2005 the ESRI, recognising the problem, said that there was 'exceptional dependence on the building and construction industry to fuel economic growth. No other economy in the EU is anywhere near as exposed as is Ireland in this regard.'[14] It pointed out that 40 per cent of direct employment was involved in the construction industry or its ancillary services; plus an amazing 28 per cent of the price of every new housing unit went to the state in various taxes and charges. The effect of this becomes apparent when one looks at where the job growth was coming from during the 2003–6 period, as shown in the graph below. It is clear that the source of the problems now impacting on the country were being firmly entrenched in the economy.

In spite of the ESRI's final conclusion that 'the Irish economy is basically robust', it did emphasise this over-dependence on the building industry and stated that '… the nature and dimensions of the risks that the economy is likely to face over the coming decade suggest the need for public policy to take action to promote a soft landing In particular, the very success of the building and construction sector holds the seeds of future potential problems. Economic policy needs to manage the exposure of the economy to any future crisis in the building sector: to reduce the possibility that a crisis may occur and to provide a buffer of resources to deal with the consequences of any future shocks.' The government could have halted, or at least contained, this property bubble—as it was advised to do—with some simple actions, such as reducing the tax benefits to the building industry or controlling the banks' lending policies through the banking regulation system or even through an aggressive taxation policy, rather than harvesting the excessive prices through stamp duty. The government was ultimately the guarantor of the banking system and should have taken a firm hand in controlling its activities. It could have used the regulator or a statute to limit the amount of credit. It could have avoided the need to nationalise banks by a much less draconian credit policy forced on the banks over the last decade. It chose not to do so, and the problem continued to escalate. In the broader economy, real productive

14 ESRI, Medium Term Review 2005.

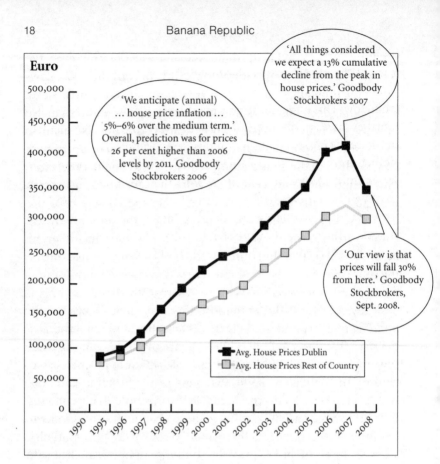

Fig. 5: Financial opinions change as quickly as Irish house prices. (Data source: DEHLG)

growth had stopped and resources were being diverted into building houses and apartments that everyone wanted to buy for reasons that often had little to do with living in them. It became a classic asset bubble as consumers chased prices higher and higher, convinced they were rising forever and they had to jump on the bandwagon now; they were followed into the fray by amateur and professional speculators, all seeking to make a quick fortune. John Kenneth Galbraith, the famous American economist who lived through many such speculative episodes as gripped Ireland in 1999–2007, has sagely noted that 'not only fools but quite a lot of other people are recurrently separated from their money in the moment of speculative euphoria'.[15] He summed up what occurs in situations like this: 'the price of the object of speculation goes up. Securities, land, *objets d'art* and other property, when bought today, are worth more tomorrow. This increase attracts new buyers; the new buyers assure a further increase. Yet more are attracted; yet more buy; the increase continues. The speculation building on itself provides its own momentum.'[16] He also explained why investors and purchasers are drawn into such events, usually against their own best judgment: 'they will be required to resist two compelling forces: one, the powerful personal interest that develops in the euphoric belief, and the other, the pressure of public and seeming superior financial opinion that is brought to bear on behalf of such belief.'[17] Similarly, in Ireland this euphoric belief abounded in financial opinion and it was all very optimistic indeed, that is until the market turned.[18]

As the decade progressed consumers were lent money against the notional value of their properties—misleadingly called 'releasing equity'—and this was pumped into the economy so people could live the Celtic Tiger lifestyle. Furthermore, this credit was often dangled temptingly in front of people rather than consumers actively applying for it. Newer house buyers were lent increasing sums over ever-lengthening time periods to try to 'get their foot on the property ladder'—an all-consuming national pursuit; others were lent money just to speculate on property in various guises, such as buy-to-lets or fly-to-let foreign properties. The financial institutions had to lend increasing amounts of money to keep the vicious circle going: prices had to keep rising to justify the previous loans they had given. This borrowed money, and the migrant workers it attracted, flooded the Irish economy, distending and distorting it, obscuring the fact that Ireland could not yet adequately serve its own population. The immigrant population was sold as some permanent bonus of the economic boom, yet as can be seen from the population growth chart below, the permanency of any migration into the country is questionable. It is on this point that

---

15 Galbraith, *A Short History of Financial Euphoria.*
16 *ibid.*
17 *ibid.*
18 *Irish Independent,* 2 September 2008.

much of the confusion rests: where did the population growth come from and how permanent is it?

Looking at it very simply, which is always the best way, people live in houses, therefore population drives housing demand. It is clear that 60 per cent of the population increase in the critical 2002–6 period was driven by inward migration.[19] However, this tells us little about the 'viscosity' of such migration for the future. This factor is vital because it was upon population predictions that the financial community based its forecasts regarding housing demand and price rises. It also factored in what it called the SVR factor, i.e. second/ holiday, vacant and replacement homes. This served only to compound the confusion because it was too easy to assume that a vacant home is a holiday home when, in fact, it could be a speculative investment or stock being held back from the market or a property unable to sell; the statistics provided by the Central Statistics Office (CSO) are not clear on this. Even the experts were never sure and had to make do with well-educated guesses.

An examination of the opinions being declared in 2006 clearly shows that overall estimates of demand were inaccurate and that this was to prove the Achilles' heel of the Irish economy. In the Goodbody Stockbrokers report of that year, after analysing all the factors, it was concluded that 'Our analysis suggests that demand for homes amounts to an average of c.68,000 p.a. over the period 2006–2011'. Allowing for migration, the report examined a wide range of scenarios and concluded a worst-case scenario of demand for 49,000 houses, with a best-case scenario of 74,000 per annum. Yet even by Goodbody's figures the market was supplying too many homes[20] in 2006—close to 90,000 in that year. It is this over-supply that led to the current huge overhang in the market, which in turn drove down completions substantially in 2008 and beyond. In effect, much of the economy had wrapped itself around the construction

---

19 *Irish Construction Economics*, Goodbody's Stockbrokers, October 2006, p.42.

20 The phrase 'houses' was replaced by 'homes' in the early 2000s because much of what was constructed comprised duplexes, town houses and large apartments rather than what could be called houses. People were encouraged to buy these smaller dwellings as a first step into property-ownership. The pervading logic was that renting was 'dead money' and you had to get onto the property ladder, no matter what the cost.

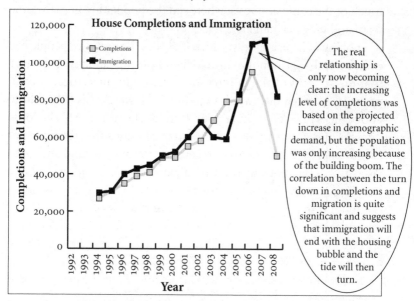

Fig. 6: If You Build It, They Will Come: the building boom was based on an increasing population, which itself was a function of the boom and its associated credit—an ever-increasing upward spiral until it turned and then began to reverse downwards. With house-building predicted to grind to a halt in 2010, immigration will likely end and emigration resume. This is fatal for any NAMA-style exercise as property prices cannot rise with the house-buying population falling. (Data source: DEHLG/CSO)

industry: rather than being a group of separate variables, everything was tied together, which meant it would only need one thread to come loose for the whole to unravel. It was a self-perpetuating fallacy: people were migrating to Ireland because of the construction boom, but the boom was ultimately built on people migrating to Ireland.

Thus here stood the Irish economy, in the mid-2000s, tied to a construction industry that was keeping the boom afloat, but was itself anchored only by a belief in continual demand for what was being produced. If the jobs related to the construction industry disappeared, then the migrant workers would leave in search of work elsewhere. By 2008 the flow outwards had begun and foreign governments were in Ireland at a FÁS-run jobs fair, trying to attract their own people home again along with Irish workers who had repatriated during the boom.[21] If the large numbers of migrant

21 *Morning Ireland*, 8.26am, 13 April 2008: interview with Kevin Quinn of FÁS.

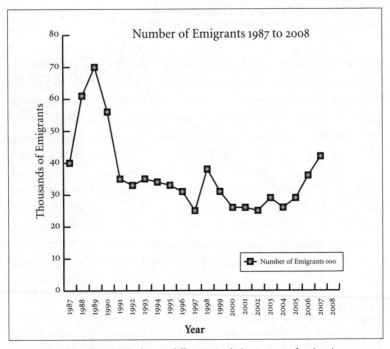

Fig. 7: Net emigration shows a different population pattern of emigration,
with the figures beginning to rise again around 2005. (Data source: CSO)

workers continue to leave, then net migration may very well not just
shrink but begin to contract again, especially when one considers
that between 2006 and 2007 alone, 213,000 people migrated into the
country. This creates a new level of volatility. Furthermore, and
contrary to what most people might believe, emigration from
Ireland began to rise in 2005 and hit an almost twenty-year peak in
2008;[22] this runs counter to belief because it was disguised by
massive immigration, resulting in a high net migration figure. In
short, population growth is highly unlikely. In fact, extrapolating the

22 Detailed in the *Irish Independent*, 8 September 2008, based on 'Population and
Migration Estimates', a report released by the Central Statistics Office in August
2008. This showed that emigration bottomed-out in 2004 and that by the year to
April 2008, 45,300 workers had left the country. This figure was last exceeded in
1990. Although it is reasonable to assume that this figure has increased substantially over the last twelve months, whether it has yet exceeded the figure of 70,600
reported for 1989 is unknown. If it had, then in 2009 Ireland would be looking at
the highest net emigration figure in twenty years. This would not be unusual,
however, considering that almost 700,000 people immigrated into Ireland over the

available data, it is likely that the population is already contracting. If the population starts to decrease, it will undermine much of the foundation of the housing industry and the Celtic Tiger, i.e. that Ireland had fundamentally changed and was attracting a permanent population shift back to its shores. It will also undermine NAMA, which is predicated on price rises over ten years for it to succeed.

The economic commentators glossed over much of this in the mid-decade. Their endless optimism with regard to the housing sector and repeated assertions that prices could never fall propelled the country blindly into indebtedness as many, many people chased the dream of quick profits. Property prices became a function of the debt provided by the financial institutions. Whilst much of this money was borrowed voluntarily, it was also lent recklessly[23] by institutions whose experience should have alerted them to a situation that was a textbook asset bubble. The government could have stopped this. The fact that it did not do so was due, in part, to incompetence, but it was also due to a desire to deflect attention away from the various tribunals into the corrupt practices of previous Fianna Fáil governments, thereby ensuring good election results.

At the peak of the property bubble in 2006/7, 23 per cent of the country's GDP was composed of construction: Ireland was building twenty-one housing units per 1,000 population, compared to a quarter of this in the rest of the EU; one in eight employees in the state was directly employed in construction.[24] If you stripped out the public service workers and added in those servicing the construction industry, then its effect was even more disproportionate.[25]

last ten years; if we assume that the majority of these were migratory workers, then we could easily see 350,000 people leave Ireland in a very short period if there is no work for them. As a percentage this figure would not be a historic high, but the difference now is the swiftness of these moves and the impact these moves have had and will have on Irish society.

23 How else could one describe giving forty-year, 100 per cent, variable rate mortgages at a time of historically low interest rates, historically high house prices and using multipliers the equivalent of six or seven times salary? Even less rational was the provision of 'interest only' mortgages, which were also variable rate. Such products are dangerous not only for the borrower but also for the lender. Repayments can rise significantly, the value of the property can fall significantly, yet the borrower might never even begin paying back the capital sum.

24 Construction Industry Federation, 282,000 employees, 13.2% Q3 2007.

25 Goodbody Stockbrokers' report, see fn 20.

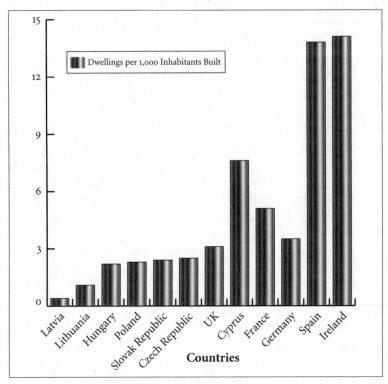

Fig. 8: Number of dwellings built per 1,000 inhabitants. Even as early as 2002 it was clear that a disproportionate amount of housing was being built. This had not changed substantially by 2007. (Data source: DOE Housing Developments in European Countries)

Various statistics all the way up the level of completions demonstrated that we were potentially building too many units. In 2002 we had the highest rate of completions per capita (see Fig. 8); by 2005, according to the European Housing Review (EHR),[26] Ireland was still building more housing per head of population than any other European Country and the volume being built was still rising. According to the EHR's data, Ireland was building 4.5 times as much housing as the UK—and the UK was also experiencing a housing bubble. The output did not peak until 2007, when we were pushing out 90,000 units. The argument presented in the media was that this was to fulfil natural demand subsequent to population growth and increased prosperity. Yet, only the following year did the stories

26 Published by the Royal Institute of Chartered Surveyors.

about 'ghost towns' began appearing; you don't have to drive too far from the capital city to find these now-vacant streets.

In an article entitled 'Welcome to the ghost-town, Ireland 2006',[27] one resident of a so-called ghost town said: 'When these houses were built we thought it would be good thing for the area, bringing people in, but it has actually made the place lonelier, since they are virtually empty almost all year round.' Many of these 'holiday homes' were built under the Seaside Resorts Scheme, which was presumably designed to inject life into remoter regions. Instead, in spite of its aims, it really only served to fuel speculation. After 2007 it became clear that there were many similar ghost towns and apartment complexes closer to the major cities.

It therefore seems highly unlikely that, as was often claimed, Irish builders were simply responding to a natural demand in the economy. In reality, the only reason it looked like it added up was the fact that migrants were occupying the new houses and apartments that were being built at such a ferocious rate.

Asset bubbles have deceived the greatest financial minds into believing almost anything—remember the dot.com debacle? Internet companies that lost money and had no prospect of ever making a profit were valued at millions of dollars at the height of the dot.com bubble. The same is true in Ireland: property valuations became so absurdly distorted that in a short number of years we could be facing a situation where hundreds of thousands of empty houses and apartments are dotted around the country. Even more worrying is the fact that most of these were built on borrowed money and if they cannot be sold or leased, the builders will not be able to service the loans, which means those monies will not be repaid to the people who unknowingly provided them, i.e. the depositors of the major financial institutions, a.k.a. the ordinary people of this country. Where this leaves the banks will be discussed later, but suffice to say that at present, if pushed to repay their loans to depositors,[28] the

---

27 *Irish Independent*, 28 October 2006.
28 A depositor lends his money to the bank: this is the only way to view the banking relationship. Banks borrow from depositors and other sources, then lend to their customers. The weakness of all banks is that they borrow short and lend long, i.e. depositors can demand money back instantly or at the end of the term deposit, but most loans are for very long periods.

banks could not do so. For the next two or three years it will be easy to argue, by those who wish to boost house prices, that fundamental demand will recover because there is simply a 'backlog' of supply that has to be worked through before prices rise again. The quantity of that 'backlog' is, I suspect, much higher than anyone knows and once there is no more building work, the 'fundamental demand' will leave and go back home or elsewhere in the EU. The stark truth is that many houses and apartments were built in response to false demand and were funded by credit that will never again be available in the same quantities.

WHAT HAPPENS NEXT?

If Ireland follows the well-worn path of other economies that have experienced similar events, then the deflating asset bubble will severely impact the economy as many consumers realise they have been living on debt or that their jobs have been funded by it. The government's budgetary surplus will evaporate and the deficit will rise rapidly, with unemployment following quickly behind. History teaches us that the fall in prices after a bubble is commensurate with the scale of the rise in the first place. In Europe in recent years this has ranged up to 50 per cent, as Fig. 9 shows.

These figures can be used as a guide to what lies in store for the Irish economy, but it must be factored in that the pace of speculative growth in Ireland outstripped that of the economies listed above. The rule-of-thumb approach suggests that the fall could be equal to two-thirds of the gains. This is being borne out even now: in 2009 price reductions of 40–50 per cent are routinely seen in the media by those who obviously have to sell, no matter what. It must also be noted that property prices tend to initially fall at a slower rate than other asset classes, but nonetheless my own forecast is that property will fall 80–100 per cent.

I am well aware that those figures will seem preposterous to some readers, so I would like to explain how I have arrived at that conclusion. Let's start with precedent: had someone predicted a 40–50 per cent fall in prices two years ago, he would have been dismissed as unrealistic. Yet this is what has already happened. The prediction of a fall of 80–100 per cent from peak prices in 2006 is

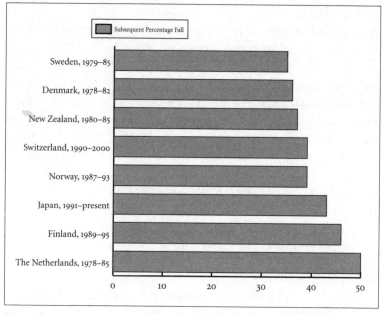

Fig. 9: Subsequent property price falls in recent asset bubbles. Ireland is likely to surpass even the worst of these because the bubble was so extensive. Furthermore, the average period of declining prices was five to six years; in Ireland, prices have been falling for only two years. (Data source: M. Kelly Report, UCD)

based on a number of factors that will affect the supply and demand of property in Ireland. First of all, it is important to accept unreservedly that Ireland's property bubble was a classic asset bubble— there still seems to be some resistance to this fact. Let me be quite clear about this: what has happened in Ireland will be used in economic textbooks for decades to come as the quintessential example of how asset bubbles form and burst. One feature of asset bubbles is that during the bust phase, when the asset price is falling, there is a belief that the worst is over, that prices will somehow stabilise at what are perceived to be realistic levels. The same experts who once said that prices could never fall change tack and announce that prices are reasonable, therefore it is a good time to get in; it rarely is. Prices tend to overshoot on the downside by as much as they previously did on the upside. In short, there are four factors that I believe will drive prices down by such high percentage amounts.

1. Supply Side

As discussed elsewhere in this text, the 2006 census showed that there were 266,000 empty properties in Ireland.[29] In 2006/7, a further 170,000 housing units were built. Whilst it is impossible to calculate the number of empty properties in real time, I think we can say it is very substantial and that the massive increase in properties available to rent is a reflection of this. Those trying to sell property will of course ply the 'last few choc-ices!' argument, but I choose not to believe too much of what desperate estate agents and developers are saying. As more builders and developers go bankrupt, there will eventually be forced sales as liquidators sell off property at any price. In short, there is a huge oversupply of property all over the country. NAMA may try to store, or freeze, supply from the market to prop up prices, but, ultimately, available supply always floods a market.

2. Credit Availability

House prices and land purchases were driven by the availability of credit. The function of house prices moved from a rational basis to simply how much a bank would lend a borrower to buy a property. There were little or no fundamentals behind the price of property save the ability of the purchasers to raise finance to buy it. Now, of course, the banks' lending criteria is much stricter and, furthermore, some of the major banks are on the verge of being nationalised and possibly being declared insolvent. In such circumstances the amount of credit available is going to become very limited, which will in turn drive down the price further.

All of the major banks and building societies are being propped up by virtue of a state guarantee that is itself now being questioned. Stricter credit conditions and/or no credit will push prices much lower. Consider the now feasible scenario that all of the major institutions are nationalised and the government is simply unable to borrow any more money. At what price would property then be transacted? I am of a piece with Paul Krugman, the Noble Laureate prize-winner, who ranks Ireland as the developed country most likely to 'go broke'.

29 These were not new builds, but an empty house is an empty house that has the potential to come on the market. The 'holiday home' excuse simply does not fly anymore.

3. Market Dynamics

Ireland is only two years into a declining cycle, the average length of which is five years or more. Contrary to what many might think, thus far Ireland has been reasonably fortunate in certain respects, for example interest rates have fallen because of global economic conditions. The global credit crisis may have triggered Ireland's problems, but it is not the underlying cause of them. There seems to be a belief that if the rest of the world recovers, Ireland will ride up on its coattails. This is more a blind hope than a logical conclusion. Should the rest of the world recover and/or inflation rise due to quantitative easing, the European Central Bank (ECB) will begin to raise interest rates. If this happens, the impact on mortgage-holders will be enormous. A major part of Ireland's problem was created by the wrong interest rate policy, i.e. the economy was out of step with ECB policy. The reverse side of this situation is that many people are now exposed to variable rate interest mortgages or short-term fixed-rate mortgages. This means that it is if and when interest rates rise that the real pain will be inflicted on Ireland.

There were strong similarities between the rise in the price of Irish shares and the price of Irish property, referred to as 'stocks and blocks' by Irish stockbrokers. Both rose by roughly similar amounts during the Celtic Tiger. The ISEQ has already fallen by approximately 80 per cent, while in some cases individual banks have fallen by 95 per cent. The trading of shares is much more liquid than property because they are homogeneous and the stock market ensures a price will be set, no matter what. The property market is less liquid, but there is an argument that the stock market is a leading indicator for what will ultimately happen in the property market.

During the bubble phase, speculative purchases were substantial. People invested in holiday homes and buy-to-lets, parents bought houses for their kids in university and single people bought property rather than waiting to purchase as a couple, later in life. This, of course, is an essential feature of asset bubbles: the compression of future demand into shorter time frames. The consequence of this behaviour is that it digs a big hole in future demand because people have bought forward their purchase decisions. Furthermore, those interested in purchasing property already see prices falling and will react in the opposite way, as people did during the bubble phase, i.e. if prices are already falling, then why should I buy now, why not wait another month? This short-term behaviour drives the market down further.

4. Demand side
The basis of many of the arguments for the property prices was a continued increase in population. As we have seen, while it is true that more than 200,000 people came to the country in 2006/7, the population is now likely to contract. A shrinking population means less natural demand for property, which will push even more supply onto the market. It is possible that we could see 100,000–200,000 people leave Ireland over the next couple of years, and this would of course push substantial amounts of accommodation onto the market. So even if the builders build nothing, supply will still increase.

In summation, Ireland now has a property market that is hugely oversupplied, a contracting population and other factors that will limit demand, compounded by serious credit availability problems. From a situation where prices are already down 30–40 per cent, this suggests even more substantial price falls are coming down the line. At this point, in mid-2009, there is as yet little real panic in the market or large-scale forced sales of units, but these are inevitable as developers go to the wall. There is anecdotal evidence that the financial institutions have been propping up the big developers to avoid such sales—time will see that strategy tested.

So, to return to the argument on price decreases, a drop of 80 per cent may seem enormous to those who purchased homes near the peak of the boom,[30] but bear in mind that in 2006 even the merest

---

30 The price of housing alters significantly in a falling market because the actual market where the housing is transacted also changes. In a recent BBC documentary the headline fall in prices *per* the Halifax Index (similar to the IP/TSB index) was compared, showing a fall of approximately 15 per cent. The reporter then went to a distressed property auction and compared the prices at which the property was sold with the land registry prices. This revealed falls of, on average, 50 per cent and in some cases 60 per cent. In a market collapse those who have to sell property do so at enormous discounts. So you end up with two prices: what the owner believes his house is worth and what it would fetch if he had to sell the house. But the value only matters if you have to sell, so in many ways fretting about house prices doesn't matter unless you are in business and must value your property for accounting purposes.

suggestion of house prices falling was dismissed as wild speculation. Thus the prediction of 80 per cent is, in my opinion, realistic. All it means is that at some point property will transact at these levels, i.e. distressed sales or forced sales. What cannot be dismissed is that house prices are a function of demand and credit availability, and both of these are fast evaporating while there remains a huge reservoir of supply to draw from. Whichever way you look at it, at best a generalised fall of at least 40–50 per cent from the peak would not be unusual. This may occur over two years or ten years, depending on a number of factors that will be discussed later, but by mid-2009 it was clear that price falls of more than 50 per cent were already happening, although this data was described by the *Irish Times* as 'secret'[31]—a clear indication that there will be resistance to even reporting the reality of the property bust. Whatever is reported or whispered, I think it is safe to conclude that those with liquid resources in 2010, 2011 and 2012 will most certainly obtain excellent bargains compared to 2005–2008.

One of the causes of this decline, the act of joining the Eurozone, will actually limit Ireland's ability to ameliorate the consequences of this projected fall in house prices. We have lost the 'tools' of currency or interest rate adjustment that we could have used to help ourselves. Furthermore EMU deficit requirements will effectively limit our government expenditure: as tax revenue falls away, the government will be obliged to cut spending, creating a spiral of falling public *and* private expenditure. The interest rates payable on the national debt will be set by the European Central Bank and conditions prevailing in the open market, which means they will probably bear little resemblance to what the Irish economy needs. It is ironic that what Ireland needs most is for the rest of the EU to descend into recession as well, so that rates might be cut. Of course, thanks to the Credit Crunch it appears there will indeed be an EU-wide recession, but all this will really achieve is to reduce demand for the goods produced in Ireland. It might be stating the obvious, but Ireland is a country that depends on a strong global market for its exports. If you don't have a job to service your mortgage, then it does not matter a whit if interest rates are high or low.

31 *The Irish Times*, Property Supplement, 8 May 2009.

The Irish government is staring down the barrel of contracting growth, rising unemployment, falling house prices and the need to borrow very large sums of money. It is inevitable that credit availability will contract, which is bad news for a country that has become dependent on easy credit. In most other asset bubbles the subsequent fall in prices created a wave of bad debts rippling into the balance sheets of financial institutions, and in many cases those institutions faltered and some failed. In the wake of the Finnish property bubble, for example, many major financial institutions were rendered insolvent and the Finnish government nationalised some if its biggest banks.[32] The Irish government has already had to nationalise one bank (Anglo Irish Bank) and it is likely that this is only the beginning as the reality of bad lending decisions destroys the capital base of the Irish banking system. Fiscally, this has backed the Irish government into a corner whereby it not only needs cash to prop up the banks but also needs it to stimulate the economy. The problem is that cash is simply not available and the government is falling into an all-too-predictable economic trap: splurging when it has the money and then purging when it runs out of cash, but failing to tackle the core problems of misspending and mismanagement. This isn't the first time this mistake has been made, but this time it's much more onerous as the country is now in a position where it needs to borrow extensively, at precisely the time when borrowing is going to be expensive and difficult. The government has responded by setting up the National Asset Management Agency (NAMA), but the function of this body—its exact constitution aside—is to obtain money from the ECB in order to re-float the banking system and the government itself. The creaking edifice of the post-2000 Celtic Tiger was built on a foundation of debt, and we are going to pay a severe price for this error.

In short, our politicians have managed to sail the economy into the 'perfect storm' with their mismanagement of the public purse. Now, at the tail end of Ireland's economic 'miracle', we are one of the most personally indebted nations in the developed world, the government has commenced a borrowing spree that is going to raise national debt levels back to the worst days of the 1980s and public

32 'The spectre of nationalisation', *The Economist*, 22 January 2009.

services are grossly inadequate by any modern standards, yet our political leaders are amongst the highest paid in the world. It is time to apportion responsibility for this unacceptable and avoidable situation.

There are two distinct groups in Ireland: the political classes, which continue to prosper regardless of what happens in the economy; and the non-political class, which comprises the vast majority of people working productively in the economy. These are the people who juggle their lives between working, sitting in traffic jams, runs to crèches and schools and ensuring their mortgages and myriad other bills get paid on time and in full. It is this group whose efforts created the economic success because it was their abilities that attracted international firms and it was their salaries that paid the taxes to run the country. It is the former group, comprising government ministers, the upper echelons of the public service and the major government quangos, that supposedly manages the economy. The truth is that they have failed to do their jobs competently, have squandered what was given to them and will seek to evade responsibility by spinning stories that essentially boil down to 'it isn't our fault, blame world events'. There are many ways to spin a story, but sometimes a simple fact can give the lie to all the spin: in 2009 the Irish government will borrow €18,000 per family[33] in order to bridge the gap between what it promised it could deliver and what it ultimately can deliver to its beleaguered citizens, plus three to four times more to fund NAMA. It perfectly elucidates the mechanics of the failure that has plunged Ireland into economic freefall: spend limitlessly, borrow endlessly.

---

33 *Sunday Business Post*, 2 November 2008, p.M2: €4,500 per adult and child.

Chapter 2

An Introduction to Economics and Finance

Economics was once described as 'the dismal science'[1] thanks to the work of Thomas Malthus, who predicted that most of the human race would starve to death. His basic theory was that food production, no matter what its initial size, could only increase arithmetically, that is one field at a time, i.e. 1, 2, 3, 4, etc., but that any population living off it would grow geometrically, that is by 2, 4, 8, 16, 32, etc., therefore the population would ultimately exceed its ability to feed its members. Even if technology allowed accelerated production, Malthus did not believe it could keep pace with population growth.

Malthus was both right and wrong, depending on which continent you live on. The veracity of his theory was not the problem, however, it was the fact that it was gloomy and offered no solutions—characteristics that are often said to define modern economics. Economists also often employ mathematics and its dense terminology, which immediately alienates many people: 'an inverted yield curve is impacting the …' that's the point when most people switch off. It gives the impression that special qualifications are needed to understand how modern economies function, but this isn't in fact true. The intricacies of the subject may be complicated,

---

1   D. Levy, *How the Dismal Science Got Its Name* (Michigan University Press, 2002), p.112.

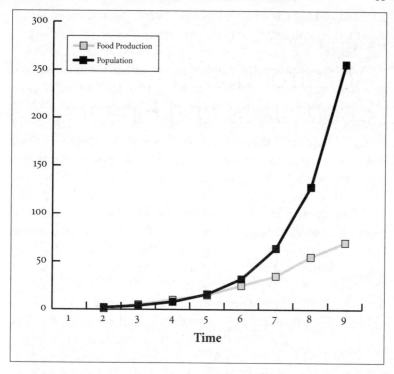

Fig. 10: The Malthusian Trap.

but the core forces that drive and shape modern economies are straightforward and compelling. Nonetheless, many people do not understand these basic forces, so in this chapter I shall explain these concepts so that the reader can fully grasp the various issues raised in the book.

1. WHAT MONEY IS
(AND WHY IT IS THE BASIS OF A SUCCESSFUL ECONOMY BY PRODUCING SPECIALISATION)

One of the key factors in any modern economy is so fundamental that most people don't even think about it: money. Although we might be very preoccupied with how much of it we do or don't have, few people ever stop to ask themselves what money really is. In short, it is the basis of every economy and is probably the greatest unsung invention of humankind. That might sound strange, but it is crucial that money is understood for what it is: a tool that was invented, just like the wheel. Money has become so important in our lives that we have forgotten the broader purpose of it, and by forgetting this we have started to make some very expensive mistakes—personally and nationally. In order to remember, we must go back in time to explore how it was invented and for what purpose.

Let's imagine a simple Stone Age village, where a group of three families lived in some reasonably comfortable huts. Each family struggled to provide the basics: they all grew some wheat for bread, caught some fish and raised some chickens to provide meat and eggs. They were surviving, but were still struggling because they had to provide a variety of foodstuffs for their families. As it happened, each family was particularly good at one task: the first family were really good at catching fish; the second family were good wheat farmers; and the last family had mastered the art of chicken farming. Yet each family had to spend time doing the other tasks at which they weren't very adept. This was highly inefficient and a waste of time, which, they came to realise, was a valuable resource.

Eventually one of the group had an idea and got all the families together to share it with them. He suggested that each family specialise in what they were good at and use their excess production to barter with each other. This worked initially, as the total amount of fish, bread and eggs increased. The fact that each family specialised in what they were good at meant they became even better at it and produced more goods, which was good news for the village, which now had more of everything. The only problem was the bartering. If, for example, the Fisher family had an especially good day fishing and wanted to swap the excess for lots of wheat and eggs, they were dependent on the other families having also had an especially good day. If this did not prove to be the case, the extra fish might go to waste. Furthermore, at times choice was extremely limited. For example, the farmer might have loaves of bread and want eggs, but there might be only fish available. The whole thing quickly became a bit of a mess as people dragged eggs, bread and fish back and forth in the village, looking to trade with one another. Not only did you need to find someone who wanted what you had to barter, they in turn had to have what you wanted to gain, in other words there had to be a 'coincidence of wants'. Quite often this didn't happen, which led to dissatisfaction and much wasted effort.

Eventually the head of the Farmer family had a good idea. He had the greatest difficulty operating the barter system successfully due to the infrequent nature of his harvests and his limited ability to store the wheat to make bread. However, now he remembered that he had a large bag of unique sea-shells that his children had collected from the beach and of which there were no more. His idea was to convince the other families to accept one shell for each fish or egg they gave him at the times when he did not have any bread to swap with them. Then in the months after he harvested his crops, they could return and exchange each token for a loaf of bread. It was a great system for keeping tally of what he owed them and vice versa. The Fisher family ran with the idea and took it one step further: whenever they wanted eggs from the Poultry family and didn't have fish, they gave them a shell instead. The Poultry family accepted the shells because they knew they could use them to get bread from the Farmer family, or to get some fish from the Fisher family when there was an abundant supply. This system allowed all the families to build up a little store of buying power with which to purchase food in lean times. And on it went, each family started using the tokens (shells) to exchange for the goods they wanted. This not only allowed them to adjust and vary their daily purchases but also allowed them to build up a store of wealth. The shells had lubricated the whole exchange process in the village and made the dealing in goods much easier.

Soon other families joined the village because they had heard about this system. A stonemason came, as did a blacksmith and a cooper. The village became very successful simply because each family knew they could provide for themselves, even allowing for the vagaries of their work schedule. In addition, by allowing families to specialise in one task, the goods became of higher quality and there were more of them. There were other spin-off benefits to the system: families could take holidays from work because they could build up a supply of shells and it allowed people to 'shape' the exchange they wanted to make, for example one loaf of bread might not be worth one chicken or one fish in December, but by using the shells then, the farmer could say he wanted three tokens for a loaf or two eggs for one token. Each person decided the value they placed on something and if the other party agreed, then the deal was done.

Effort was also saved in searching for people with whom to barter because it didn't matter whether you had eggs and the other villager had something you didn't want because when you accepted shells for your goods, you knew that you could get what you wanted from someone else because they, too, would accept shells. Thus time and effort were saved in transacting goods, and this time could be spent producing more goods.

2. INTERNATIONAL TRADE:
HOW DID MONEY LEAD TO JOB SPECIALISATION AND CREATE MUCH OF MODERN TRADE?

The funny thing was that the shells did absolutely nothing, they were intrinsically worthless, yet as a token system of keeping track of the value they were superb and made the whole village more efficient through specialisation. The introduction of job specialisation led to specific trades arising, such as the blacksmith, the baker, the carpenter, etc. As people focused on the same task all day, it led to more efficiencies and to what could be termed scientific progress in particular fields. The longer a blacksmith made horseshoes and ploughs, the better he became at it and the better he learned to refine metals. The longer the baker made bread, the more he learned about yeast and how to produce bread more efficiently, and so on.

In time, these tokens became money. Money is intrinsically worthless today, but it is in limited supply and is accepted throughout the economy, therefore can be used as a token system to facilitate exchange. Money was the key to growth in every civilisation, along with the wheel. Any civilisation that lacked a money system failed to develop—not because it did not have money *per se*, but because its citizens could not specialise sufficiently, therefore did not prosper and were eventually overcome by those societies that did prosper. It was economic specialisation, facilitated by money, that allowed craftsmen to emerge in Europe and that ensured Europe pioneered and dominated the world for so long. Europe had the headstart and exported this to North America; together, they still dominate much of the economic world.

There is, of course, one important point that has been overlooked so far: historically, how was it decided what was going to be used as money? In the example above we used shells because it was convenient, but in reality the first money was usually in the form of gold or silver coins. The reasons for this were fairly simple. Precious metals were intrinsically attractive and already used as adornments, so had some intrinsic worth. Furthermore, they were relatively easy to carry, were durable and, importantly, were malleable, which meant they could be shaped into coins of varying size and weight. The critical factor, however, was that gold was limited in supply because it was naturally rare and difficult to extract from the ground. It is absolutely essential that the item designated as money is physically limited, otherwise it becomes pointless. The amount of money must equate roughly with the amount of goods being produced so that efficient exchange can take place. Money is rather like oil in your car engine: there is a right amount of it, and either too much or too little can cause problems. It is this point that is absolutely crucial because it explains exactly what has been occurring in Ireland over the last decade. But to return to our thread of thought, how was the leap made from gold to paper money?

As society progressed and expanded, the frequency of purchases meant it became very inconvenient to drag around bags of gold and silver coins in order to transact business. This inconvenience was exacerbated by the high likelihood of the theft of one's precious metals. For this reason people began to deposit their gold coins with goldsmiths. The goldsmith had a secure storage for his own gold, so storing someone else's gold was not too difficult and produced a nice bonus for him in the form of storage fees. It was very convenient all round: you would take your gold along and give it to the goldsmith and he would issue a slip of paper stating, 'I have X ounces of gold belonging to Mr Y'. Whenever you wanted your gold back, you would go to him and hand over the receipt and take back the gold—simple as that. However, even this became too much work for some people. Soon, if a goldsmith had established a good reputation in a town, then Mr Y might simply say to a supplier, 'Look here, just take this receipt from the goldsmith, it is as good as gold'. The seller might also know of the goldsmith and have a good opinion of him and therefore be happy to accept the receipt for the gold instead of the gold itself. A goldsmith's reputation thus became very valuable in itself as it gave his receipts a wide currency and acceptability.

Over time fewer people went back to collect the gold, instead trading in receipts. Thus began the move to transacting pieces of paper backed by gold rather than transacting gold itself. Eventually the goldsmith decided there was more money to be made in the 'banking' business. It had become apparent to him that most people were not bringing back their receipts because they trusted him. People treated his receipts almost as 'real' money and were willing to transact them because they were as limited in supply, the same as the gold to which they referred. This is how banknotes developed; starting as a note from the 'bank' that it had some gold to guarantee a receipt. Many banknotes still carry the phrase 'I promise to pay the bearer', which is a historical throwback to the promise to pay out gold to the bearer. By the by, upon this very simple trading pattern was built the modern, complex banking system.

It has been noted that the crucial factor in the trading of money is that it is in limited supply, which gives it worth. However, our clever goldsmith soon hit on a means by which he could create money through his banking endeavours: why not write new receipts for gold, without there being any actual extra gold behind them? He could then lend out these receipts to businesses or private individuals and charge interest on them. Eventually he began to pay interest to people to lodge their gold with him—the forerunner of modern deposit banking. The people receiving the banknotes had no idea there was not enough gold behind them to guarantee them, but as long as they didn't know this and he issued just the 'right' amount, the wily goldsmith was safe. If, however, there was a panic and everyone wanted their gold back quickly, which was known as a run on the bank, the goldsmith would have a serious problem as there were more banknotes than there was gold. In fact, the whole banking system was a bit of a confidence trick, but it did not matter as long as there was enough gold to give out to the few people who demanded it back. The bank provided the critical extra 'money' to allow an economy to grow; remember, the more goods and services that were produced, the more money was needed to facilitate their exchange. So when an economy sought to grow, the banks facilitated this expansion by releasing more money into the economy, which they did by lending out 'new' receipts to buy the new production.

The key thing was, of course, to avoid a run on the bank, as that would dispel the finely balanced illusion upon which all parties relied. Throughout the seventeenth, eighteenth and nineteenth centuries 'runs' on banks occurred on a regular basis, which adversely affected commerce and trade. These runs were often caused in part by the fact that rival private banks, which all issued different banknotes, would try to cause runs in order to eliminate the competition. It was not unknown for one bank to spread rumours about another bank in order to try to start a panic. It was healthy rough-and-tumble capitalism, but it nonetheless created too much instability for money, which was an important component of the economy. For this reason governments stepped in and began to regulate the issuing of banknotes, eventually establishing government and controlled central banks that regulated and policed the right to issue notes backed by gold.

Over the last 100 years practically all central banks have come off the 'gold standard', in other words they have removed the right to demand a fixed amount of gold for a note. Thus the link was severed and paper money became money in its own right. While the concept of gold backing a currency is now something of an anachronism, there are still currencies backed by gold. The Swiss Franc has a gold reserve behind it, as do many other central banks, and Fort Knox stores the national gold reserves for the USA. There are also many gold coins still being produced by countries such as Canada and South Africa. The historical desire to cling to something that is physically limited in supply is also still present, so that in times of uncertainty or worry about 'paper' money or the economy, the price of gold will climb partly because of such investors,[2] who want what they see as 'real' security.

Whilst the attraction to gold might seem antiquated, it is not unfounded; the success of paper currencies has been varying. The difficulty with all paper money is that it is not connected with a physically limiting factor. With no physical limitation on its supply, governments have often taken the easy route and just printed more of it when they needed to—as the USA is currently doing to combat

2   Technically, gold is not really an investment as it does not produce an income stream or any form of return.

the Credit Crunch—whereas gold is limited by nature. Like the greedy goldsmith who issued too many receipts, some governments printed too many banknotes in order to buy their way out of trouble. This has happened quite frequently throughout history and classic examples include Germany during the Weimar Republic (1919–33), when notes for higher and higher face value were issued, until eventually they were worth only the paper on which they were printed.

The same occurred in Zimbabwe over the past decade. Ten years ago the Zimbabwean dollar was on par with the US dollar; in 2008 the exchange rate for a US dollar was 650 billion Zimbabwean dollars and yet the government kept printing more money. The more pieces of paper were printed to exchange for 'real' goods, the higher climbed the exchange rates between the real goods and the pieces of paper, i.e. the price went up. In other words, the more money there is available to buy that which is limited in supply, food, etc., the more of those pieces of paper are needed to exchange for them.

This brings us to the most important point in this chapter: the question of what happens when too much money is put into circulation in an economy. Going back to the seashells example, if, for whatever reason, the number of shells had doubled overnight from 100 to 200, the exchange rate between shells and bread/fish/eggs would have shifted considerably. Instead of one shell, for example, being needed to exchange for one fish, it would rise to two shells per fish. The reason for this being that there would be twice the amount of shells in circulation, and so the various buyers and sellers would adjust quickly to this new amount of tokens. When this occurs with money, it is called widespread inflation.

When there is too much money in an economy, the price at which the money is exchanged for the real goods rises. The price will continue to rise until the money and real production in the economy are equated. This was evident in Weimar Germany and in Zimbabwe, where prices have grown as fast as the printing presses could print the money. Real goods must be produced with effort, but money can be created instantly with a printing press or by adding a zero to a bank balance. This point is critical because it leads to an understanding of what general inflation is. Widespread inflation is a sign that there is literally too much money in circulation in an economy for the amount of real goods behind that money, while deflation is caused by a reduction in the supply of money. It is easy to fall into the trap of seeing money as the benchmark value because you earn it and therefore equate it to your efforts. This tends to set everyone's reference point as being money. But it is the human effort behind the money that is of value, not the money itself. Despite the simplicity of this basic rule, this is the very confusion we often fall into when the amount of money in an economy rises. When we see the price of something rise, we assume it's worth more, we assume an increased worth based on an increased demand. What we can forget is that it is also possible that the increased price is due to extra money being put into circulation and that it is money that is devaluing rather than the value of the good rising. The idea of 'too much' money is difficult to grasp because people earn money, but there are economic players in the economy, such as the banks, who can literally create money and put it into the economy. The effect of this is to slowly devalue the actual exchange worth of money, in an economic 'disease' that decreases the effectiveness of money as a tool.

3. INFLATION

When we hear people talking about inflation, it is most often in the sense of rising prices. This is only the tip of the iceberg, however, as rising prices are simply an indication of inflation. In fact, inflation causes significantly more problems in an economy than just increasing prices—it damages the core functions of money as a tool and it does so without many people even noticing.

Inflation distorts people's ability to compare prices and leads them to 'misallocate their resources', i.e. to spend money on the wrong items. One of the main functions of the price of something is to allow consumers to allocate their incomes. The actual price of something sends a signal to the consumer and gives him quite a lot of information. If a loaf of bread is €2 and a pint of milk is €1, then he can decide whether he derives twice the utility from bread as he does from milk. Obviously people don't walk around the super-market making continuous utility calculations, but they are roughly aware as to the relationships between prices, be it for cinema tickets, houses, cars or whatever. When widespread inflation occurs, prices often begin to rise unevenly and as a result the consumer becomes more uncertain about the relative value of what he is buying. In the real world it means people can be ripped off very easily because the reference prices they use to establish relative values are changing so quickly, they simply do not know the value of things. This creates confusion for the consumer and he begins making assumptions about the price quoted, for example that it must be reasonable because everyone else is paying it.

Inflation also sends out confusing signals to those who save money. Saving is usually a productive activity: people save so as to store wealth for future needs and to give them stability. However, inflation can quickly erode the value of the money saved unless it is compensated by higher interest rates. If it isn't, then savers will make the rational move of ceasing to save and instead start spending in order to avoid losing the value of their money. In other words, one of the main functions of money, as a store of wealth, is eroded and it becomes a less useful tool. Furthermore, people usually spend their money on that which is showing the highest gains in relation to inflation, often assets such as land, shares, etc. The undermining of the value of money makes people alter their behaviour in quite startling ways.

Inflation also leads to more inflation, which is one of its most insidious characteristics. When prices rise, the various economic agents react by raising the prices they charge for their labour and goods, which in turn causes other prices to rise and so on. This behaviour can often become anticipatory and entrenched when prices are 'index-linked' or inflation-proofed. It is these secondary effects that signify that inflation is becoming established. As no one wishes to be the one left out in the cold and not get 'their' price rises, workers demand higher wages, employers then raise their prices and goods go up in value again. Once inflation becomes ingrained in an economy, it tends to become persistent because everyone wants to get one more price rise to compensate their losses.

Inflation benefits those who can react quickly to rising prices, but penalises those on fixed incomes, such as pensioners, who cannot react because they are paid a fixed amount of money that they usually cannot adjust. So, for example, a self-employed tradesman can react to inflation by raising the price he charges for his labour from one day to the next, but a person on an annual pension cannot effect any changes to their income.

Inflation causes unemployment in the medium- to long-term, which is probably its most damaging effect. It does this in a number of ways. First, inflation begets inflation and causes the price of labour to rise, making exports more expensive. If an exporter can no longer compete, jobs will be lost. Inflation also creates boom–bust cycles, whereby labour employment rises and falls rapidly in a cycle rather than staying at a steady rate. Inflation also creates asset bubbles, which suck resources from the economy into one specific area as people chase speculative gains in order to keep up with inflation. Once the speculative episode collapses, as it inevitably will, unemployment rises as labour finds it difficult to transfer back quickly to the productive economy.

Finally, when prices begin to rise, it is rarely recognised as a problem due to the quantity of money in circulation. There are usually very specific reasons found to explain why prices are rising and these arguments generally revolve around claims that the supply of the product has reduced or that demand for it has increased. While it is true that there will always be fundamental shifts in demand for one specific item or asset class, such arguments never fully explain the occurrence of real widespread inflation reflected by general price rises. If the supply of money is constant, then as people spend more money on one product they must spend less on another and the price of that should fall. Real inflations can only be explained by more money being in circulation, causing all prices to rise.

The problem is that widespread inflation is usually preceded by narrowing individual inflation on a small number of goods. This is the classic route to an asset bubble: rational price rises occur in an asset class due to fundamentals. Take, for example, the housing market in Ireland. There were initial price rises due to demographic factors creating more demand. This led to more money being loaned out, thus injecting new money into the economy. The price of houses rises further due to this new money, not because of fundamentals but because people still believe it is rising based on fundamentals. The gear change is seamless and smooth; the rational becomes the irrational. More money is borrowed and put towards buying the asset class, laying a circular motion: people buy the asset because the price is rising, which attracts more attention to that asset. Fear then pulls in more demand as people shift their purchasing decisions to the present, fearing having to pay higher prices in the future because prices will continue to rise. So in the Irish example, there were parents buying houses for their university-age children, to avoid those children having to pay truly astronomical house prices in the future—at least, that was the thinking. Out of fear comes greed, which pulls in speculation as vendors try to profit from the vicious circle everyone is now operating within. The money then spills out of the asset class into the general economy, causing a general rise in the price of goods. Those with savings see others making huge gains and decide to stop saving and begin chasing the particular asset upwards, while other people start borrowing because the cost of money is lower than the anticipated rise in the asset class—'a sure thing', in other words. The asset class becomes, in effect, the route by which more money is injected into the economy, creating widespread inflation. The banks create credit, and hence money, to buy more housing and don't even realise it.

Every central banker knows the damage inflation causes, which is why they work vigorously to control it. Most consumers, whilst annoyed at rising prices, rarely see fighting inflation as the top priority because they often feel they are insulated from price rises or can adjust to them by demanding higher salaries. Accordingly, nobody is willing to fight inflation by foregoing their pay rises. Most responsible central bankers know differently, however, and understand the damage inflation can wreak on an economy, which is why they are overly concerned with controlling it.

We have mentioned 'increasing money supply' and it is worth reinforcing the point of how more money is injected into the economy. As we all earn money, it can be difficult to conceive how more of it is created instantly. Yet this happens in much the same way as the goldsmith created more money by writing new receipts without the backing of gold. Bankers can literally create money by increasing the lending in an economy; if banks lend more money in Ireland than is borrowed abroad, then there is more money here. They can also create money by lending out more money than they have on deposit; governments can do much the same, as can the central bank, which can print money,[3] if need be. In modern banking the use of cash has become relatively unusual for high value purchases, with most consumers opting to use electronic transfer of one kind or another. This is the next step: just as we moved from gold once, we are now in the process of switching from banknotes to electronic balances and exchange these using debit cards, bank transfers, etc. This allows the supply of money to change with little control, or even understanding, on the part of those in charge.

As highlighted above, in a speculative bubble the asset class becomes the route by which this money is pumped into the system. As the banks are willing to lend more and more money to buy what is essentially the same product, they are injecting this money into the economy. The seller spends this on wages for builders, on taxes and professional fees, etc. Like an overflowing champagne fountain, the money pours out of the asset class and into the economy. It is 'earned' by people, but because there is more money than labour, these people can charge more and therefore earn more, and so on it goes. Yet people are never sure if they have more money because they are producing more or because there is more money generally. If the latter is true, then all goods will rise in price, a rise that is unrelated to any fundamental factor.

The ECB has only one mandate: to keep inflation at 2 per cent or less over the medium term. In its brief there is no reference to promoting economic growth or creating jobs, its sole concern is to ensure price stability, i.e. a low inflation rate. The reason for this is that Germany, the biggest economy in the EU and the one that was essential to the success of the Euro, knew from experience that a successful economy was based on strong, stable money that worked effectively and that if inflation was allowed to blunt the effectiveness of money, it would distort the economy and create inefficiencies.

---

3   Modern banks do this by other methods, but they are effectively creating money out of thin air.

There is no escaping the fact that a weak economy can create a weak currency, but it is also true that a weak currency can create a weak economy by damaging it with inflation. Germany knew that some other countries in the potential Euro area had 'weaker' currencies and was therefore at pains to ensure that history did not repeat itself. It knew that politicians in these 'weaker' countries would try to put pressure on the ECB to skew interest rates one way or another for political reasons, and that it therefore needed to prevent this by mandating that the control of inflation was the sole concern of the ECB. The ECB, and other central bankers, know from experience that inflation can be controlled by raising interest rates because a rise in interest rates removes money from the economy. This removal occurs in a variety of ways, including making borrowing more expensive and making saving more attractive. There are arguments about the effectiveness of such moves, but in general higher interest rates do slow inflation. These positive effects notwithstanding, politicians dislike independent central bankers because their rate rises can be unpopular with their citizens and can occur at the wrong time, i.e. just before an election.

Ultimately, Germany's concerns have been proved right. It became clear that certain governments, particularly France, were trying to pressurise the ECB to broaden its mandate beyond the control of inflation. Thus far these pressures have been deftly resisted, thereby increasing the credibility of the ECB as a truly independent central bank. Yet the ECB has one rather large dilemma in meeting its brief: it must set an interest rate for the whole Eurozone, even though that area is composed of diverse economies. In theory the economies should all converge, but in reality there is a wide spectrum of economies within the area and, without political unity, there is little chance of any real convergence. The reality is that when some countries are booming, some are 'busting' and others are in-between, nonetheless the ECB, in theory, looks at the Euro area as a single entity, using average figures. The difficulty is that the ECB governing council is composed of national representatives from the various countries, who always have one eye on their own country's situation and needs. (If this was not to be the case, then it would be staffed by a governing council made up of the most talented people drawn from the Euro land area, irrelevant of their country of origin, just like the Bank of England or the Federal Reserve.) This is the paradox at the heart of the EU: all of the Member States have one eye on their own country and one on the Euro area. This is evident in the one unusual aspect of the ECB: it does not release the minutes of the meetings where interest rates are set. This precludes the public from seeing who voted which way. (According to Jean-Claude Trichet, the current president of the ECB, they don't really need to vote, just reach a general consensus, but eventually there must be a vote if consensus cannot be reached.) It is not logical to assume that members can convince each other they are right. This leads on to the likely reason as to why there are no minutes released: if there were, it would explode the myth that rates are set for the Eurozone because it would become clear that each national member argues for what is best for his/her own country. The Bank of England and the Federal Reserve do release the minutes of such meetings precisely because they are not concerned about this issue.[4]

This national bickering aside, the regional differences have been contained very well to date and Monsieur Trichet has proven to be an able and impartial central banker. The question remains, however, as to how well the governing council will hold up in the face of a real crisis. What will happen if one of the Euro countries is in real difficulties or if there is stagflation or deflation or a serious economic crisis that forces the ECB to take tough decisions that do not have the unanimous consent of the Member States? That will be the ultimate test of the ECB. In short, the ECB needs to disprove one key argument that has always been directed towards it: that there has never been a successful monetary union that was not also a

---

4 The narrow national issue is further evidenced by the fact that the French almost sank the Euro project at its inception by holding out for the guarantee of a French head of the ECB, ultimately agreeing that the first head of the ECB, Wim Duisenberg, should resign after half his term was up and be replaced by a French candidate. This was an open secret and is, in fact, what happened. The Germans wanted the ECB in Frankfurt, near the Bundesbank, if for no other reason than to convince their own people that the ECB would—by some form of osmosis, presumably—be a successor to the popular Bundesbank. Either way, Ireland is just along for the ride, so we can only hope that the interest rate policy will suit us.

political union. All monetary unions have fractured because ultimately the control of money is political rather than economic. Ireland and England shared a common currency until 1979, but split because Ireland was more interested in tying itself to Europe via the old Exchange Rate Mechanism. Europe is not an entity like America, rather it is a collection of sovereign states, each with its own agenda, and in the medium to long term the test for the ECB is to avoid being drawn into political battles.

4. WHAT GOVERNMENTS ARE AND WHAT THEY SHOULD DO

We all complain about our politicians breaking election promises or raising taxes or not providing enough public services, but what exactly is a government supposed to do? The following scenario will help to explain it. Imagine you went to your local supermarket to do your weekly shopping. With list in hand, you approach the main entrance, only to be intercepted by an employee of the supermarket. He takes your list and your money and says he will do your shopping for you, that it's a new service. You wait for half-an-hour and he reappears, but you soon discover that there are a few problems. First, not all the goods you wanted were available in the store, so the helpful shopper decided to buy what he thought were good substitutes. Some of these substitutes you actually dislike, while others are more expensive than what you originally wanted to pay. He also considered three bottles of wine too extravagant, so he only got you one. Finally, not only is the total bill much higher than what you would normally have paid but your helpful shopper demands that you pay him 20 per cent on top as payment for his services. This sounds like a strange way to do business, but this is essentially how governments work, just on a larger scale.

Governments collect money, through taxation, from the people who have earned it. The government then spends that money on what it believes the citizens want it spent on or on what it believes the citizens need. Governments create nothing, they simply spend taxpayers' money in an attempt to increase the efficiency of the economy. This sounds logical enough, but there are a number of serious deficiencies with this model. Governments have to pay civil servants to collect the taxes, pay someone to account for the money, pay others to ensure that the taxpayers comply and ultimately pay to enforce the tax laws if the taxpayers do not pay what they owe. Once all that has been done, they must pay other Departments to spend the money collected and to account for the spending of it and investigate any misspending. It's a very costly way of spending money efficiently, since that is the objective of the exercise.

A government's real dilemma, however, is that it must decide how to spend the country's money. This is where the real inefficiencies take hold. Governments don't know what their citizens really want. Yes, they have a rough idea based on the broad set of policies they presented to the electorate that secured their election, but this is rarely helpful when it comes to micro-managing large blocs of taxpayers' money. Secondly, governments have proven time and again to be soft touches when it comes to pet political projects or convoluted schemes with which they have become enamoured. This is down to the primary focus of re-election, which requires that they remain popular with a majority of the people, especially in marginal constituencies. Ideally, that popularity should peak around election time, which can lead to 'election-fever economics', whereby money is allocated on the grounds of political gain, without consideration for best, most efficient use of funds. Governments also have a long history of involving themselves in areas where they shouldn't be operating, such as airlines, telecommunications, steel production, mining, forestry, hotels, car production … the list goes on and on. Governments usually become involved in such areas because these are 'strategic' industries and supposedly in the public interest. But in the end these enterprises usually become furnaces for taxpayers' money. The precedents are there to prove the point: conveyor belts of money were fed to state firms all over Europe without achieving even minimal returns. If they had been operating in the private sector, these firms would have prospered with competent management or else suffered the fate the free market inflicts on inefficient firms, with the labour and capital eventually being diverted to more worthy ends. When it's a state firm tottering on the brink, however, the usual response is to divert yet more funds to the lost cause.

Finally, most governments suffer from OPM syndrome: they spend Other People's Money with less care than they do their own. This explains why governments spend so much money on everything they buy compared to private citizens. For example, if you want to buy a flight to New York, you will search the internet and find the best value option, even if it means suffering a little inconvenience to save some money, such as taking an early morning flight. Governments, on the other hand, will buy the exact flight they want because it makes no difference to them—they are not really paying. Equally, if you want to buy a new computer, you will do some research before deciding on what you believe to be the best computer to suit your needs, and more often than not people make reasonably good decisions. By contrast, a government will hire a consultant to recommend which model to purchase, and it's quite likely a second consultant will be brought in or perhaps a committee formed to make sure that the first consultant is giving the best advice.

In the final analysis, governments usually understand little of what they are actually doing and therefore are easily led astray by salespeople and consultants. And on it goes, with the money raised through taxes slowly being whittled away, to no great effect. Vast bureaucracies grow up around the various government depart-ments, sapping more and more resources. Without the rigours of the free market and financial self-interest to guide them, govern-ments squander their citizens' hard-earned cash. Take, for example, the much-maligned public health service in Ireland, which now employs over 100,000 people and consumes every single penny of income tax and all the excise duty collected.[5] In spite of this massive funding, it is an accepted fact that it is a sub-par service. This is not because of the medical staff, but rather because there are cadres of administrators and managers, led by politicians, who have no strategic direction and are continuously fighting short-term fires. In short, then, governments are inefficient and waste resources. Which naturally raises the question of why we have governments at all? The answer is that we do need governments, but only efficient ones.

5   Statement of Exchequer Surplus/Deficit, Department of Finance, 31 August 2008.

Governments can do much good and a successful economy needs good governance, in fact a successful economy is totally dependent on good governance. Governments are the defining factor that separates us from more primitive societies, and a good government can multiply and leverage the work of its citizens. This is because there are many services that are vital to a nation's existence, but which private citizens simply cannot buy in the normal sense because they do not operate according to the normal market rules of supply and demand. The police force is a classic example of this. A citizen cannot buy police services as needed; instead, a police force is there to ensure the law is obeyed at all times. The police force must apply the law without fear or favour, whether the 'client' is rich or poor. As such, it cannot respond to signals from the market. It is one of the fundamental services that ensures a free society and also that the free market functions as it does. Other examples include the emergency services, environmental agencies, monopolies commission, public schooling, road-building, public healthcare, foreign policy, etc. In other words, citizens need their governments because the work of a government is essential to the good of society.

A good government creates a successful foundation from which its citizens can prosper and from which private business flourishes. A bad government interferes to such a degree that the market does not work and the economy eventually fails. On the one extreme were countries like the Soviet Union, where there was centralised planning of all services and the demand/supply signals from consumers were ignored. The government attempted to anticipate all of the needs of all of the people, but in the end there was no incentive for the public to excel at what they did because there was no personal gain in it for them. This was communism and it failed. On the other extreme are free-market economies like America, where the government performs the most basic public services and leaves the rest to the free market. This obviously works, broadly speaking, but it often leaves behind the weaker members of society and fails to develop many essential services, such as public transportation, outside of the main cities.

In Europe there is a spectrum of middle-way, 'social market' solutions, ranging from the more American style prevalent in the UK and Ireland (remember Mary Harney situating the country closer to Boston than Berlin) to the more interventionist style favoured in France. There is no ideal or correct solution. These are political decisions that depend on what the citizens of any given country demand, prefer and are used to. Democracy exists precisely to allow us all to make this choice. Nevertheless, it is clear that over the last two decades European governments have been attempting to bring in more of the American approach and reduce what they do. In the wake of the Second World War various governments became heavily involved in all areas of business, including mining, airlines, steel production, car production, telecommunications, etc. Much of this occurred by a process of nationalisation of already privatised industry by socialist-oriented governments that felt they were doing the right thing. By the 1980s, however, the folly of this route was exposed as growth faltered in the wake of US success and state enterprises consumed resources and distorted the market through protectionism. Governments—beginning with the Thatcher government—began a process of privatising (or re-privatising, as the case often was) these industries. This was a difficult and, in the case of the UK mining industry, a violent process as workers had become used to what were relatively highly paid and stable jobs. These high salaries and job stability were being paid for by other taxpayers, however, and this simply could not continue. This experience demonstrated yet again that the longer such enterprises are propped up by governments, the more difficult it is, socially and economically, to wean people off these industries.

Ireland pursued the privatisation path quite late compared to other countries and with varying degrees of success, yet it succeeded better than some other European countries. In Europe companies such as Alitalia, for example, have been haemorrhaging taxpayers' money for decades, but the Italian government lacked the ability to tackle the issue until 2008, and even then lost its nerve and poured more money into the company rather than let it go bankrupt and risk the ire of union members. In Ireland much the same has happened with 'privatised companies': in order to placate the unions, chunks of privatised enterprises were handed over to the workers, while in some cases, such as Aer Lingus, the government retained a large bloc of shares for reasons that were never fully clear. This created a quasi-privatised entity that still leaned on the state and ultimately cost taxpayers even more money.

In the 1990s Aer Lingus, whilst still technically a competent airline, had really become simply a benevolent fund for its employees. Machiavellian politicking ensured that world-class managers were lost from the airline prior to and after it was privatised. Aer Lingus now exists in a twilight world, like many quasi-business entities in Ireland: if it didn't exist, no one would create it, but because it does exist it is propped up by the state. There is little doubt that if Aer Lingus disappeared tomorrow, most Dublin, and Limerick, politicians would breathe a sigh of relief because in their clinics they would no longer have to deal with the problems it creates. The airline is still identified with the state and when flights or jobs are cut, it is the politicians who get complaints about it. In 2008, whilst it was a substantially slimmed-down version of its former self, Aer Lingus still faced the need to cut another €100 million in costs. One has to ask why it has taken so long to do this and whose €100 million have they been wasting year in and year out? If they could cut €100 million in costs in 2008, then why not in 2007? Or back in 2005? In the end, Aer Lingus will find it difficult to remain independent or viable with its current cost base. It is simply a relatively small airline with thirty-odd planes, a large cash reserve (being depleted) and one of its most valuable assets: legacy slots at London's Heathrow Airport. In short, Aer Lingus gives us an excellent example of what happens when governments get it wrong.

In the final analysis, a government can propel a country into the world class or it can condemn its citizens to penury. Governance is an art form, the essence of which is in knowing what to do, when to do it, doing it well and, critically, knowing exactly what not to do. What good governments should and should not do can be summed up in the following six points.

What Governments Should Do

1. Define the rules of how the socio-economic system functions and enforce these rules, but not actually take part in the game unless absolutely necessary.

2. Ensure that economic tools, such as money, do not create inflation or deflation and instead simply lubricate the economic exchange process.

3. Control the amplitude of the business cycle so as to avoid excessive peaks and troughs.

4. Provide social 'safety nets' for the unemployed and the disadvantaged to the degree the electorate wants, but not use the public services to become an 'employer of last resorts' and draw resources from the more productive private sector.

5. Ensure that there is a strong correlation between taxes collected and services provided, e.g. motor tax is spent on roads, PRSI is spent on social insurance, etc. Taxes should not become a mechanism to raise more money for the general aims of the government, but rather a process by which to achieve the stated aims of those taxes.

6. Ensure that the Budget is balanced so that debts are not passed on to future taxpayers. Deficits or surpluses are symptoms of governments that lack efficient control and forecasting mechanisms.

Chapter 3
The State of the Nation

Before we delineate the current state of play in Ireland, first let's think about where we started. Up until the late 1980s Ireland was widely regarded as an economic disaster zone, with crushing levels of unemployment, ongoing emigration and corruption in high places. The new era that was ushered in the 1990s came about due to a combination of economic and social factors: the liberalisation of the economy, an ending of endemic and open corruption, improvements in the infrastructure, transfer payments from the EU and a reduction in the corporate taxation rate. Once the path had been cleared, the economy began to grow rapidly, leading to a reduction in unemployment and a subsequent improvement in the government's finances, i.e. more money was being received into the Exchequer than was being paid out of it. The government used this surplus money to pay down the national debt, which released more money to the Exchequer in the long-term. The favourable economic conditions and the highly talented workforce attracted many international high-tech firms to Ireland, which further reduced unemployment and increased the overall disposable income circulating in the economy. Thus for the first time a virtuous circle was created of lower unemployment and higher taxation revenue.

The unprecedented success of the Irish economy attracted international attention. The phrase 'Celtic Tiger' was first used by

Kevin Gardiner of Morgan Stanley in 1994 in a report describing the burgeoning Irish economy. It was adapted from the term 'Asian Tigers', which was used to describe Asian economies that had experienced periods of rapid growth. With the new economic success came prosperity and more people had more disposable income. More disposable income meant that house prices began to rise as people competed to buy their desired houses—a natural free market phenomenon. People who had emigrated began to return to Ireland and those who might have emigrated did not, which in turn created even more natural demand for housing. Life was not perfect, but it was good and getting better. Irish society and economy was expanding quickly, and much of that growth, up to the end of 1999, was fundamentally sound and based on the efforts of the Irish workforce.

There was a larger economic event occurring in the economy, however, and this was Ireland's commitment to join the EMU and adopt the Euro. One European currency meant one European Central Bank, and that institution would set one interest rate for Europe. Interest rates are one of the main tools by which the Central Bank controls an economy. In very simple terms, central banks raise rates when they believe an economy is overheating and lower them when they wish to stimulate a sluggish economy. The basic rationale is that higher interest rates means that borrowing money is more expensive, therefore less borrowing occurs, which slows down expansion and limits inflation. It is somewhat of a blunt instrument, but interest rates can nonetheless have a very powerful effect and are therefore frequently employed by all central banks as a means of influencing the shape and flow of the economy.

With the advent of the single Eurozone, there would be one interest rate applicable for all the Euro economies and it would be handed down by the ECB. It was this that caused the Irish economy to come unstuck. The problem, ironically, was that the economy was booming and unemployment levels were dipping rapidly. In theory, the Irish Central Bank should have been holding interest rates steady or raising them. Yet as the date approached to join the EMU, 1 January 1999, the Irish Central Bank was forced to reduce interest rates substantially in order to converge with the lower rates being applied by the ECB. The American central banker William McChesney Martin once described the function of a central bank as being to take away the punch bowl just as the party was getting going.[1] What happened in Ireland in 1999, to extend the metaphor, was that the Central Bank was obliged to add even more alcohol to the punch bowl. In effect, it was required to over-stimulate the economy.

There is little doubt that the ECB understood that such problems could occur, but there was little it could do. The head of the ECB did warn the head of the Irish Central Bank about the threat of over-stimulation, but that was all he could do.[2] Realistically, it is likely that the ECB was not concerned by any potential economic problems within 1 per cent of the economic area; it was more focused on successfully launching the new Europe-wide currency. Nevertheless, the ECB did clearly warn all Member State governments that if they wanted the benefits of a common currency, there was a commensurate responsibility to control their economies by other means. By this it was recommending that individual governments should uses taxes and other policy instruments at their disposal to steer their economies safely through the EMU channel. This was not 'rocket science' by any means; the policies necessary to achieve this would have been easy to construct by an economist given the authority to do so.

In Ireland's case, this did not happen. The government pursued economic policies that further stimulated the economy by reducing taxes and letting the property market accelerate on foot of reduced interest rates. This was not modified by the interest rate policy pursed by the ECB in the early 2000s. In spite of the warning bells that had been sounded, the government never took the necessary steps to ensure that the lower rate policies did not distort the economy.

The consequences of the over-stimulation were already evident at the turn of the millennium as the economy started bloating outwards and straining the physical factors that limited it. At this stage the government should have applied the brakes with various

1   P. Navarro, *If it's Raining in Brazil, Buy Starbucks* (McGraw-Hill Professional, 2004), p.192.
2   *The Irish Times*, 19 May 1998.

fiscal measures. Instead the economy was effectively accelerated over the edge with a 'hope for the best' attitude. This was compounded by financial liberalisation, which saw the introduction of new credit instruments, such as those that 'released equity' (formerly known as re-mortgaging), 100 per cent mortgages, interest-only mortgages, forty-year mortgages and the plethora of other instruments with which people could indebt themselves. At the pinnacle of the Celtic Tiger unapplied-for loans were sent by post to pre-approved candidates, often to parents encouraged to indebt themselves to provide a deposit to facilitate their children assuming their own mortgage. The number of new products by which people could indebt themselves was truly impressive. Credit was available on a 'whim', according to the head of the Money and Budgeting Service (MABS).[3] In fact, bank employees reported that they had set targets of loan volume;[4] the banks were literally forcing credit into the economy. The economy and the financial institutions should have been tamed, growth should have been shaped and controlled so as to benefit people, but these things simply did not happen. The party was allowed to rage on and as a result now, in the throes of the mother of all hangovers, there is a bitter realisation that the over-reliance on credit is going to prove our downfall.

By 2000 the signs of overheating were evident everywhere and parts of the national infrastructure were straining at the seams. Dublin Airport became chaotic and overcrowded; it simply was not designed to cope with the number of travellers who now began using it to enter and leave the country. Similarly, the streets were flooded with new cars, which created traffic chaos. The economy was allowed to expand too quickly: cars could be imported rapidly, but roads could not be built at the same speed. This might sound like gloomy economist-speak, that we should have put a dampener on the 'good times', but it's not that. The point is that those tasked with leading the country should have been taking the wider, long-term view. The government should have expanded its services commensurate with the private consumption that was occurring, but it failed to do so.

3   *Sunday Times*, 19 October 2003.
4   'Liveline', RTÉ Radio 1.

THE IMMIGRATION EFFECT

There was another way, too, in which the government failed to perform its duty properly, and that was by allowing uncontrolled mass immigration to distort the economy still further and compound the problems already created. As the Celtic Tiger roared, hundreds of thousands of people poured into the country from abroad, all seeking work and a chance to improve their lives. Initially the influx was partially composed of returning migrants, who had left during the doldrums of the 1980s, and what were called 'asylum-seekers', many of whom were in fact economic migrants. Regardless of what tag you give them, this latter group have contributed enormously to the Irish economy. Some were drawn by the fact that children born in Ireland obtained residency and an Irish passport, which automatically bestowed residency rights on their parents. There was nothing wrong with exploiting such 'loopholes'; the Irish

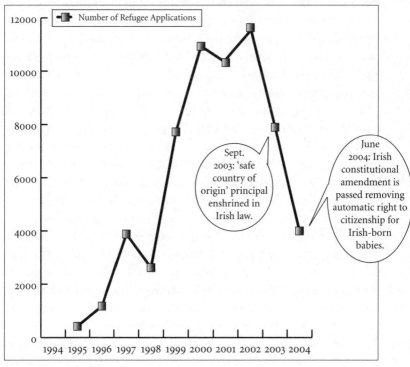

Fig. 11: Applications for asylum in Ireland, 1994–2004. Once the government takes the appropriate action it can control and shape its immigration policy.
(Data source: Office of the Refugee Applications Commissioner)

have being doing so for many years in other countries. But it demonstrated the need for a structured immigration policy rather than the less structured procedures that were in place. The reason they were less structured was that Ireland never had to deal with a real, large-scale desire by other people to migrate to the country. The absence of any policy or management of what was contributing to our economic success keeps arising in relation to this period. Eventually, two legal amendments were put in place to limit this form of immigration (Fig. 11).

Since 2004 the migrant population has largely been composed of legal immigrants from other EU Member States as the Employment Permits Bill, enacted in April 2003, granted free access to the ten EU accession states from May 2004.[5] The economy was growing so fast that it needed labour to do the jobs Irish people could not or would no longer do. This only compounded the fundamental problem, however, as the new arrivals entered into an economy that could barely service its own population adequately. The immigration in itself created more demand for housing and ancillary services and presented complex legal problems, for example enforcement issues against foreign drivers. This immigration stalled somewhat after 2002, but then surged after 2004, as can be seen in the graph below.

The issue was not the immigration, which in many ways enriched Irish society, but rather the fact that there was no clear immigration strategy in place nor any method of enforcing one. Everything was being done 'on the fly'. The level of immigration that was occurring required experienced social management because it had an enormous impact on the economy. At the stroke of a pen, in 2004, the government had given 40 million people the right to work in Ireland[6] without any analysis of what might be needed in preparation for this or any selection process. Compare Ireland to Australia, where there are strict guidelines stipulating who is allowed in, based on economic needs. The Australian Minister for Immigration and Citizenship, Senator Chris Evans, said in a speech recently that 'Strong border security and humane and risk-based detention policies … are both hallmarks of a mature, confident and independent

---

5   www.oireachtas.ie.
6   Employment Permits Bill 2003.

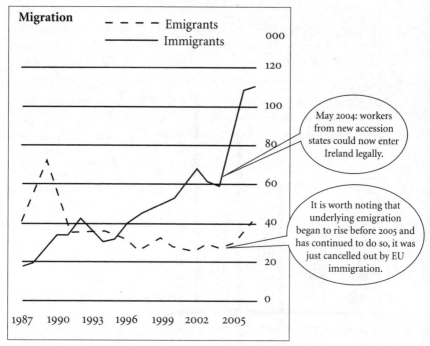

Fig. 12: Immigration to Ireland between 1987 and 2005. (Source: CSO)

nation.'[7] It is not a question of racism, but of deciding what skills are necessary for the betterment of a particular country. Accordingly, most other EU countries strictly limited access for a number of years to allow a managed policy of immigration that would benefit the native population as well as the incoming population.

There is little doubt that Ireland should have been bringing in people from all over the world, with selected skills, who planned to make a home here permanently. The lack of such an approach was clear in a 'snap shot' picture of a FÁS office on one day in 2008. It found that 52 per cent of those seeking employment services were non-nationals from ninety-four different countries. Yet at that time FÁS Director-General Rody Molloy was arguing that Ireland needed 500,000 more immigrants. The inference is that there was no policy in this area at all, just a short-term, myopic view of the situation.

7   www.minister.immi.gov.au.

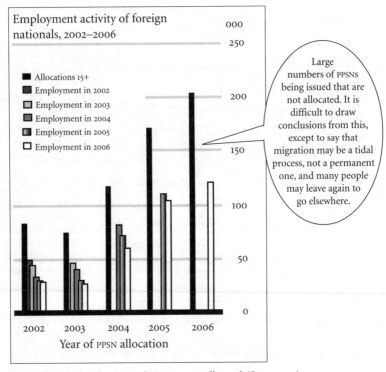

Fig. 13: Employment figures in relation to PPSNs allocated. (Source: CSO)

Where has that led? A suggestion has now been mooted that we pay the unemployed immigrants to leave.[8]

Furthermore, only 50 per cent of those who were given a PPSN (Personal Public Service Number) in 2006 were in employment in 2006.[9] This does not mean they were doing nothing, they may have been working illegally or in employment that was not 'insurable'; tax law implications aside, this is still indicative that they were needed. But then again, they may not have been working because they did not have the right skills or, indeed, they may even have left the country. This is the crux of the problem: we simply do not know the answers because there is no mechanism by which to assess accurately the volume of people in the economy, let alone what they are doing.

8   *Evening Herald*, 5 September 2008.
9   Finfacts.ie.

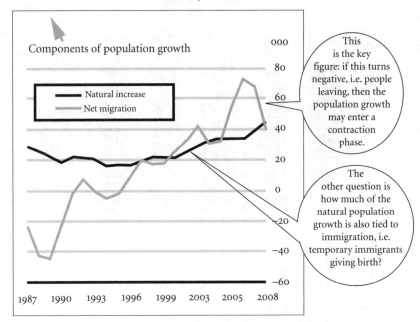

Fig. 14: Breakdown of population growth in Ireland between 1987 and 2008. (Source: CSO)

In the Central Statistics Office (CSO) publication on migration to Ireland,[10] the word 'estimate' or 'estimated' is used twenty-six times, the document is even entitled, *Population and Migration Estimates*. This means that even those with their finger on the pulse cannot accurately tell us what is going on in our population figures. What we can say is that by 2007 Ireland had the fastest-growing population in Europe for some years[11] and that two-thirds of that population growth was the result of immigration, although that could be an underestimation as migrants from previous years would also have been having children. It is simply too difficult to pin down what has been and is happening, although the preliminary figures available for 2009 do show that the trend has turned down and the population may already be contracting. How far the tide now turns is also difficult to tell. In 2006, when the last census was compiled, there were 420,000 foreign nationals living in the country[12]—how sure can we be that these people will not leave as the economy declines?

10 www.cso.ie/releasespublications/documents/population/current/popmig.pdf.
11 CSO.
12 CSO.

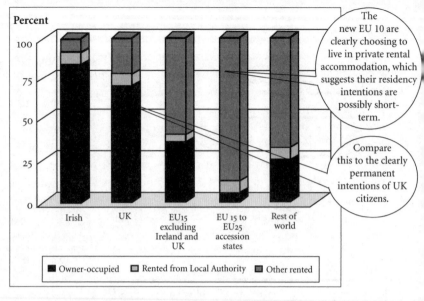

Fig. 15: Accommodation figures. (Source: CSO)

This is the biggest short-term issue regarding immigration: the question of permanence. A society cannot function if hundreds of thousands of people join the economy and then leave abruptly a few years later. Just as schools, hospitals and other social infrastructure cannot be built overnight, neither can they be dismantled quickly. If the immigrant population, who are embedded in our communities, contributing to the economy and to society in general, decides to move on, it will leave a gaping hole in every facet of Irish society. This is exactly why other countries have well-thought-out immigration policies—to avoid this sort of adverse reaction. In Ireland, however, where no such mechanisms were put in place, there are simply too many variables to allow a reliable prediction of future population changes. What seems most likely is that the population rise will slow substantially, then possibly begin to decline as the economic downturn continues to slide. This is a crucial question, but when all that's available is anecdotal and out-dated statistical evidence, it is impossible to divine the answer. In 2008/9 circumstances changed so fast, it served only to underline how inadequate the available statistics are. For example, Fig. 15 highlights the fact that many immigrants are living in rented accommodation versus owner-occupier, particularly the new 'EU 10' immigrants.

In conclusion, one can say that immigration was in large part what fuelled the boom from 2004 onwards. While it is almost impossible to measure exactly—researchers are forced to rely on peripheral, unrelated statistics to get a feel for what was and is occurring, such as the RyanAir route pattern and where and when it is cancelling flights—it is arguable that it was just unfortunate happenstance for Ireland that at exactly the wrong moment, when we least needed it, we permitted vast numbers of people to come to the country legally. While these people wanted to come to Ireland and contributed hugely to Irish society, this influx gave a shot of unhelpful adrenalin to an economy that badly needed to stabilise, not expand. It is also arguable that had immigration been exhausted, the bubble would have deflated sooner and with less damage to the overall economy. Although it is equally possible that other, non-EU labour would have been found to fuel the boom or it would have happened anyway via illegal immigration, as happens regularly in the UK and the US. Should the tide of immigration turn backwards now, the population will contract dramatically, which will deliver a knock-out punch to Ireland, economically, socially and psycho-logically. Most of all, it will puncture the hope that Ireland has weathered the worst of the storm because the Celtic Tiger was based on an expanding population. When that cornerstone is taken away, the whole edifice starts to teeter again.

THE EMIGRATION EFFECT

Migration figures are made of immigration minus emigration figures. The focus thus far has been on immigration because the numbers have been so large. However, the figures in the migration graph (Fig. 12) clearly demonstrate that emigration has been rising since 2005. By 2008 it had hit a near twenty-year high as over 43,000 workers left the economy.[13] This story was 'below the radar' because the immigration figures disguised it. In terms of destinations, Australia and New Zealand were the countries of choice for the majority of these emigrants. Apart from the sheer volume of people

13 CSO.

choosing to leave, the most perturbing aspect of this for the Irish economy is the fact that, unlike the 1980s, the profile of today's emigrants is couples in their thirties and forties with children. One possible explanation for this is the level of opportunity available elsewhere. As an emigration consultant noted: 'New Zealand has reported high demand for both skilled and unskilled workers, including agricultural and fishery workers, labourers and freight handlers as well as administrators and managers.' In other words, it is not just professionals who are in demand around the world, which might make emigration attractive for some people. There is another factor, however, that makes it positively irresistible.

A large, comfortable family home in a middle-class area in New Zealand can be had for €250,000, while any detached family home in most areas of Dublin could have sold for at least €750,000–€1,000,000, capital gains tax free as the primary residence, over the last number of years. If people thought about it—and many obviously did—the potential was enormous. Couples who bought their home ten or fifteen years ago and whose mortgages were almost non-existent could sell their home in Ireland, emigrate to New Zealand and buy a better house for €250,000, and still have €500,000 left over to put in the bank. Working through the figures, it becomes even more attractive. One could have gotten 7 per cent[14] deposit on money in New Zealand, which would equate to NZ$70,000 in interest per year on the remaining €500,000 left over from selling the house in Dublin. This equates to a good professional salary in New Zealand,[15] where the cost of living is much lower than in Ireland. It would create a very nice cushion for the new emigrants, or possibly even a reasonable retirement income.

Scenarios like this explain why emigration hit a twenty-year high. Non-professional people with average salaries could literally alter their lifestyles forever by selling and emigrating. Even better, if your house was worth €1–€2 million, then you could have retired on the income of a solicitor in New Zealand and bought a palatial home just from selling a decent home in a desirable area in Dublin. These sorts of comparisons not only elucidate the emigration figures, they

14 Source: RaboPlus Bank, New Zealand.
15 www.emigratenz.org.

also highlight the irrationality of house prices during the Celtic Tiger years. Contrasting the information taken from one estate agent in Auckland and one in Dublin, you could sell a reasonably modest home in Dublin and move to New Zealand to buy a substantial house and invest residual income at 7 per cent to generate NZ$224,000 per year, every year, in perpetuity.[16] It's very easy to see why emigration had become a viable option for thousands of Irish people.

THE FINAL MIGRATION EFFECT

In the final analysis, it is the question of permanence that is the key issue in terms of migration. As we have already discussed, it is very difficult to get solid information to allow accurate prediction on this score, but one way to figure out the possible trend is to examine the intentions of the largest bloc of recent immigrants to Ireland: Polish people. According to CSO figures, there are approximately 65,000 Poles living in Ireland.[17] These highly talented, well-educated migrants were welcomed into the economy, but will they stay now that the economy is faltering?

A Polish newspaper asked this very question and studied blog sites to try to ascertain the intentions of its departed population.[18] A few sample comments reflect the general view of migrants in England and Ireland: 'if this keeps up, I'm staying, unless things start going wrong here, then I'll look for another place' … 'You just got to be where it's good. It's good here now, so why should you move?' With the Polish economy improving, some had another strategy: 'I'm coming back [to Poland] in March, because I want to give it a try myself, and if my business succeeds, I'll stay in Poland, and if it doesn't, I'm back in the UK within 8–9 months tops.' What these examples demonstrate is that for many Poles—and by inference other nationalities—migration is economic, therefore if things turn down, many might leave. This is confirmed by the temporary nature of the 'new EU 10' living arrangements (see Fig. 15) and also by the

16 Obviously one would have to allow for inflation, but there is no point in complicating matters.
17 This is the official figure; the real figure is likely to be higher.
18 www.polishworkers.pl/polishworkers/1,60747,4916646.html.

fact that 90 per cent of Poles came to Ireland after 2004,[19] when it was legally possible.

We don't know how many or when, but it seems clear that a high percentage of the immigrant population will move on if the Irish economy nosedives. It is a vicious economic circle: if things get worse, migrants might leave; if migrants leave, things will get worse because they will vacate property and remove demand from the economy. The vast majority of this section of the population is living in private rented accommodation, which was no doubt bought by investors. The more people leave, the more vacant property will be pushed onto an already laden market. The whole house of cards depends on population growth, but if the economy contracts, it is likely population figures will do likewise, compounding all the problems and digging the hole still deeper.

The government's role in this should have been one of monitoring and effective planning, but instead immigration was misread as a permanent mass migration that would continue. As a result, it was erroneously factored into formulas to project house prices or the economy ever upwards. What now has to be accepted and understood is that this flow of people can be reversed, at huge cost to the Irish economy. The figures from the CSO are suggestive of this: emigration rose and immigration fell in 2008, whilst net growth in the population is slowing.[20] If this continues, then in one to two years the population will begin to contract again. The prognostications of fundamental demographic demand made in 2006 are simply inaccurate now.

The government must bear responsibility for not checking the flow of immigration in any way. By failing to establish any meaningful controls or measures, it allowed an already over-stimulated economy to be further distorted—it was like a shot of adrenalin to an already exerted athlete. The more the economy expanded, the more immigrants arrived, with 122,000 coming in the six months prior to the census in April 2006.[21] But it was all an illusion—the house of cards was already starting to sway, but no one

19 CSO.
20 CSO.
21 'Census reveals extent of migration to towns,' *The Irish Times*, 13 July 2007.

was paying any attention. Now, as the world faces a recession that looks bleak indeed, the Irish economy may be hit a blow that could have been avoided: a quick drop in population leading to a severe drop in demand across the board, which will have a significant impact on house prices and indeed on all elements right across the economy. At a time like this, one begins to wish fervently that the government had played its cards right.

THE MULTIPLIER EFFECT

The effect of inward migration on the economy in the mid-2000s cannot be underestimated: it not only encouraged the building of more residential property but also put great pressure on an already inadequate infrastructure. Of course, the higher property prices rose based on false assumptions about demand, the less the rises had to do with economic reality. People bought property because prices were rising; prices were rising because people were buying property. The economic facts were stretched to fit the new 'utopia' of Celtic Tiger economics, assuring punters that all was well. Many economic commentators needed to provide good explanations as to what was occurring because it was their banks who were lending the money and their auctioneering firms who were profiting from the sales. These commentators most certainly believed what they were predicting, there is no suggestion of anything else, but they were wrong, and they were wrong at the worst possible time.

There is nothing particularly unusual about all this—history shows that the peak of every economic bubble sees the most confident predictions. There were some notable exceptions to this rule, however, such as Rossa White of Davy Stockbrokers, who wrote an excellent article in 2006[22] questioning much of the pricing fundamentals in the property market and warning that it had become a 'frenzy'. White described as 'fundamentally unsound' the arguments being used by estate agents, who were encouraging buy-to-let investors to focus on the potential for capital appreciation rather than income. He stated that 'The evidence summarised ... refutes the theory that supply shortages are leading to rocketing prices in desirable areas.' He accurately concluded that 'property is

22 'Davy on the Irish Economy', Davy Stockbrokers, 29 March 2006.

a risky asset, like equities, corporate bonds and commodities. Net yields of 1.5%, which are commonplace in Dublin, look ridiculous compared with a risk-free rate of 3.5% on ten-year gilts' and that 'fundamentals suggest ... an adjustment in prices, rather than rents, that will eventually bring valuations down to more realistic levels'. White was a lone voice against a swelling chorus of extravagant promises, although, following the Persian maxim that 'success has a thousand fathers and failure is a bastard child', I suspect that in a couple of years time you will not be able to find anyone who said it was a good idea to buy property in 2006/7.

Where Ireland goes from here will be discussed in detail later, but suffice to say that the government has sailed the country, in a sub-standard, leaking vessel, into the greatest economic storm ever to hit the globe. The Celtic Tiger, if it ever existed, disappeared around the turn of the century and the country gorged on cheap credit. It wasn't an economic strategy, it was a cul-de-sac. Whilst boasting that we were now a rich, competitive country, the truth is that we were carrying excess weight, so to speak, and becoming uncom-petitive. It is at the peak of this economic obesity that the country is now being asked to run an economic marathon that demands high levels of stamina and preparedness. Unlike other booms, in this case the country literally risks economic bankruptcy and a loss of fiscal sovereignty. The responsibility for this falls squarely at the feet of the Irish government.

Chapter 4

The Government's Role

I t's a question that is repeated often, on radio, in pubs, in homes, in newspaper articles, in blogs—how did the government fail to improve the general quality of life in this country when it had billions of Euro at its disposal to do so? Why have we ended up pretty much back where we started in economic terms, with our economic independence severely under threat?

Examining the circumstances in which Ireland found itself, it is difficult to pinpoint where the rational economic growth stopped and the irrational growth began. This tends to be the case with bubbles, it is tricky to disentangle events and say that one phase stopped here or one started there because rarely is there one definitive point. Nonetheless, we shall try to do so.

If we define the Celtic Tiger as rapid growth driven by an export-led boom, then the Celtic Tiger ended with the slow-down in 2001/2[1] and credit took over as an important driver in the economy. National personal debt levels rose from €39 billion in 2000 to €134 billion in 2006, and all other types of debt followed suit, rising rapidly during this period. Debt was now being used to fund the property market and a boom in consumer goods. Ireland had gone from being a productive economy to one built on debt, which

---

1 'Fruit of the boom years squandered', *The Irish Times*, 20 November 2007.

should have triggered the alarm for economic commentators. They seemed oblivious to it, however, instead focusing solely on rising property prices, which in turn made people feel as if they were wealthier and encouraged more property transactions. The attitude was a casual and careless one, as the *Irish Times* pointed out: 'The likelihood is that we will continue on our merry way, aware that our houses are probably overvalued but accepting it. Buyers will just load up the borrowing wheelbarrow and buy their dream home in the expectation that, in a few years, it will be worth a lot more. And why should they think otherwise?'[2]

Property had become so grossly overvalued that some buyers were stretching themselves beyond the point of financial pain, certain that if they did not buy a property now, they would never own one because the prices would keep rising. Furthermore, incentives like 'equity release' products allowed a person to write a cheque and have it subsumed into his mortgage. These financial products allowed people to go on a holiday or buy a car today, but the repayments might stretch over twenty to thirty years. In other words, the boom was compressing more and more money into the current timeframe from the future periods, and the cash-happy consumers were ignoring the fact that it would all have to be paid off, presumably long after the object borrowed for was gone. This was financial recklessness of the highest order on a personal level, but the wider impact was that the increased money supply caused prices to continue rising, keeping the whole vicious circle turning. When too much money chases too few fixed goods it results in widespread inflation, which is exactly what happened in Ireland as prices floated upwards on a tide of borrowed cash.

Ireland had become the most indebted nation in Europe[3] and yet nobody stopped to ask the obvious, simple question: why do we need to borrow so much money? A successful economy should make its citizens wealthy without forcing them to resort to personal borrowing. In a successful economy, no one should have to borrow heavily to partake in society nor be required to rely on the intangible, transitory valuation of their home as the basis of their

2 'Bubble intact despite high house prices', *The Irish Times*, 18 November 2005.
3 As measured by the ratio of personal debt to GNP.

wealth. Of course, the fatal flaw in economic theory is the human being, who is capable of acting in his own worst interests and disobeying all the principles once money enters the equation. As more and more people appeared to become wealthier and wealthier, many fell victim to social pressure to keep up and they did so by borrowing. Often, the borrowing was used to fund speculative schemes, by which the borrower planned to become rich and get 'his' slice of the cake. This is borne out by the fact that speculation was reaching reckless levels. It is now evident that people were borrowing money not only to buy speculative property but also to buy shares in property investment funds.[4] Borrowing money to buy shares—especially at an all-time high—is a sure recipe for financial disaster. In doing so, the borrower exposes himself to enormous risks of rising interest rates and falling prices on the underlying investment, which is exactly what happened. This was in turn compounded by the fact that many of the funds imposed long waiting periods or onerous penalties on withdrawing. Therefore the quoted price on these funds is pointless—why have a price if you cannot realise the cash?

Still others were pressured by family and friends to stop paying 'dead money', i.e. rent, and get in quick before housing became completely unaffordable.[5] This led to a sense of panic, which led people to take out more onerous mortgages in order to get on the 'ladder', such as interest-only or 100 per cent mortgages. There was an incredible level of self-delusion in all this: taking out an interest-only mortgage to buy an apartment that could fall substantially in value and locking yourself into it even as your lifestyle changes, e.g. children arrive, is a far more dangerous situation than the oft referred to 'dead money' being spent on rent. When interest rates start to rise, repayments on the mortgage also rise, which simultaneously drives down the 'value' of the property. Thus you end up paying more for something that is worth less and less, and yet cannot even begin to pay down the capital amount owed

---

4   'Property throw away the keys', *Sunday Tribune*, 31 August 2008.
5   I always wondered at the logic of such statements: who exactly did people expect was going to be purchasing property when it arrived at the point where 'no one could afford it'?

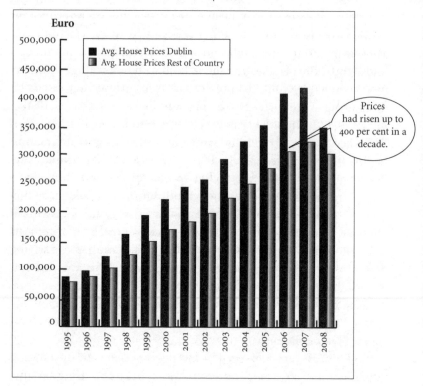

Fig. 16: House price trends between 1996 and 2008. (Data source: DEHLG)

because you are struggling to keep up the increased interest bill. It is impossible to extricate oneself from this and 'move up the property ladder' as planned because to do so would require selling the apartment for the original asking price, which has now become impossible. So while you may have gotten your foot on the first rung of the property ladder, there it will stay, firmly glued, for the foreseeable future.

Investors and consumers colluded in chasing prices upwards with various property-related schemes. In a classic asset bubble pattern, the rising prices attracted more buyers, eager to get in on the action. Increasing prices meant increasing speculative interest, which reinforced the pattern. The two main drivers of the asset bubble were firmly in place, fear and greed—the fear of one set of people that they would never own a home, the greed of another set of people to make a quick profit from the rising prices.

Looking back on it now, from the vantage point of the economic mess we find ourselves in 2009, it all seems quite incredible. A staggering level of national resources was being diverted into house-building. In 2004 80,000 units were built, and this figure would rise to close to 100,000 units before the peak. This volume was defended by figures suggesting that we were simply 'catching up' with the European housing stock, which seemed a persuasive argument. But if it was a simple correction, why did we have to indebt ourselves so much to do it? The impression one got was that there were people aimlessly wandering the streets of Ireland, homeless, earnestly waiting for a house to be built for them to live in. In the short term the irrationality of building such a huge volume of houses was explained away with spurious arguments, including that our population was growing permanently. The graph above shows that this was blind optimism. The house-building figures stand out in comparison to most other countries experiencing similar bubbles, such as Spain and the UK, and was clearly out of control. Nonetheless the government was still providing the tax breaks that encouraged more construction.

By 2006/7 the asset bubble was feeding on itself: developers were building houses and apartments in anticipation of more migrants arriving; migrants were arriving only because of the economic activity produced by the building industry. Even worse, the national frenzy was now being exported as the Irish started buying property all over the world, their pipe dreams funded by eager Irish financial institutions. Those properties bought by private individuals were often described as holiday homes, but if that was the case, why did the marketing literature keep referring to capital appreciation? Who would care about capital appreciation if a purchase was for enjoyment reasons? And who would risk their primary residence by re-mortgaging it to buy a holiday home?

I suspect that in many cases 'holiday homes' provided a convenient figleaf to allow people to engage in a little speculation. The economics of buying a foreign holiday home in the first place are questionable—what do you do with the other forty-six weeks of the year? Who maintains it? Who ensures that it is secure? Conveniently, those selling the homes offered management services

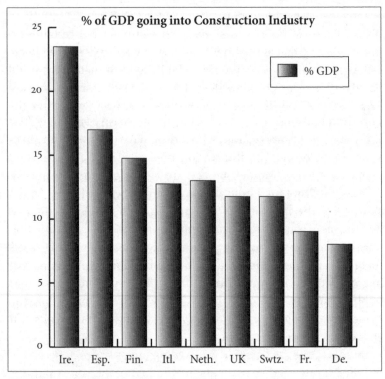

Fig. 17: Percentage of GDP allocated to the construction industry during the boom. (Data source: Euroconstruct)

and various rental guarantees, etc., but if it was such a wonderful investment, why didn't they keep it for themselves? Why were property developers suddenly seized with a socialist conscience? To be fair, some advertisements were quite up-front about their intentions and did not bother with the 'holiday home' charade. At the peak of the boom, people were encouraged to buy property in countries they may never even have visited, such as India, and about which they knew even less. The urge was to make 'easy money' and catch the 'next wave' upwards, where it was assumed property must be cheap because it was cheap compared to Ireland—but then, almost everywhere was cheap compared to Ireland. Rental properties are difficult to manage at the best of times, but purchasing apartments in countries a long way from Ireland, both spatially and legally, is extremely challenging indeed. Many such purchasers are already regretting the wisdom of such decisions. They are coming to realise that their 'investments' were pure gambling, but certainly no one was saying that at the time. Ordinary people, PAYE workers, were encouraged to play games of financial Russian Roulette that could have very serious consequences, but it seemed normal because everyone else was doing it, too. For some reason, even after the lessons imparted by the Telecom Éireann shares fiasco, people saw mass participation as a comforting reassurance. In another instance, at one of the ubiquitous foreign property shows that characterised the boom years, it was advertised that credit cards could be used to pay for deposits on foreign properties. And how was the final amount to be paid? Easy, by 'releasing equity' from your personal residence, i.e. re-mortgaging your family home.[6]

The property market had become a casino and the financial institutions were facilitating the purchase of the chips. Banking had gone from being a fundamental process of taking deposits and lending them to industry for the purchase of homes, to lending more and more money to 'shoot craps' at the property table. This is something Irish banks have come to regret, but I think it is their depositors who will ultimately come to regret it even more.

WHAT OF THE REAL ECONOMY?
It is crucial to remember that those speculating in property at this time were in the minority, as were those borrowing beyond their means. The Foreign Direct Investment (FDI) that Ireland had attracted in the first instance was still yielding returns, and these companies were expanding and being joined by other companies. There was a significant element of the economy that could be called the 'Celtic Tiger': the economy was doing well and many people were truly prosperous. The government was running a huge surplus, so much so that it could even afford to save money in the National Pension Reserve Fund (NPRF). However, as with the sub-prime crisis in America, the actions of a minority were affecting the majority.

A sizeable number of people were engaging in speculation and other activities, and were being encouraged to do so by the financial institutions that were funding the big gamble. The actual extent of

6 'Cheaper destinations draw Irish investors', *The Irish Times*, 16 September 2004.

this group will be revealed as the bubble unravels. Whatever its size, the actions of this group were undermining the long-term health of the economy in a number of ways.

First, the incessant demand for property was sucking in resources that could have been deployed elsewhere. The building of hundreds of thousands of housing units, hotels, shopping centres, etc., was hijacking resources from building and infrastructure. There is only so much a country can physically produce, no matter how quickly it expands. Therefore, expansion should be controlled so that it occurs on a slow, pro-rata scale, incorporating houses, social facilities, roads, transportation, etc. For growth to be viable and sustainable, the mix has to be right from the start, which should be the government's job.

Secondly, the banks became laden down with property-related debt to a degree that affected their viability; in some cases, financial institutions had 80 per cent of their loan books in property. The long-term effect of this will be discussed later, but it is unlikely to be a positive outcome and I suspect that more financial institutions will fail and need to be nationalised and rescued by the government, just as has happened at Anglo Irish Bank. However, this 'solution' simply shifts the problems to the government and, ultimately, outside funds will be needed if the banking system is to continue in a similar form. When the Credit Crunch hit the international markets, the Irish banks were caught very far out on the proverbial limb and the consequences of this will be felt for well over a decade to come in the banking system. The Irish banking system survives by virtue of the state guarantee issued by the government, but the government is simply the next domino and it must find cash to recapitalise the banks. Whoever does this will likely extract a high price.

Thirdly, human resources were also drawn into the construction frenzy. Those who might have continued in third-level education or trained in other fields were attracted to construction because of the highly paid jobs available. It is likely that a number of people trained as bricklayers, plumbers, carpenters, etc., on the basis that construction would boom forever. With any fall in construction, they will be unemployed and will have to retrain in other fields, or might simply choose to emigrate to where their skills are in demand.

Fourthly, incomes across the board were increased by the general increase in prosperity that was tied to the property boom and its related borrowing—the rising tide that lifts all boats, as the pundits love to say. A person might be selling paintings and believe he has nothing to do with the construction industry, but trace the money a couple of steps back and it is very likely to be causatively linked to construction and/or the taxes generated by construction. Although many did not realise it, the credit generated by the building industry permeated every corner of the economy.

Lastly, and most significantly, the government became dependent on revenue generated by the property boom. This is painfully evident in the speed with which the government's budgetary position eroded following the fall-off in the number of new houses built. Nothing else indicates so clearly to what extent the government was relying on the property bubble. The government spread this largesse around in give-away Budgets, with this money seeping into the economy and giving lie to the illusion of permanent wealth, its recipients all the while unaware that it was connected to construction or anything unstable. If the government gives some form of income to an individual, be it a salary to a civil servant, a grant or some kind or a tax-break, one tends to assume that it is reliable and stable. The key understanding regarding the next five years is that nothing is stable, nothing is secure and everything you thought of as such you must revaluate.

WHERE WAS THE GATEKEEPER?
Looking at all the information and statistics, the obvious question is: where was the government in all this, why didn't our experts and ministers recognise the problem that was growing and take steps to avert disaster? It seems the gatekeeper had abandoned his post, and the barbarians flooded in.

In the heady days of 2006, predictions abounded and few questioned the long-term sustainability of what was occurring because few attempted to assess the level of immigration or motives driving it. For example, in 2006 Goodbody Stockbrokers predicted that completions in 2008 would be 70,000–80,000, yet barely two years later the real figure was revealed to be 45,000, with the same

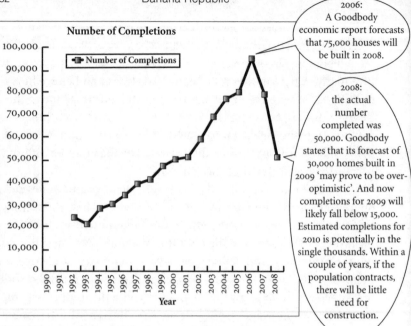

Fig. 18: House completions in Ireland, 1992–2008. (Data source: DEHLG)

economist admitting that his revised estimate of 30,000 for 2009 might not be accurate (see Fig. 18). It is now clear that house-building for 2009 might stand at 15,000 or even lower. This was the informed opinion of an experienced economist, working for one of the largest stockbrokers in the country, with access to all the analytical data available, yet his forecast was very wide of the mark. Why? Because of the volatility of what was the fundamental driver of the economy.

As the economy moved into 2007 and 2008, many commentators and government ministers simply did not seem to grasp that the government finances had become tied to the construction sector. Such misunderstanding is not unusual; it has been seen during previous, similar euphoric investment episodes. What happens is that economic diversification disappears and is replaced by a presumed diversification. It is presumed that the economy can be pigeon-holed, with a section for construction, a section for services, a section for car sales, a section for retail and so on. But during Ireland's bubble, many of these barriers, as we will see, were removed and everything became tied to property. The government failed to understand this, which is why the surplus evaporated after the housing market went into decline. The speed of its decline is quite staggering, however: in 2006 the government had a €2.3 billion surplus over what it spent compared to what it took in; by 2009 the predicted deficit was close to €20 billion.[7]

The government and many commentators seemed at a loss to understand how this could happen. The catch-all phrase 'economic downturn' was repeated endlessly so as to give it a name, but it wasn't an explanation. The 'Credit Crunch', international conditions and rate rises were all paraded before the public, in the hope that nobody would peel away the layers of labels and enquire about the root cause. But it does not take too much analysis to find out why the government finances imploded.

At base, the balance sheet was out of kilter. Outgoings were too high because the government had let spending get out of control. On the income side, taxation revenues declined with the fall in house-building and the general decline in economic activity this precipitated. The construction boom was credit-fuelled and much of what had been defined as 'growth' was simply borrowed money being pushed through the economy. This was taxed, which produced the surpluses. Once the torrent of building activity began to falter, many rivers downstream were slowly starved as the cash drained away.

THE 'BIG BANG'
Like all property bubbles, the illusion could not be sustained forever. It is difficult to define precisely what caused the bubble to eventually burst, but it was likely a combination of rising interest rates and a slow realisation that many middle-aged people in Dublin could retire on the sale of their houses (and I'm sure some did). But if a specific point along the timeline has to be identified, then I think the publication of the 2006 census figures in 2007 was a significant turning-point, allied with rising interest rates making deposits more attractive. The census report contained one simple yet telling

---

7 Such is the current volatility of the situation that the final deficit is very difficult to predict.

statistic that was devoid of any hype and that clashed jarringly with conventional wisdom: 266,000[8] housing units were vacant on census night in 2006. Even allowing for those who claimed that 20 per cent of these were holiday homes, it was still a figure well over 210,000 vacant housing units. It was like the little boy pointing at the naked emperor and stating the obvious. To be honest, 210,000 empty units might not be abnormal in a society like ours, but this was at the height of the frenzy, when people were clamouring for property 'before it was too late'. Prices had been falling a little at this stage and I suspect investors looked at these figures and then remembered that 94,000 units were built[9] in 2006 and 80,000 were predicted to be built in 2007, did some quick arithmetic and promptly came to the conclusion that something was fundamentally wrong with the market. This was confirmed in 2008 when there were claims that there was a three-year over-hang of supply of apartments in Dublin[10] and in 2009 when the rental price of property began to fall sharply.

The drum beat in the media in 2006/7 was that there was massive demand for housing and this would continue to grow due to the surging demographics (see Fig. 19), but the critical questions in many an investor's mind must surely have been: if there is such massive demand, why are there more than 200,000 empty units? How many of these are new? How many are being held back in the hopes of higher prices? There was simply no way to tell from the raw statistics. Vacancy rates varied from county to county: in Leitrim, for example, which was a popular spot for speculative builds, vacancy rates reached 30 per cent, nationally 15 per cent of properties were vacant, but there were 46,000 empty units in Dublin alone. These figures were met with the usual counterattack from the cheerleaders of the property market and a blizzard of statistics snowed down on investors to dismiss any concerns of a collapse in prices. However, now there were also people like Rossa White who were questioning the very fundamentals of the market.[11] At this

8 'Economy to weaken more than previously anticipated', *The Irish Times*, 6 October 2007.

9 'Attitude to empty properties will shape the market', *The Irish Times*, 10 August 2007.

10 'Down to Business', NewsTalk 106–108FM, 6 September 2008.

11 www.davydirect.ie/other/pubarticles/econcr20060329.pdf.

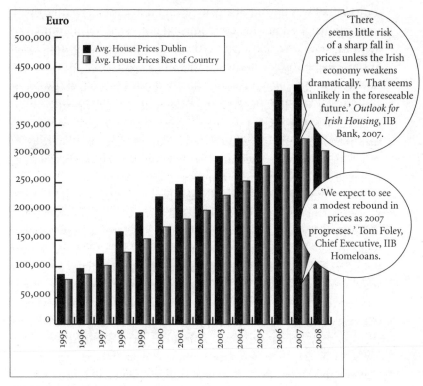

Fig. 19: Predictions on house prices. (Data source: DEHLG)

stage a significant number of shrewd investors decided now was a good time to get out, and they started to sell; this included the banks, which had been selling off their own premises on 'sale and lease back' agreements. As a result of this movement in the markets entering 2007, the ship began to list ever so slightly. It is an interesting sidebar to look at the words used at the time to describe the falling prices.

Once the prices started falling, the tone changed slightly. In the media, economic commentators lined up the by now standard culprits and pointed their fingers at them. In the *Irish Times*, Austin Hughes stated that price drops 'owe a great deal to higher interest rates. However, the fiasco surrounding stamp duties and some doom-laden predictions have also had a significant impact.'[12] He

12 Austin Hughes in 'Head to Head', *The Irish Times*, 8 October 2007.

concluded that once 'confidence improving' measures were taken in the upcoming Budget, then 'a modestly improving trend in house prices in a more stable market should become evident during 2008'. Hughes, who is a very experienced and talented economist, broadly represented the general view espoused at this time, which sought to soothe the market by arguing that a slight easing or a small correction in the market was healthy, but things would resume their upward trend quickly enough once supply was cut. There is no doubt that these commentators truly believed their predictions and could produce the figures to support their assertions.

It is striking, however, how similar these comments were to those made during initial share price falls in 1929 by the renowned economist Irving Fischer, who said that 'stock prices have reached what looks like a permanently high plateau'.[13] There is a common belief in many asset bubbles that fundamentals have altered so much, the mechanism that defines prices has changed forever and granite-like fundamentals hold up the market, which means prices can rest or pause before resuming the climb upwards. This is called the paradigm shift theory and while it is a very reassuring metaphor, it is completely erroneous. In 1929, just prior to the collapse, the equally prominent Princeton economist Joseph Lawrence said that 'stocks are not at present overvalued'. Those who were wrong about the Irish asset bubble were in equally eminent company.

That said, I don't believe the media commentators discussing the property market realised the position they held in the financial community. The people who were constantly interviewed by the media on the matter were assumed to have not only superior knowledge, which they do possess, but an oracle-like ability to predict the future. Their words were listened to closely by many buyers and investors, who took them as gospel. The experts can change their opinions within a very short period of time based on market fluctuations—and they are entitled to do so—but those who bought property cannot change their positions so quickly. Buyers and investors were owed no duty of care, of course, nothing of the sort. We each make our own decisions, and the many economic

13 Galbraith, *A Short History of Financial Euphoria*, p. 80.

commentators who spoke about the housing market were giving an opinion based on the fundamentals as they existed at the time. Unless they had lived through a similar asset bubble, they had no reason whatsoever to question their calculations.

Interest rates, as we have seen, contributed to the decline in house-building, along with many other factors, including what could be called 'buyer exhaustion'. So many buyers joined the property market in the past ten years that it came to the point where there were very few consumers left. Added to this was the effect on buyers of realising that property prices *could* fall, after being told they simply could not fall—it planted a seed of doubt. Thus the property illusion was partially exposed and speculative sellers began to move towards the door.

Worldwide economic events accelerated the decline, but strangely the bursting of the credit bubble in America was viewed as some external shock that could not have been predicted. I believe Ireland was part of the whole process. What occurred in Ireland was exactly what was happening in the US and in the UK, albeit in a different guise. Put simply, property created a debt bubble that imploded on itself when prices turned down. There were constant assertions in Ireland in 2007/8 that 'sub-prime' was not an issue here. This betrayed a complete misunderstanding of the situation. In its broadest sense 'sub-prime' described loans made to people who potentially could not afford the payments. In exchange for taking this risk, the bank charged a higher interest rate—a normal reflection of the risk versus reward theory. Understood this way, interest-only loans could be classified as sub-prime: why would a person take such a loan other than because they could not afford to repay the capital from the start of the loan? Lending money to people over a forty-year period raises the same issue: if the borrower cannot repay a loan over a thirty-year period, should a bank be lending the money? In effect many of the loans were sub-prime (as shall be demonstrated over the coming years) because the durability of the income streams relied upon to repay them are questionable. Offering a forty-year loan to a borrower who is relying on renting out a room and getting 'bonuses' in order to repay it is not good business.

And so the decline continued. In 2007 prices fell by varying degrees of between 0.2 per cent and +1 per cent per month, according to the TSB/ESRI figures. However other figures, which focused on asking prices, suggested that prices were falling further and faster; it was generally accepted that over 20 per cent had come off houses by 2008, and by 2009 that fall accelerated as official statistics struggled to reflect the true state of the market. The problem with measuring house prices using sales indices such as the ESRI is that they only measure sales. So if a house were on the market for €1 million and is then reduced to €700,000 and again to €600,000, this would not register, even though it is now not likely to sell for the original asking price of €1 million. The absence of sales volumes means valuations become difficult and the published statistics inaccurate.

In an alternative approach, the website *www.irishpropertywatch.com* tracked asking prices on the *www.myhome.ie* site. It was an ingenious process that allowed price reductions on homes on the major property sites in Ireland to be monitored. For the first time consumers had access to real-time information on the housing market and did not need to rely on retrospective announcements from the more established indexes, so they could see for themselves what was happening in the market, without any spin. However, *www.myhome.ie* later decided to alter its website so that prices could not be tracked, which Sherry FitzGerald also did on its site, although *www.daft.ie* did not follow suit. Whilst it was the website owners' absolute right to do so and they may have valid reasons unrelated to the above argument, it was a worrying sign and it sent out the suggestion, whether intended or not, that those selling houses did not wish people to know how fast the prices were falling. Furthermore, in mid-2008 the *Irish Times* included a warning on its property pages that it could not guarantee that the prices given for house sales were accurate. This warning was incorporated into the property pages after several sellers contacted the newspaper to say that the final selling prices of their houses were lower than those being reported to the media.

The key to any market is transparency. Once any hint of opaqueness descends on a market, it introduces panic. If people feel they cannot trust the figures, the collapse becomes more protracted and extensive. As 2008 progressed, prices fell further; some houses were reduced in price by 25 per cent, 33 per cent and even higher.

CONFUSION

At this stage in an asset bubble it is the norm for confusion to enter the market because the market no longer knows what to do as the forces underpinning it have now come into question. In one part of Dublin 4 prominent hotels, which were bought for over a third of a billion Euro, were closed down in order to redevelop the sites and turn them into apartments and commercial units. The entire contents were stripped out and sold off. At the same time, in another part of Dublin 4, the owners of the impressively designed Gasworks project could not sell them as apartments and instead applied for planning permission to have them turned into hotels. The owner of the

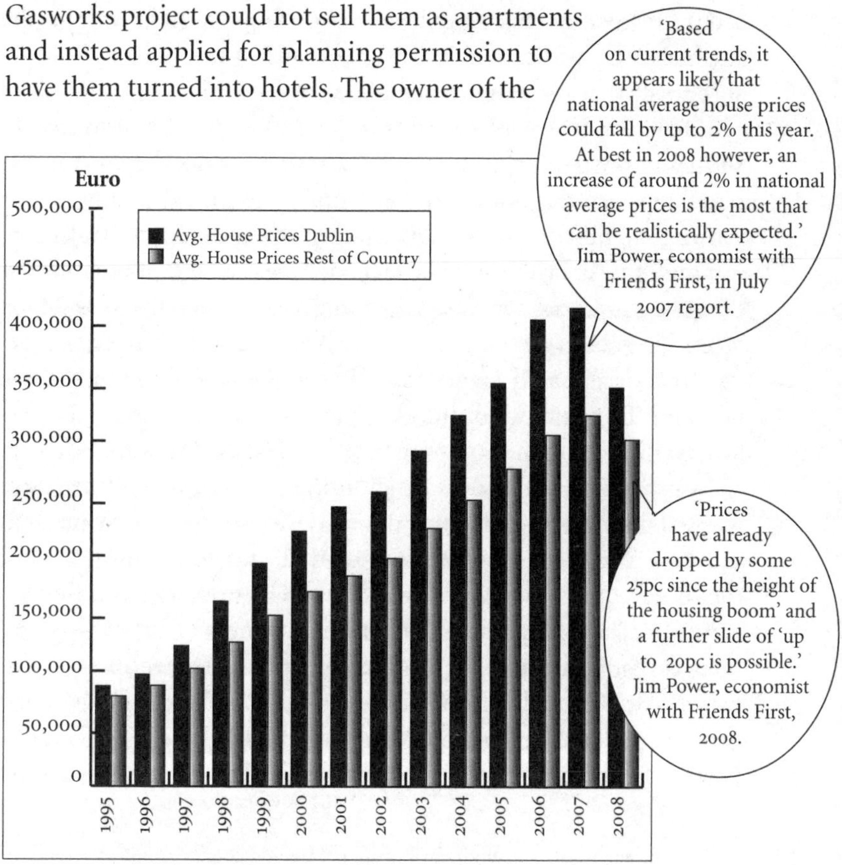

'Based on current trends, it appears likely that national average house prices could fall by up to 2% this year. At best in 2008 however, an increase of around 2% in national average prices is the most that can be realistically expected.' Jim Power, economist with Friends First, in July 2007 report.

'Prices have already dropped by some 25pc since the height of the housing boom' and a further slide of 'up to 20pc is possible.' Jim Power, economist with Friends First, 2008.

Fig. 20: Comments changed with market movements.

Ballsbridge hotels then did an about-turn and re-opened the hotels, pending planning permission for the mixed-use development he wanted to build. Something was wrong with the market, and the infallible suddenly became fallible. The economic commentators were not impervious to this confusion either. Reactions varied, ranging from very frank U-turns, to assertions that prices would fall 45 per cent, to claims that once builders cleared excesses, prices would rise again because of 'fundamental demand' (see Fig. 20).

The predictions altered again somewhat as 2008 went on, emphasising that fundamental demand still existed, but pointing out that negative sentiment and falling prices, plus the lack of credit, were now encouraging people to wait out the market.[14] The explanation given for this was that people were choosing to rent and sit on the sidelines. This was plausible, in fact, because it was the only way the absence of supposed fundamental demand could be explained. The rationale was: if people are not buying, they must be renting. In September 2007, Jim Power said: 'There is strong demand in the rental market, suggesting that potential buyers are deciding to rent rather than buy due to the uncertainty about the future trajectory of house prices.' However, the facts demonstrated that the number of rental properties available was rising and actual rents were falling by an annualised rate of 14 per cent[15] by the second quarter of 2008, and this accelerated into 2009. How did this tally with the big demand for rental accommodation from people who were lying low, waiting to pounce on property? It just didn't add up.

In my opinion, those commentating in 2007/8 could not have realised that the 'fundamental' demand was tied to the construction industry and was not only anticipatory but could evaporate once the construction industry slowed down. The reason I point this out is not to cast aspersions—I am in the business of predicting and forecasting myself and all prognostications are susceptible to what Harold McMillian described as 'events'—but rather to highlight the necessity for each person to take responsibility for his own finances. Economists make the best assessments possible with the information

14 'Jim Power's positive outlook for housing market in county', *Munster Express*, 21 September 2007.
15 www.daft.ie.

available, but it is far from an exact science, and never will be. When an asset bubble is distorting all the figures the fog of confusion descends and many commentators simply cannot believe what is occurring.

ANGLO IRISH BANK SHARE COMMENTS TIMELINE:

February 2007: '5% placing a massive vote of confidence; raising our estimates and target' Target Price: €16.50c, Davy Stockbrokers. Share Price = €16.00[16]

September 2007: 'Raising our target price to €17.60', Davy Stockbrokers.
Share Price = €12.95

November 2007: Target price reduced to €13.50, Davy Stockbrokers.
Share Price = €11.66

January 2008: '2008 will ultimately prove a fruitful year for investors in Irish financials', Davy Stockbrokers, January 2008.
Share Price = €9.39

May 2008: 'First half year "outcome suggests model is proving very resilient"'—comment on Anglo Irish Results.
Share Price = €8.40

July 2008: 'Recognising that the macro environment has deteriorated considerably in recent months, we are changing our target price methodology … hence, we are cutting our ANGL target to 750c', Davy Stockbrokers.
Share Price = €5.12

October 2008: Anglo Irish shares fall below €3.

November 2008: Anglo Irish shares fall below €1.

December 2008: Anglo Irish shares fall below 0.50c.

January 2009: Anglo Irish is nationalised by the government and the shares effectively become worthless.

The net effect of all this instability was a severe impact on stock-market prices during 2007/9—it was, to all purposes, a stock-market crash. The falls occurred because stock markets are liquid markets, where shares can be bought and sold in seconds, which means it

16 End of Month Share Price used in all instances.

quickly reflects market opinion. Property, on the other hand, is less liquid and takes longer to move with the times. The share price falls of the banks, builders and suppliers—whether overdone or not— reflected the real concern being experienced. Of course, with the builders and banks went the entire stock-market index, because they now made up so much of it. This highlights again just how tied up all the asset classes were in the property market. For example, the pensions of people who had never bought or sold a house in the past forty years were now dependent on the fortunes of the asset bubble. It was a recipe for unmitigated disaster.

So, what exactly was the government's role in all this? Wasn't this incredible situation the fault of reckless banks and speculators who were caught short by the Credit Crunch? Yes, this is true, but at the core of the problems were two key government failings: an inability or lack of desire to control the economy and a regulatory system that simply was not regulating.

In terms of controlling the economy, the government should have recognised the dangers of an asset bubble forming; there were sufficient warnings from academic and professional sources. It could have controlled the excesses as early as 1999, but instead was too interested in populism to implement any of the harsh measures that were necessary. The function of a government is often akin to the function of a parent: it has to exert authority in the short-term to deter behaviour that it knows will lead to long-term problems. In Ireland, it was a case of fun and games today and forget about tomorrow. The government made matters worse by giving generous tax breaks, which inflated the bubble still further. The reason for this was simple—the unashamed desire to be a popular government. It would have been hugely unpopular to attempt to curb economic growth because growth is seen as a good thing. As we have seen, however, there is well-paced growth and there is reckless growth, and it should have been obvious to the government that Ireland fell into the latter category.

On a micro level, the regulatory system established to regulate the banks failed absolutely, as evidenced by the enormity of the banking crisis that the country entered in 2008. For example, a competent banking regulatory system would have prevented Anglo Irish Bank and Irish Nationwide from building up loan books that were so skewed towards one segment, they were catastrophes waiting to happen. A competent regulatory system would have attempted to limit loan amounts being made available and would have ensured that mortgage applications were scrutinised in detail. It is clear now that many mortgage applications were over-optimistic, at best, concerning incomes and, at worst, based on a fraud driven by desperation. The government actively seeks to regulate when and where people consume alcohol and tobacco, yet it allowed credit to be consumed voraciously, apparently without limit or control.

Chapter 5
The Likely Outcome

Although it is clear that economists often get it wrong, it is nonetheless necessary to try to work out what the future might hold, to divine how the markets might behave in the coming years. So, what will happen next in Ireland's economy and housing market? There are a number of possible scenarios that must be explored. Before we do that, however, it is worth addressing one other issue briefly, so that it can be removed from the equation.

Some commentators have been accused of talking 'doom and gloom' and RTÉ's former Economics correspondent, George Lee (now a Fine Gael TD), appears to be the lightning rod for this accusation. This is hard to fathom as I think most economists and financial experts would agree that his analysis was very balanced and responsible. He told people the facts; whether they liked them or not, there was nothing Mr Lee could do to alter them. There seems to be a sort of superstitious belief that those who speak plainly and point out the serious predicament Ireland is facing are somehow drawing the wrath of the gods upon us. This is an irrational reaction to the facts and the fact-givers, although it does seem to be part and parcel of the speculative episode. Galbraith noted that 'There are, however, few matters on which such a warning is less welcomed. In the short run, it will be said to be an attack, motivated by either deficient understanding or uncontrolled envy of the wonderful process of enrichment.'[1] One noted economist, Roger Babson, who gave a stern warning on stock market prices in September 1929, was so fiercely lambasted in the press that Galbraith described it as 'a lesson to all to keep quiet and give tacit support to those indulging in the euphoric vision'.[2] Babson's work was denounced as 'notoriously inaccurate' and his motives as 'gratuitous', at best. This was the fate of many who predicted problems for Ireland when it was unpopular to say such things. This only compounded the problems, however, by making it appear to the general public that there was uniformity of opinion, except for a few 'begrudgers'.

Recent events in Ireland prove that, as Galbraith says, financial history repeats itself endlessly. The reaction to the RTÉ documentary *Future Shock*,[3] which was an astute and tellingly accurate piece of journalism, was very similar to that experienced by Babson. One newspaper reported that:

> RTÉ's Future Shock was very much a shock tactics programme and many within the property and construction industry have already labelled it irresponsible, partly inaccurate and wholly sensationalist while lacking sufficient balance—elements that call into question its credibility and authority[4] ... It also, regrettably, has caused distress to many recent purchasers and has also put off many young buyers who were intending to purchase their first home in the near future.[5] Even if only a few people took it at face value, the programme still did much damage to market confidence.

Some parties even complained to the Broadcasting Complaints Commission, alleging that 'the programme intentionally set out to undermine the confidences of those thinking of buying residential property. Mr. D'Alton believes that the programme was dishonest and reckless in its portrayal of the Irish property market.'[6]

1   Galbraith, *A Short History of Financial Euphoria* (Penguin, 1994), p.2.
2   *ibid*, p.8.
3   *Future Shock*, RTÉ, transmitted at 9.35pm, 16 April 2007.
4   *Irish Independent*, 20 April 2007.
5   These people are no doubt thanking their lucky stars now that they tuned in that night.
6   Complainant David D'Alton: Broadcasting Complaints Commission, Reference Number 120/07.

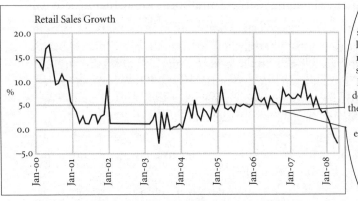

Fig. 21: Retail sales trend between 2000 and 2008. (Source: CSO)

It is almost incredible that in a developed democracy someone attempting to counterbalance the drumbeat of 'buy … buy … buy property' should have been treated as if he was misinforming the public or shouting 'fire' in a crowded theatre. There seems to be an almost medieval belief that if you speak the words, it will happen. It is worth exploring this for a moment because I suspect it will be used as a 'get of jail free' card for those who predicted nirvana for the Irish economy. One highly competent and respected economist echoed these concerns, concluding his economic analysis of the situation by saying that 'there is a major caveat to this, but one well within our control, and that is confidence. Thanks to uninformed pessimism, it's taken a battering of late.'[7] The premise appears to be that a strong and fundamentally sound economy could be brought to its knees by somebody asking simple questions or raising legitimate concerns or, to put it more bluntly, pointedly making the blindingly obvious statement that perhaps indebting yourself for forty years to buy a shoe-box apartment at the tip of the largest property price rise in the history of the state might not be a shrewd financial idea.

The fall in consumer confidence and retail sales in 2007/8 (see Fig. 21) might have been due to the fact that 75,000 people lost their jobs over a one-year period. They lost their jobs not because of words but because of economic reality. Similarly, the 50 per cent fall in share prices did not occur because of negative sentiment, but was

7   *Sunday Independent*, 31 August 2008.

due to rapidly changing market conditions. To say that negativity, or 'doom and gloom', causes economic problems is akin to saying that putting up an umbrella causes rain to fall from the sky. The truth is that people put up umbrellas when rain starts to fall; there is a link between the two, but it runs one way and not the other. The loss of confidence was connected to real economic concerns people were experiencing, not commentators pointing this out.

BANKING ON THE BUBBLE

One of the big post-bubble questions is what will happen to the banking system. We are witnessing an unprecedented series of events in Irish banking in 2009, but what will the future bring? There are two possible outcomes, which we shall loosely call the ostrich scenario and the flush-the-system scenario. The latter is an American-style solution, whereby the banks admit it was a speculative bubble and begin writing down the debt and flushing the system of bad and impaired loans. It is a cathartic process that seeks to find where the real demand for property lies and to let those businesses that made bad economic decisions fail. No more time wasted talking about negativity or gently-gently, softly-softly, it's a case of assessing the situation coldly and realistically and then taking the hard decisions. It is a painful process, but it reinvigorates the system and allows the economy to move on.

The former is a Japanese-style approach, whereby the banks stick their heads in the sand and prop up those economic participants in order to continue the illusion. The problem is that asset bubbles become so fundamental to the economy, the government tries to keep all the plates spinning or, worse, to shield economic participants from the consequences of their actions. That is why Japanese share prices started falling in 1991 and are still lower seventeen years later. Without a cathartic flushing of the system the market never recovers because people do not believe that the worst is over, therefore confidence is destroyed. The banks perpetuate the myth that it was not an asset bubble at all, and therefore do not realistically mark down the true value of their loans. Instead they tinker around the edges, hoping things will improve, and find someone, be it the government or the ECB, who will agree to prop up property companies for fear that if they fail, it will make matters worse.

So, which way will the banks go in Ireland? History suggested that the banks would try to save face and brave it out, which would ultimately lead to serious problems within the financial system— and history was proven correct. The banks never fully admitted the nature and extent of the problem until it was too late, when depositors had begun to flee and funds were drying up on the international markets. The government then had to get involved and provide state guarantees for all the monies owed by the banks. By early 2009 it was clear that not even this was sufficient and amidst a national outcry, Anglo Irish Bank was nationalised and yet more money was given to the banks to prop up their capital base. The next step, albeit an apparently confused one, was the setting up of the National Assets Management Agency (NAMA). This agency has the potential to be either of the two scenarios listed above. If NAMA values the property portfolios realistically and executes the exchange process swiftly, it will bring economic reality to the market. However, economic reality would likely mean that all the banks would be declared insolvent because their capital base would be eliminated by the realistic valuations of the property. Remember that the banks don't have the depositors' money anymore—it is gone. The recognition of a bad debt figure is simply the recognition of the fact that this money can never be recovered. This in turn will trigger insolvency as the liabilities, i.e. the money owed to depositors, will exceed what the banks are owed. Thus it is likely that NAMA will use an artificial value in order to provide enough money for the banks to survive.

The professed aim of the government is to save the banks, so the idea that there would be tough negotiations with the banks is facile. Tough negotiations would provide a market value to property, and the banks would fail. The apparent aim of NAMA is to somehow take over all the property loans and then drip-feed the property into the market over the next ten years. This will serve only to keep the market depressed and to keep investors out because every time property prices rise significantly, NAMA would sell. In truth, however, I don't think there is a coherent, cogent plan at work here—as evidenced by the comments made by the head of NAMA, Dr Michael Somers, to the Dáil Committee in May 2009, where he said that he remained unclear as to how the agency would operate. Yet looking past the precise details, the key aim of NAMA is to access ECB cash because the ECB is the only entity in this equation with cash.[8] The core function at the heart of NAMA is that the banks will be given government bonds in exchange for their bad property loans and they can then use these (even though the market might never buy them) to tap funding from the ECB. What the government is doing is not only risky but cynical. It is forcing the ECB to choose between bailing out the Irish state or letting the economy default and thereby threaten the stability of the Euro. The ECB may acquiesce in this, but only because it has no other option. Should the ECB, at any stage, turn off the flow of cash to the banks and to the government, then both would likely be bankrupt. In the short term, however, the government may have found the perfect benefactor, who appears willing to risk money when others will not.

The banks and the financial institutions fuelled the asset bubble by increasing the amounts of money they would lend out to customers, yet it appears they did not actually understand what they were doing, or at least, not until it was too late. There is one simple fact about the Irish housing market that needs to be borne in mind: the vast majority of people could afford to buy a property only by borrowing from banks or building societies. It was the process of lending more and more money to customers to buy a fixed commodity that caused the prices to rise. The more prices rose, the more the financial institutions lent out, until finally they were authorising 100 per cent mortgages. The impression was given that the value of a house was solid, reliable and an economic necessity in a person's life. This rationale simply indebted people more in order

8   The bizarreness of this situation is highlighted by reports in the *Sunday Business Post* (17 May 2009) that the Irish banks are also purchasing up to one-third of the government bonds to finance the soaring deficit. The banks are then immediately using these as collateral to access emergency funding from the ECB. It appears that the government and the banks have formed a tag-team and are drawing billions of Euro of funding from the ECB, even though the ECB is not supposed to be lending to governments. The Irish government is running rings around the ECB and converting government bonds, which the markets would never buy, straight into cash—and the ECB can do little about it whilst attempting to provide emergency funding to others.

to own the same asset. If, for example, an institution lent every potential buyer an extra €50,000, then within days house prices would rise by €50,000 as those borrowers competed to bid on properties and the reverse now applies as prices are falling.

You might well ask, how could all of the bankers have been wrong, surely these people are trained professionals? If we look at every other speculative episode, the answer is clear: bankers, too, get carried along with the euphoria and start to believe that there is some fundamental paradigm shift taking place in the economy. From the banks' point of view, it must have looked like rational investment because as prices rose, their loan books looked very healthy as the security they had over previous loans kept increasing. So, paradoxically, the more money they lent to people to buy houses, the more 'secure' previous loans looked. We now know this to be wrong, but in the midst of a boom it is difficult to argue against this. Nobody believes they are in an asset bubble; they believe price rises are fundamental.

When viewed another, more realistic way, however, it is clear that during an asset bubble the value of the asset is like a children's bouncy castle—it needs air blown into continuously in order for it to stay inflated. Similarly, the housing market in Ireland needed massive amounts of credit fed into it to keep prices up. The causative link is never 100 per cent, but it is obvious now that as the banks provide less money, prices will fall and the more they fall, the less money the banks will provide. The irrational house prices existed only as long as a sufficient number of people did not want to sell their properties. Yet by offering products that 'released equity', i.e. re-mortgaging, banks were effectively telling consumers that they could capture this transitory value of their house. It is revealing that there was a link from the homepage of the Permanent TSB/ESRI house price index to a page offering viewers a chance to assess the possible current value of their home, then suggesting the figure they could borrow against it. This will all come to an end as house prices fall and easy credit ends. Bankers are often described as people who offer you an umbrella in case of a rainy day, then demand it back once it starts to rain, in other words they often give you credit when you don't need it and withhold it when you are desperate for it.

At the moment buyers are in the envious position of being paid to wait. With prices falling every month, each month a buyer sits tight can potentially save him thousands of Euro. The price falls are self-reinforcing in the same way as the rises were, and people will react accordingly unless drawn back into the market. Where does this leave the banks? I believe it leaves them in a very precarious position.

Banks acquire money from three main sources: from depositors, from shareholders and from other institutions in the inter-bank market.[9] Banks repackage this money and lend it to their customers at a slightly higher rate than the rate at which they borrowed it. This is how a bank makes a profit, along with charging fees for its services. It may seem strange, but when you deposit money with a bank, you are in fact *lending* your money to them, in other words you are their creditor and you depend on their ability to make good loans, so that the bank is in a position to pay your interest and refund your deposit. It is critical to state the obvious at this juncture: the banks do not have the vast majority of money deposited with them because it is lent out in turn to other parties, keeping the cycle of money moving all the time. Thus your money has been converted into property or holidays or whatever, and has been exchanged in return for a promise of repayment.

Normally this system works well and there is little to worry about. The reason why it can work smoothly is that depositors leave their money with the bank, and do not all try to get their money back at the same time. This is essential because the banks do not have the cash. Furthermore, in normal times people just move their money from one bank to another; depositors don't particularly care because they presume the banks are solid and are managing their loan books well. In the abnormal setting of the property boom, however, the banks were lending out higher and higher sums to more and more people whilst shaving their margins to the bone in order to compete with each other. Now, with property prices falling and unemployment rising, it is not too difficult to see that loans will become impaired and may have to be written off.

---

9   It is more complicated than this, of course, but these are the three core sources of funds.

The fact that property prices are falling is irrelevant initially because it is the ability of people to make repayments on their loans that counts. There is a media preoccupation with 'negative equity', but this is of little concern unless you wish to sell your house or refinance your loan. If the banks have secured those loans on property, however, then it may end up with the underlying security. But banks do not want houses or hotels or apartment blocks because they deal in cash and do not want to have to make forced sales. What was slowly dawning on the banks in 2007/8 was that they had created 'the market', they had provided the liquidity and while prices were rising and it all looked like an economic utopia, the reality was that everything was flowing smoothly solely because they were lending so liberally. Once this changed and prices started falling, everything changed because the banks restricted lending. If, therefore, a developer had a hotel or a block of apartments, the market for these was dependent on the banks.

The banks are caught in a 'Catch 22' situation and it is they who are driving down the very asset of which they 'own' so much. The banks are driving down the value of their own security because short-term survival mentality demands that they do this. The stricter they become on loans, the further prices will fall. What happens if depositors *en bloc* realise what the stock market realised very quickly about their difficult situation? If this realisation dawns on those who fund the banks, then nothing short of a clear and direct statement from the ECB that it stood behind the Irish banks might save them.

The first bank to fail in Ireland was Anglo Irish,[10] but many others are already insolvent or dependent on the state guarantee and without this support, they too would fail. However, the Irish banks have yet to see a real run on them, i.e. where ordinary depositors all demand their money back. Over the longer term, the question has to be asked, who has the resources to save and recapitalise the Irish banks beyond the ECB, i.e. to make good their losses? If the general public and investors perceive that the government is not solving the banks' trouble, then a run on a financial institution is increasingly

---

10 The bank still exists solely because the government nationalised it and put its resources behind it.

likely and the government simply has nothing left to offer in the form of a guarantee. The state would then be dependent on the ECB as the only real source of funds, which would turn the whole problem into a political one rather than just an economic one.

Upon the foundation of the Euro, its opponents said that, ultimately, the weaker countries would have to be bailed out at the expense of countries like Germany. This now looks set to happen, although the ECB is unlikely to want to admit this as it does not wish to look like it has been out-manoeuvred by a small country like Ireland. It is no victory, however. After sticking up the proverbial two-fingers to Europe and rejecting all criticism over the last decade about the economy, Ireland now has to go to them for a bail-out. It is an ignominious end, but our politicians appear to be unabashed. I have spoken to many German people who are becoming increasingly angry about this and the sentiment is clearly that the EU would be a better place without Ireland. This expulsion could not be implemented, of course, but the sentiment reveals a hardening of attitude against a nation that is viewed as a truculent teenager.

CONSUMERS AND THE GOVERNMENT

Ireland's housing bubble is so enmeshed in the nation's finances that as house prices fall, it will bring down a section of the economy. The basis of all financial crises is an inability to understand just how dependent everything has become on one factor—property, in this instance. In the case of the Celtic Tiger, property was in turn dependent on immigration, which is like building a house on shifting sands. So there are two seams—property and immigration—and one very large faultline in the form of the government's over-reliance on one sector to generate money.

As a result of the government's myopia, the demise of the property sector and a simultaneous decrease in the immigrant population threatens the entire economy because it means the banks face insolvency. The solution that now seems most likely is that the government is going to try to borrow its way out by funding its budgetary deficit with borrowings and issuing more government bonds to save the banks. The government's hope is that a recapitalised banking system, over which it would have *de facto* control, would recommence lending in an attempt to get the economy going again. The government would hope that, somehow, the economy would become productive through this process and thereby allow it to pay off the national debt. This is the path of least resistance and may engineer a second, smaller boom, but only at the cost of national sovereignty because we would be facing a depression a couple of years hence due to the volume of debt that the State, on behalf of the citizens, would have assumed. Debt is the genesis of this problem so more debt will not solve the matter. Instead, what's needed is a dismantling of the inefficiencies that led to the acquisition of so much debt.

Ireland fought to get into the Euro in order to prove that we, the citizens, were good Europeans and that we had changed permanently. In the first instance, breaching the debt criteria dictated by the EMU will lose us credibility, no matter how many countries have done so previously. This in turn will drive up the price of debt and limit our borrowing options further. Eventually the government will simply run out of options and hit the wall at the end of the borrowing cul-de-sac. Government debt could hit €100 billion in 2010 and continue growing, and this in the face of 15 per cent + unemployment. Ultimately, if the ECB is unwilling to fund the government via the backdoor of the banks borrowing with government bonds, then the only source of funds would be the IMF. This is not a happy prospect as the IMF would impose draconian terms and conditions. The IMF is not a benevolent friend; it is the lender of last resorts, the one who comes in to sort out the fiscal problems that governments have proven themselves incapable of resolving. In short, the Irish government can sort out its own problems, or the IMF will have to do it, its way, in two or three years time. Unfortunately, the budgetary exercises in 2009 proved that the government simply cannot make the cuts it needs to make, which is why the state is currently borrowing €500 million a week.

The IMF would make the cuts the government has shied away from. It would not be a case of negotiating with public service unions or pandering to vested interests. The IMF would simply say to public servants: there is a 33 per cent pay cut and that's it. It would likely slash the minimum wage[11] and social welfare payments

11 It is clear that the minimum wage is going to create unemployment or a new

and slice off the inefficient elements of the state. Its stance would be simple: there is no more money and you can take it or leave it; you can go on strike or protest, do whatever you wish, but it will not make any difference. Whilst painful viewed from the short term, this course of action would ultimately prove beneficial. Already one economist has all but welcomed the day the IMF comes in because the Irish government has proven to be so weak in its attempts at controlling the deficit. Nonetheless, if the IMF did become involved, it would scar the reputation of the country for decades to come and lead to a drastic reduction in living standards and a surge in emigration.

A COMPARATIVE CASE

It always helps to look at comparative cases when trying to determine likely future outcomes. Finland provides an interesting case in terms of the Irish economy. In that case, a period of prosperity saw property prices rise by 'just' 225 per cent—compared to 300–400 per cent in Ireland—over a decade-long boom that also saw massive growth in credit. The property prices peaked in 1989 and then began to fall, causing the banks to cut credit. Property prices fell substantially in line with the falling credit, in a vicious circle. Whilst house prices fell, unemployment went from 3 per cent to a peak of 18 per cent over a short three- to four-year period and the growth in GDP went from a positive 5 per cent to a negative 5 per cent in the same timeframe. The consequences for the Finnish banks were dire: most had to be rescued with public funds, some closed down and others were merged together in shot-gun weddings. Shareholders of the banks received nothing because it was their businesses that went bust. While instructive, this comparison is of limited use because Finland had the resources to bail out the banks, whereas Ireland does not—which is why the government is tapping the ECB for funding. The difficulty in the Irish case is that the control and the responsibility have been separated. The government can likely corner the ECB into giving the

group of illegal workers. With people eager to work and deflation present in the economy, the minimum wage is a serious impediment to getting Ireland out of this mess.

banks tens of billions more in cash, but it appears that the ECB will not be able to control what the banks or the government are allowed to do with that money. Again, it demonstrates the fatal weakness of monetary union: there is no real political union, nor is there ever likely to be in the EU.

In summation, the likely outcome for the Irish economy is more serious than many people yet realise. The belief is that once the economic well-being of the EU and the USA take a turn for the better, then all will be well with Ireland. But even assuming this happens, the problems with Ireland are more structural, plus the country has lost the competitiveness that made it a beneficiary of US and EU growth.

The truth is that the government must retrench because it has no money and is faced with difficult decisions in trying to raise it. Emigration will rise if the EU and the USA recover, and the population possibly contract, making housing look even more over-valued. The trough of house prices, in line with the peak, will reach 80–90 per cent. Industrial strife will take hold as the money will not be available to pay higher and higher salaries, even though many workers are going to need pay rises to keep going. The net result will be industrial unrest on a scale we have not seen for some time.

The only real solution that will cure the problem quickly and effectively is if property is pushed onto the market and sold off; let the market find the real price of this asset. If banks begin to fail, so be it—go to the ECB/IMF for help, merge some banks, close down others, deal with the reality on the ground. It would be a sorry mistake to waste more money by pouring it into a deflating bubble; this has been tried numerous times before and it always fails. Now, more than ever, the government needs straight thinking, straight talking and imaginative problem-solving in order to turn this 'likely outcome' into an opportunity, rather than the crippling disaster it threatens to become.

Part Two

Chapter 6
The Key Issue: Quality of Life

W here does Ireland find itself now, at the end of the first decade of the twenty-first century? Over the last decade Ireland has quite often been described in the media and by its politicians as a wealthy country, a claim that is usually supported by figures showing that GDP (Gross Domestic Product) rose by some impressive amounts per year in comparison with other countries and that average incomes appear higher than other European countries. The impression was given that Ireland had 'arrived' and was now playing in the premier league of countries, and that this welcome turn of fortune was the result of gifted politicians' skilful stewardship of the economy. Those same politicians basked in the reflected glory and rewarded their own efforts with enormous pay rises in 2007. There is now the potential for the Taoiseach to receive a salary of €310,000 per annum, which surpasses the pay packets of the German Chancellor, the President of the United States, the British Prime Minister and the President of France.[1] When one considers that Ireland is a country of only 4.2 million people and Germany, for example, has a population of 75 million people and exports more than any other country in the world, the imbalance is staggering.[2] Does the leader of Ireland

1 *The Times*, 29 October 2007.
2 *The World Fact Book*, Central Intelligence Agency.

deserve to be paid so much to manage such a small country? One could argue yes if he has done a superb job, but can that be said of recent incumbents?

First, let us ask the pertinent question: is Ireland really a wealthy country, has that been achieved for and by the populace? The answer might have been 'yes' on paper, but it is a resounding 'no' if wealth is valued in terms of quality of life. Ireland came last in the 2008 European Quality of Life Index.[3] How can these two measures be squared? How can we be told, on the one hand, that Ireland is one of the wealthiest countries in Europe, yet at the same time have the lowest quality of life? The answer must be that Ireland is not a wealthy country in the full sense of that word. The use of GDP, or any metric based on it, to measure a modern quality of life is not only questionable, it is misleading. To quote a prominent EU commissioner: 'Quality of life depends to a degree on the type of goods consumed, good access to healthcare, quality of education, family relations, the integrity of our public officials and the state of our environment.'[4] The measure provided by GDP is, of course, important, but not as important as might be generally believed. If you borrowed money to buy a breakfast roll, then the GDP would rise by the value of the breakfast roll, but does that really mean anything?

In modern Ireland the average citizen is earning what would be considered a good salary in many parts of the world, but he is trapped in a country where this money cannot be converted into a higher quality of life either because that life is not available or because the price of obtaining that life remains beyond his means. It is my contention that Ireland's citizens have been misled by their politicians and have been seduced by the media coverage trumpeting the country's economic success. Furthermore, whilst taxpayers have worked hard to provide massive funds to the government for the good of the economy, the government has grossly misspent this money and proved itself unable to convert that money into improved quality of life for the populace. This failure is difficult to comprehend as this is a fairly simple process:

3   RTÉ Business.
4   Environment Commissioner Stavros Dimas.

Citizens work and generate tax revenue → Government spends tax → Quality of Life reflects government's spending

The function is simple: the government turns your tax money into public services. The efficiency with which it does this is the measure of its success.

The Irish economy deviated from this straight path over the last decade and became an economy of two parts. The first part was rational and productive, driven by Foreign Direct Investment and Irish entrepreneurial talent, which created productive jobs and real growth. The second part was driven by a speculative property bubble that sucked resources from the other part of the economy. It will ultimately imperil the real growth Ireland has achieved. The government has led the nation into the cul-de-sac of a speculative property bubble, fuelled by credit that is fast becoming scarce. The effect of this on the real economy has been startling, but it has also had other, seeping effects that threaten the stability of society itself. When one examines the key public services and the general experiences of the public in their daily lives, one can only conclude that Ireland is a poor nation in many fundamental ways.

PUBLIC TRANSPORT

An important measure of a country's wealth is its public transport system, and Ireland shows up very poorly indeed in any comparisons on this score. The only purpose-built transportation system produced in Ireland in the last decade is the over-ground light-rail system that operates in Dublin City, known as the Luas. And the fact that people marvel at this shows just how starved the country is of real transport alternatives. Widespread, dedicated transportation systems simply do not exist in Ireland's cities. It remains one of the few countries in the world whose capital city does not have an underground rail system, a disadvantage that makes real commuting next to impossible. If you are in Castleknock, for example, and wish to go to Blackrock, the public transport options available are almost farcical—it would require steely determination and great mental dexterity to figure out a viable route. The same is true if you wish to travel from any part of the city to the airport—a route one would think would be straightforward given that so many people need to use it.

The problem is that while there is the DART (Dublin Area Rapid Transit), the Luas and the Arrow and lots of QBCs (Quality Bus Corridors), there is no single, co-ordinated, integrated system whereby a commuter can descend into an underground station in one part of the city and emerge at another part within twenty minutes. This is the case in London, Frankfurt, Paris, New York, Munich, Vienna … everywhere but here, it would seem. The lack of such a system condemns commuters to sitting in traffic jams for hours[5] as they navigate their way around roads that were not designed to cope with the volume of cars using them, listening all the while to politicians on radio shows berating them for not using public transport and being 'un-green'. In 2003 the government was advised by an experienced head of the Madrid Metro, who was also a civil engineer, that Dublin could have a basic metro system functioning within thirty-six months for an outlay of €1.5 billion.[6] Six years later, there is nothing to show for it but plans gathering dust, while the price now quoted for just one part of that metro line (Northbound) is close to €5 billion. And of course now that the public purse is rattling with loose change, it looks unlikely that a metro system will be built in Dublin anytime soon.

Outside of the capital, the picture is even gloomier. Those living in rural communities often find themselves isolated because of the lack of even the most basic public transportation service. The country has long been in desperate need of infrastructural developments beyond the major motorways, but this has not occurred.

The irony is that several decades ago, Dublin did have an excellent public transport system, courtesy of the Dublin United Tramways Company (DUTC), a private company. The electrified tram system was initiated in the 1890s and was eventually expanded to cover most of the city. The DUTC had routes running from Nelson's Pillar (now the Spire in O'Connell Street) to Dalkey, Terenure, Sandymount, Palmerston Park, Rathfarnham, Drumcondra,

5   Not everyone would use public transport, but an efficient system would take enough cars and buses—and bus lanes—off the streets to increase the flow of traffic.
6   *The Irish Times*, 20 June 2003.

Donnybrook, Phoenix Park, Park Gate, Lansdowne Road, Howth, Sandymount, Dartry, Clonskeagh, Dolphin's Barn, Glasnevin, Kingsbridge, Inchicore, Westland and Ballybough.

The tram company paid Dublin Corporation a fixed rent per mile of track laid on the streets. It was run efficiently and expanded as necessity demanded. The efficiency of the system was impressive. By the year 1900 the DUTC reported that its trams were covering 2,180,832 miles of journeys in Dublin every six months; compare this to approximately 1,300,000 miles on the LUAS every six months. Furthermore, during the nineteen days of Queen Victoria's visit in April 1900, the DUTC carried 3,157,352 passengers,[7] a staggering figure which represents a higher capacity than today's average Luas figures.

Many people might be perplexed to hear tell of this successful system and rightly wonder what happened to it. Well, the Transport Act 1944 was passed in the Dáil and it incorporated the formerly independent DUTC into the newly formed Coras Iompar Éireann (CIÉ). By 1951 the last tram was gone from the streets of Dublin, replaced by buses. By the late 1950s the Harcourt Street line was closed down and that was it: the government had eliminated the last rail-based public transport system in Dublin City. In short, at the beginning of the last century Dublin had an extensive, LUAS-type transport system that was in private hands, made the taxpayer a profit and provided an excellent, efficient service. The government actively assisted in its demise and dismantling and then, fifty years later, asked the taxpayer to pay €770 million to replace a small portion of it. The two Luas lines currently in operation have a total length equalling 14.5 miles, which works out at a highly inefficient €53 million per mile. It's a travesty of epic proportions.

The upshot of the loss of the city rail system and the construction of its less efficient modern counterpart is the huge volume of cars on Irish roads. Once the boom provided the means, the people voted with their wallets against an unreliable public system by embracing the car. Aside from the emissions issue, the leap in car-ownership created a big problem because the infrastructure simply wasn't there to cater for the volume of traffic. The government had

7   Reported in the *Irish Times*, 24 April 1900.

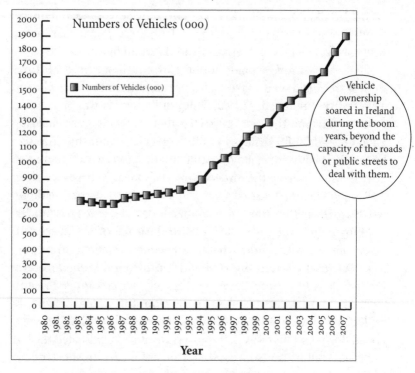

Fig. 22: Car-ownership figures from 1983 to 2007. (Data source: Department of Transport)

plenty of transport strategies, but unfortunately it had no single, workable solution for the number of vehicles on the road, which has now grown enormously with the boom.

The result of this? Predictably enough, major traffic congestion. In terms of quality of life, the real costs of the traffic chaos in Dublin, and across the country, includes the following:

- The time people spend in their cars as they sit in traffic jams is a real and substantial cost to the economy, as well as decreasing quality of life. Time lost in traffic is time that could be spent more profitably elsewhere—with families or working. An efficient public transport system would give people a real choice between car and rail/tram/underground, which would decrease the numbers of drivers and leave the streets quieter for those who want to or need to drive. The policy at the moment appears to be to force people out of their cars using the stick rather than the carrot, but to where exactly? Car drivers are over-taxed, over-ticketed, clamped and squeezed by all branches of the government in what is at base a cynical revenue-raising exercise. People often use their cars because they have to, not because they want to, so penalising them for doing this is hypocritical.

- 'Predictability' costs are incurred. A major travel website advises visitors to Dublin that 'Generally timetables are worthless as the chaotic traffic plays havoc with them'.[8] The more cars there are on the streets, the less predictable public transport becomes, thus the less used. It's a cycle that the government must break by drastically improving timetabling on public transport and by reducing the number of cars using the roads so that buses can move more freely and thereby become a real option.

- It has become very stressful to drive and park in Ireland's cities and towns. In the first place, the lack of a decent public system forces the citizen into his car, whereupon he faces congested, poorly maintained roads and frustrating traffic delays. Once he reaches his destination, he now faces the unenviable task of finding a parking space. This is enough to raise anyone's blood pressure. The number of cars in Dublin and other cities has led to the local government effectively auctioning off car-parking spaces. This has not only caused parking costs to rise but also means people are endlessly filling meters, punching out parking tickets, looking for coins for meters and looking out for predatory clampers, or just driving around looking for a parking space. This reduces quality of life and puts great stress on people who are already feeling stressed and frustrated in their efforts to get to their destination on time. Clamping vehicles, unless they are blocking a vital public service, is a waste of resources and merely a method for raising money. It has been banned in many countries on private land, being permitted by public authorities only where fire zones, etc., are blocked. In the now famous Scottish case of *Black v Carmichael*,[9] clamping was equated to extortion and theft and was outlawed on private grounds.

8   www.tripadvisor.com.
9   1992 SCCR 709.

Parking charges and restrictions are now imposed in hospitals in Ireland, which impacts people at their most vulnerable. It is these little inconveniences that accumulate and reduce the overall quality of life.

- The final cost has long-term impact: policy becomes reactive rather than proactive. Short- and medium-term solutions are sought to quell the problems rather than solving them once and for all. Government policy in this area must anticipate and shape transport solutions for the generations to come, incorporating all of the building blocks of a sustainable, environmentally friendly, efficient and reliable transport system, otherwise the citizens will be condemned to many more years of stress and lost time.

It would be easy to continue for some time on this theme, but we shall conclude with a brief look at Dublin Airport. Unfortunately, the primary airport represents a classic case of how uncontrolled growth can skew public facilities. It is easy to criticise the Dublin Airport Authority (DAA) because much of the criticism is deserved. Viewed from its side of the fence, however, within a relatively short space of time the DAA faced a situation where demand for its services exploded because the economy was left to grow unchecked. The critics will say that the problem is that the DAA is a state bureaucracy with all the nimbleness of a camel in the last stages of pregnancy, but in truth, even the most agile creature would have had difficulty responding to those growth levels. The DAA was caught on the back foot from the start, so the airport was expanded in piecemeal style, with a bit added on here and another bit there, until a confused creation sprawled out of the space where an attractive terminal building used to be. Aesthetics aside, the airport is now probably making the most efficient use of the space it has. But it will face a new problem soon: all of the expansion work may well prove unfounded if the population decreases and lack of disposable income causes a decrease in discretionary travel, e.g. stag parties in Poland.

By mid-2009 it was clear that much of the discretionary travel that had been a hallmark of the Celtic Tiger was falling off at a dramatic pace. The head of marketing at Budget Travel, Clem Walshe, announced that 'Irish tour operators have cut their collective capacity from 900,000 to about 550,000 seats'.[10] This was compounded by the fall in inward tourist travel due to the global recessionary environment. Furthermore, Aer Lingus began to cut back its scheduled capacity on long-haul routes and cancel other routes, and many other airlines followed suit.[11] Ironically, this was at a time when Dublin Airport had finally begun addressing its physical constraint issues and starting building Terminal Two. This was a classic example of the inaccurate signals the economy transmitted to its participants. Dublin in 2010 will end up with no underground, but an airport that will be able to handle two or three times the capacity that will use it.

In that event, the DAA will be facing a situation in which is has an over-capacity, rather than under-capacity. It has geared up for future demand based on current demand, but the current figures are skewed by the boom. It is very likely that current demand will fall away as the recession progresses, leaving the DAA with a large capacity airport, and less travellers using it. This is the damnable position many transportation providers are experiencing: the nature of the expansion work necessarily entailed long lead-in times, which meant they could not react quickly during the boom; now, when they have reacted and are offering an improved service, business has begun to decrease, leaving them with over-capacity.

The long-term solution for Dublin Airport is the same as that adopted by all progressive countries: the green-field solution. All legacy airports are inefficient because they are physically limited in their ability to expand, plagued by an over-regulated and unionised workforce that are often politically connected and lacking proper transportation services. Compare, for example, Kennedy Airport to Newark Airport, Heathrow to Stanstead, the old Hong Kong Airport to the new one, or the old Munich Airport to the new one ... the list is endless. Old airports are usually bad airports and as such they need to be closed down and whole new frameworks laid out to facilitate a move to a better-appointed site. In Ireland's case, however, the politics of land values, rezoning and unions have

10 *The Irish Times,* Tuesday 2 June 2009.
11 *Irish Independent,* Saturday 13 June 2009.

prohibited this to date. These stumbling blocks need to be removed to allow for the fresh vision that is needed.

THE POSTCODE PROBLEM

Ireland does not have a postal code system. That may appear a minor point, and in some respects it is, but it is indicative of the government's inability to develop even the most fundamental aspects of the infrastructure. A postal code system—and I don't mean Dublin 4, 6 or 24—assigns a unique postal code to a small block of addresses, a business, a government department or even a single building. In the UK, for example, a six-digit system operates, e.g. OX3 8NT, and in the USA a five-Digit ZIP (Zone Improvement Plan) code is used, as in Beverly Hills 90210. Postal codes indicate the geographic location of your house, depending on the system in use, to within a few houses or streets. The UK introduced its code in 1959, the US in 1963 and, unbelievably, the Germans introduced one in the middle of the Second World War, in 1941. Ireland is one of the last developed countries to be without such a system.

There are obvious savings and efficiencies achieved by using a postal code: the postal service and private delivery companies can organise their deliveries more efficiently, which saves money, time and reduces the incidences of lost letters and packages. This is vital for Ireland, where common surnames and townlands in rural areas can cause much confusion. Moreover, a postal code system assists private and public organisation in allocating services to the public because they can tell quickly where people are based just from their postcode. More importantly, emergency services would be greatly assisted in locating houses as it would eliminate any confusion.

As usual, Irish politicians have plans in place. On 23 May 2005 the Minister for Communications, Energy and Natural Resources, Noel Dempsey, announced that Ireland would have a postal code system in operation by 1 January 2008.[12] The press release stated that '*A postcode is a vital piece of infrastructure for a modern developed economy. Without an effective postcode in Ireland, there is a real danger that not only postal operators, but also consumers, business and public services will be at a disadvantage compared to our EU partners.*'

12 www.dcmnr.gov.ie/Press+Releases.

This is true, but 2008 came and went without a postal code system being introduced. The plans were shelved for more consultation— it appears that after two rounds of public consultations and working groups, more consultations are necessary—and the target date is now 2009.[13] It is now not clear when a postal code system will be launched in Ireland. If Germany can launch one whilst at war with the rest of Europe, why couldn't Ireland have launched such a system in the ninety years since Independence? Again, as with so many issues, Ireland is missing an important element of what is needed to operate as an efficient country.

PUBLIC HEALTHCARE

'Health is wealth' as the old saying goes, but the public healthcare system that is struggling to service Irish society is poorly managed, poorly performing and the prognosis is far from comforting. Whilst it employs more than 100,000 people,[14] many patients are forced to wait for months for procedures such as vital diagnostic tests. In one stark example a woman waited nine months for a test to confirm whether she had cancer; by the time her positive result arrived, it was too late to cure her.[15] If that woman had had private health insurance, she could have had that test almost instantly and would have had an opportunity to fight the disease.

In another example that was highlighted extensively on the RTÉ radio programme 'Liveline', Cystic Fibrosis (CF) patients described in depressing detail their plight at having to 'endure' the public health system and how CF patients die ten years earlier in Ireland than in other parts of the developed world.[16] It is easy to complain about waiting four or five hours in Accident and Emergency, but these are cases where people are literally killed by incompetence and mismanagement. And this is happening despite the fact that by 2006 €12 billion of taxpayers' money[17] was being spent on public health

---

13 Another round of public consultations was ordered and has yet to decide if and when the system will be introduced.
14 Department of Health and Children.
15 *Irish Independent*, 15 October 2007.
16 *The Irish Times*, 22 May 2007.
17 Department of Health and Children.

expenditure; this is up 235 per cent on the 1997 figures. To put that astronomical figure in context, if there are two million adults in the country, then the average adult paid €6,000 in taxes per year for a wholly inadequate health service.

For the government to claim that this is a wealthy country, when citizens are dying for want of simple procedures, should be a matter of public outrage. What is even more galling is that the Taoiseach could even contemplate taking a €38,000pa pay hike,[18] making him the highest paid leader in any OECD country,[19] while such inequities exist.

Where is the public outrage? The problem is that when it comes to the health service and the HSE (Health Service Executive), we have heard it all before, over and over again. People feel frustrated and hard done by, but feel there is nothing they can do about it. Instead, they buy the best private health insurance they can afford and hope for the best. They are the lucky ones, there are plenty others who cannot buy their way out of the public healthcare system. In a modern economy no person should be denied prompt basic medical services because they do not have enough money. The best private medical insurance in Europe costs less than what the average taxpayer in Ireland pays to support the public healthcare system. That is a sobering thought and one that should give us all pause for thought, and reason to petition our politicians to work harder and deliver a service that does equate health with wealth—for everyone.

At this stage, the public health service represents a serious inability on the part of the government to manage public institutions and large budgets. It is worth examining the structure of the public healthcare system in Ireland in order to tease out the nature and extent of the problems inherent in it.

The HSE, the administering body of the public health service, was established by the Health Act 2004 and came into effect on 1 January

---

18 This pay increase was deferred, but it is still available to the Taoiseach should he wish to take it up. It is unlikely he would in the current circumstances, but the point is that the political classes had reached a level of arrogance where, even though they were presiding over an inevitable disaster, they believed they should be paid as if they were the best leaders in the world.

19 Organisation of Economic Co-Operation and Development, which comprises thirty countries.

2005. It replaced the old Health Board system, which had divided the country into the care of ten/eleven health boards, each administering its own specified area. One of the problems with the old system was political interference. As politicians sat on the boards, there were instances where, for example, medical cards were sought for constituents as favours. It also led to battles to keep many services local that should have been centralised. That was all set to change with the advent of the HSE.

In theory the Minister for Health, who is appointed by the Taoiseach, is responsible for the broad strategic development of healthcare in Ireland. The Minister appoints the member board of the HSE, which in turn appoints a Chief Executive. The HSE is responsible for the day-to-day running of the health service and decides how the annual budget is allocated. It all seemed very workable on paper, but there was an inbuilt problem from the outset in that the establishment of the HSE was rushed, with no consultation carried out to find out how the administrators of the Health Boards would fit into the new system. To ensure industrial peace, the entire group of managers and administrators in the old boards were guaranteed the same level of job in the new HSE.

The transition process was not well managed, however. Some managers moved jobs, some left the health service, while those who stayed often did not know to whom they were reporting. The *Fitzgerald Report*, when describing the cancer misdiagnosis problems that beset the system, noted that there were 'systemic problems of governance, management and communication ... There were too many people involved from different levels and areas within the HSE, without clarity about their roles and responsibilities within the process ... the decision-making process was fragmented, with insufficient clarity about decisions, who was making them, why they were being made, or when they were signed off.' There were simply too many management structures—presumably indicating one layer of new management laid over the old layer, without ensuring a proper fit. The Minister for Health, Mary Harney, now appears to wish to change the system again and try to revert to a hybrid of the old system. If the health service were a private business, it would either be bankrupt or the management would have been changed a long time ago.

The impact on quality of life is obvious: Irish people face either a steep bill for private health insurance or are forced to rely on a substandard service that is capable of making fatal mistakes. Whichever side of the divide one occupies, there is a two-tier system that does not benefit anyone. It is an indictment of any society to have a situation where money decides one's fate in terms of health. That is wrong. If the government prioritised its citizens' quality of life, it would seek and find real, sustainable solutions to the health-care crisis. For that is what it is, a crisis. The stories documented in the newspapers and on radio in heartbreaking detail all attest to that—think of Susie Long,[20] Orla Tinsley[21] or Rebecca O'Malley.[22] These women are facing lives cut short by an inadequate health service. And for every voice heard in the media, there are a hundred others who could speak of similar inequities and outcomes. What we have is a system in which excellent nurses and doctors fight constantly to help their patients, but are impeded by poor management systems and unhelpful bureaucracy. What we need is a system that values its staff and patients alike.

Aside from these very real and pressing quality of life issues, the health service also presents many challenges for the government's finances. To date, those who have been harmed by the incompetence of the health service have not coalesced into a broader legal action. We live in a litigious society, however, and it will not be long before those who have suffered through negligent acts begin to claim compensation en masse. The tort of negligence has simple requirements: a duty of care to exist between the two parties; a breach of that duty of care and an occurrence of damage that is causally linked to that breach. The trouble this presents to the Irish taxpayer is that when one party is required to pay damages to another the aim,

20 Susie Long was a forty-one-year-old woman who rang a radio discussion programme in January 2007 to highlight the impact of healthcare delays on her life. Forced to wait seven months for a colonoscopy to diagnose bowel cancer, Susie Long died of her illness in October 2007.

21 Orla Tinsley is a twenty-two-year-old woman who suffers from Cystic Fibrosis and who has campaigned tirelessly to highlight the low level of care afforded to CF sufferers in Ireland.

22 Rebecca O'Malley received a false all-clear for breast cancer and subsequently had to have a mastectomy.

partially at least, is to correct aberrant behaviour and deter it. But the reality is that the taxpayer pays the government to mange the health service and if the government mismanages it, the taxpayer foots the compensation bill. Those who are causally responsible for the mismanagement are not held responsible, suffer no consequences and continue to be paid a salary by the taxpayer. Nobody is dismissed, nobody is held civilly liable or criminally liable. At worse, they retire into obscurity with a pension that is also paid by the taxpayer. There is a finite pot of money, created by the taxpayer, and the danger is that it will be depleted through payments to the problem-creators and the problem-dodgers. That will never heal the health system.

LAW AND ORDER

One of the major influences on the quality of life is crime levels. Crime imposes financial costs on people by necessitating preventative measures and increasing insurance premiums. The real impacts are more insidious, however. Crime is a creeping malaise that slowly infects every part of the social body as the fear of crime reduces the quality of life for everyone and consumes vital resources in deterring and detecting it.

Listening to the media, it would be easy to get the impression that Irish cities are murder capitals. This isn't the case. The murder rate in Ireland is lower than most developed countries[23] and if the gangland murders are removed—which in large part are internecine struggles between criminal gangs—the murder rate falls even further. Regardless of what the nightly news might suggest, the real issue affecting quality of life in Ireland is the effect of low-level personal and property-related crime.

The general level of crime has increased in recent years, as the crime statistics show. For example, 'theft without violence' rose 262 per cent between 1998 and 2006.[24] To the 'outsider' this is quite alarming, but it seems that city-dwellers in Ireland have grown accustomed to it because it has happened incrementally. I have visited Ireland frequently over the last number of years and have

23 *Irish Independent*, 16 July 2007.
24 CSO.

noticed the situation worsen each time. The average city centre at night-time is a dangerous place to be—there are fights, aggressive begging behaviour and large groups congregated in public areas. There is public vomiting and urination and repeated low-level crimes that reduce the quality of life experienced by the average citizen. These incidents are often not significant enough to merit individual media coverage or to be quantified in any statistical table, but this sort of crime is present and it is persistent. Many people I know who live in the cities have become so adept at avoiding or pre-empting such behaviour that they believe it is not as persistent as it actually is. But the truth of the matter is that there is a low- to mid-level crime epidemic in Ireland that is affecting everyone.

Before we can proceed to solutions to this problem, it is necessary to understand what is causing the problem. For this, we must examine the role of the judicial system and An Garda Síochána, along with political corruption and the prison system.

THE QUESTION OF ORDER: AN GARDA SÍOCHÁNA

The buffer between the criminals and the honest citizens is the police force. By international standards Ireland has an excellent police force, with little or no visible corruption. On the other hand, it is also an old-fashioned force with rigid military command structures. The literal translation of 'Garda Síochána' is 'guardians of the peace'. Their brief is to fight crime, but the name suggests that a permanent state of peace exists and the Gardaí are there to maintain it. It is the members of the police force who are best placed to know how the force should be changed and modernised to make it better able to do its job, yet it remains under the thumb of the political system and has not been allowed to develop independently. This whole area of the mandate and the responsibility of the force needs to be seriously reassessed and appropriate action taken to ensure we have a modern, well-equipped, proactive police force, rather than a troupe that is hindered by political interference.

The Gardaí are there to defend our quality of life, but what can they do, unarmed as they are, when they are facing an arsenal of weapons wielded by thugs who have no compunction about using them? There is a war raging between opposing criminal factions in

Dublin and Limerick, gang members who defend territory and drug profits with extreme violence. In 2007 and 2008 there were twenty-two 'gangland killings' and zero convictions.[25] Nor is this an aberration from the norm: over the last eleven years there have been 127 gangland killings and only fourteen convictions. The politicians and media commentators might criticise the Gardaí for these figures, but the underlying problem is that the force is seriously under-resourced in terms of both weapons and technology. The question needs to be asked: how can a police force enforce the law effectively and maintain order when it lacks the means to confront criminals or protect citizens?

At management level there remains a belief that 'situation management and dialogue' are the preferred methods rather than force.[26] But is this sufficient to control and combat crime when criminals are either armed or high or both? In June 2008 it was reported that officers 'could' be given pepper-spray within two months.[27] The article went on to say that 'Gardai have been complaining for years that the mixture of drink and drugs is causing greater violence and increasing difficulties in restraining violent prisoners, particularly those who have been mixing cocaine with alcohol.' As of April 2009, pepper-spray had still not been issued as standard equipment to all Gardaí. This is a standard policing tool in use around Europe, but Ireland is—as usual—last to implement it. Why is the command structure so slow to react to what the rank-and-file need? It is infinitely better to subdue criminals and aggressive drunks as it avoids the need for physical contact, which endangers the garda as well as the person being arrested.

Technology is the second issue that distinguishes the Irish police force from its European counterparts. Recent advances in technology are being used to great advantage by police forces in Europe and in North America, especially in relation to fitting out squad cars. Thanks to television, Irish people are very familiar with the standard patrol car in use in Britain, with its computer terminal that allows the police to check in real-time if the occupant of a car or the

25 Correct as of September 2008; see *Sunday Tribune*, 31 August 2008.
26 *The Irish Times*, 5 February 2007.
27 *Sunday Independent*, 6 April 2008.

licence plate of a car should be of any interest to them. The latest technology being fitted in police cars in North America is taking this to the next level: automatic licence-plate detection scans licence plates as the police car drives along, and if it recognises any plate from a predefined list, it alerts the police in the car. The systems currently in use can scan 3,000 plates an hour on cars travelling in front, behind and beside the cruising police car. The aim of the units is to match cars to those featuring on a 'hot list', i.e. stolen cars, cars being parked for later use in a getaway, cars associated with unlicensed or uninsured drivers or cars of banned drivers. It can also be used to carry out surveillance of known criminals, such as drug couriers. This hi-tech policing puts continuous pressure on criminals because they cannot move in the street without attracting immediate attention from the police force. It benefits the police by giving them knowledge that can help keep them safe as they do their job, and it seriously disadvantages the criminals, which benefits both the police and wider society.

In Ireland, by contrast, the average private car has more technology in it, in the form of communications equipment, GPS, etc., than any squad car. The average Garda squad car has a two-way analogue radio to communicate with a central location, and that's it, that is the extent of the technology in most police cars. It is well known that a scanner can be purchased that allows the listener access to the police frequency, which is exactly what the criminals do. Furthermore, these radios have problems communicating between North and South Dublin, which is a farcical situation.

A digital radio system has been promised for years,[28] but bureaucracy, mismanagement and political interference have ensured delays in delivery. A contract for the system was signed only in May 2008,[29] with full implementation in all Garda divisions to occur within the next two years.[30] The Gardaí are simply too far behind the technological curve to be able to serve the people of Ireland

---

28 *The Irish Times,* 10 October 2007.
29 *The Irish Times,* 2 May 2008.
30 *Irish Examiner,* 6 April 2009, reported that test rollouts were to occur 'within weeks' in the North Central and South Central Divisions. Full rollout in all national divisions will occur over the next two years.

efficiently. Unbelievably, Garda Inspectorate Kathleen O'Toole stated in 2008 'that almost half the Garda stations did not have access to a car'.[31] This is not technological backwardness, it is technological retardation. Bravery and dedication will only take a police force so far; they must be adequately resourced and armed in order to do their job properly and safely.

There is a very strange paradox in neutral Ireland whereby the Army, the Air Corp and the Navy are equipped with highly sophisticated weapons and communications technology, including anti-tank missiles and satellite communication equipment, but the police force is equipped with a truncheon, a radio system that Mr Marconi could repair and, if they are lucky, the station might have access to a car. Why would the government of a neutral country pour money into the defence forces and leave the police force under-funded, when it is the police force that is sent out to face down hardened criminals? If quality of life is deemed to be important, the government should quickly reassess the crime-fighting capabilities of An Garda and provide the help they so badly need to tackle serious crime. Until this happens, the quality of life of the whole populace will continue to be adversely affected by the criminals.

THE QUESTION OF LAW: THE JUDICIAL SYSTEM

At the frontline in society's fight against criminal acts of all kinds is the judicial system, but it is ill-equipped to enter the fray. It creaks along with antiquated practices that would have been suitable fifty or 100 years ago, but are proving dreadfully inadequate in modern society. Young, hardened criminals appear in what is quaintly known as 'children's court'. Petty criminals clock up many convictions before they potentially face any corrective behaviour, which benefits neither them nor the public.

In order for society to function properly all illegal acts, regardless of who perpetrates them, must be pursued and prosecuted with equal vigour. The police's role is to catch criminals; those involved in the broader judicial system are responsible for prosecuting them and incarcerating them, and also proposing new legislation to aid

31 *The Irish Times*, 10 October 2007.

and abet the police and to target enforcement of existing law. The cornerstone of any judicial system is equity and consistency. This is essential if the law enforcers and the people are to be able to trust the system to deal correctly with all cases that come before it. In Ireland's recent history, there seems to have been some exceptions made to the rules, which is a dangerous pattern to follow.

Financial Crime

Crimes are not just muggings, break-ins and car-theft, they also include non-violent actions that have a financial impact on people. These sorts of crimes can inflict as much suffering and have a similar financial impact as 'normal' crime. If your pension fund is defrauded, your retirement will be impacted. If your share portfolio collapses in value, you will suffer a lower quality of life. If you are illegally lured into buying a foreign property, this can seriously impact your life and cause huge levels of stress. Although the practitioner might argue that 'no one gets hurt', the price paid by victims of financial crime can often be enduring.

The recent property bubble has produced a long litany of figures from the banking and property industry who, whilst they may not have been convicted of any crime, have had a detrimental effect on the lives of many people. Most have simply retired with pensions and/or golden handshakes and walked away. The Office of the Director of Corporate Enforcement and the Financial Regulator appeared impudent in the face of widespread questionable financial practices that will impact citizens for decades. Yet in the now well-worn practice of Irish business few, if any, will be held to account and a committee will be established to investigate what went wrong and to explain how the door can be closed long after the horse has bolted. The tribunals were littered with tales of tax evasions, private banks, corruptions and peddling influence, and the initial emanations from the post-Celtic Tiger hangover suggest that nothing much has changed. It might be argued that there is little financial or political crime in Ireland because there are so few convictions, but that is the whole point. In view of the tribunals, the most logical assumption from this fact is not that such crimes do not exist but that they are not prosecuted.

Anglo Irish Bank had to be nationalised because of the activities of a small number of people, and Irish Nationwide looks to be going the same way. The cost to taxpayers will be billions of Euro—money that could have been used to build hospitals or an underground. What the country is facing is the prospect that potentially the biggest single crimes to be carried out in the State were committed by financiers, not thugs in balaclavas. Yet the pursuit, or even the investigation, of any potential criminal activity—and, of course, none may exist—is done at a gentlemanly pace. The low rate of conviction in such matters speaks volumes about justice; to state otherwise is to ignore the obvious. The lack of convictions is not only scandalous, it critically undermines people's belief in politicians and in politics. The landscape of Dublin was scarred by grubby dealings, yet people see those responsible as being all but immune to prosecution. Over the coming years the people will need to believe in their politicians more than ever. Leadership in difficult times is always challenging, but it is hampered considerably when there is a lack of unity between the political leaders and the people.

The Prison System

The other arm of the judicial system is the Director of Public Prosecutions (DPP), the courts and the Department of Justice.[32] It is these institutions that decide on prosecutions, carry out the trials and ultimately propose new laws and attempt to have them enacted in the Dáil. In various ways they are all responsible for one fact: Ireland has the second lowest number of people in prison in Europe.[33] This is not, as one might hope, because Ireland has a more law-abiding population or a more sophisticated non-custodial system of punishment. In fact, statistics indicate that Ireland has the same level of 'ordinary' crime, or higher, than Scotland, England or most other countries, but the second lowest rate of incarceration.

One reason that has been suggested for this seeming anomaly is a 'revolving door' policy that releases prisoners because there is no

---

32 Shortened title, I have excluded Law Reform, etc.
33 *The Irish Times,* 4 January 2008.

space for them.[34] Ireland has 72 people per 100,000 in prison, whereas in Scotland it is 141 and in England it is 147. This suggests— although there are other possible explanations—that not enough people are being imprisoned in Ireland. Why would this be the case? There are three possible explanations.

First, liberal bail laws that permit bail in situations that would not be entertained in other jurisdictions, where the alleged offender would be held for trial because of the flight risk or the risk of re- offending whilst on bail. The number of people failing to turn up for trials is difficult to ascertain exactly, but it does seem very high. According to facts presented in an answer to a question put forward in the Dáil,[35] there are 36,000 outstanding warrants for people who failed to turn up for their trials. Whilst this figure is overstated by a number of factors, it is nonetheless indicative of a serious problem. Furthermore, senior police figures constantly complain of senior criminals getting bail. This situation has been improved by a referendum ten years ago and new criminal legislation,[36] but we still have a judiciary that, when balancing the constitutional right of a person to his/her freedom because of the presumption of innocence versus the rights of society as a whole, chooses the defendant. Nevertheless, it is submitted that the presumption of innocence between a person who has never committed a crime and one with fifty previous convictions should be different. Do not the fifty previous convictions erode the present presumption of innocence in even the smallest way? There ought to be guidelines for judges with regard to defendants presenting with previous convictions, which would ideally shift the burden of proof in bail applications to the applicant where the applicant has former convictions.

Secondly, court-issued warrants are not being enforced, which leads to more crime and a casual attitude towards law enforcement in general. According to Eamon Gilmore TD there are 4,000 com- mittal orders outstanding, i.e. the courts have ordered that 4,000

---

34 *The Irish Times*, 4 January 2008. Although it should be said that the expert in this piece believes that more prison places is not the solution.

35 This information was recounted by Eamon Gilmore TD in the Dáil, based on an examination of the Garda computer system on 25 November 2007.

36 *The Irish Times*, 22 May 2007.

people should be arrested and committed to prison, but they remain at large.[37] Furthermore, according to evidence released by the Central Statistics Office in 2008, 25 per cent of all crimes committed in 2007 were committed by people on bail.[38] This included forty murders, twenty-six rapes and thousands of 'minor' crimes, such as theft and burglary. This is an increase of 1,200 per cent on 2004. It is simply not good enough that criminals who prey on the rest of the population are at large because the Gardaí cannot locate them in order to enforce the law.

Thirdly, prison spaces are very limited. If there is nowhere to put prisoners, there is little point in arresting or sentencing criminals. It is all well and good to pass legislation dictating harsher sentences, but if there are no prison places to accommodate those who are convicted, then all there can be is a merry-go-round of judges and prison authorities trying to decide who is the least danger to the public. The government has not built the prisons the country needs. It is now attempting to rectify this with a prison-building programme, but it appears to be too little, too late.

So, what do our public services and our daily experiences tell us about modern Irish society? What it says is that these are the signs of a country that had wealth on paper, but that never translated into a better society for all. These are the signs of an economy in which people earn sufficient income to provide well for themselves, but must pay significant taxes and sundry charges on their income. It is the government's job to administer and spend the public finances on behalf of the taxpayer, and it has failed to do that job. It has failed to lay the foundations of an efficient and orderly society and economy. It has failed to ensure that people are secure in their homes and on the streets, that basic healthcare needs are provided in an efficient manner, that people can buy a home for their family without taking on the burden of debt and that people can travel around their area and their country in an efficient, environmentally friendly way. These are the specific areas in which a government is supposed to provide direction and funding, yet after over a decade

37 *The Irish Times*, 6 December 2007.
38 *Sunday Independent*, 1 June 2008.

of being in receipt of the largest tax revenues in the history of the state, this government has failed to achieve these basic goals on behalf of the population. The failure lies with the political classes, not with the people.

Chapter 7
What Needs to Change?

Ireland should be a permanently wealthy and prosperous country —it has all of the necessary ingredients: a democratic state that is a member of the EU, English-speaking with an educated, highly skilled workforce that attracts high-added-value technology jobs to the country. What we have instead is an economy that has been hampered by 'roller-coaster economics' of boom and recession and population flux. Ireland produces some of the best business minds in the world, but many of them leave. Living and working in other countries, one of the things one notices is the disproportionate number of Irish people at the pinnacles of their business and professional careers. For example, Irish CEOs dominate European air transportation, yet our own, state-protected legacy is permanently on its last legs; it is trapped between union intransigence and political meddling, which block it from thriving but never allow it to die. These are just two of the factors that pull down the Irish economy and prevent it from achieving its full potential. Other problems are presented by an education system that fails to focus on pure and applied science and an electoral system that does not appear to serve the people as well as its proponents suggest. The other significant stumbling block to success is a certain, ingrained attitude that pervades the highest offices and which is all too evident in the guise of cronyism and lack of accountability. These factors need to be addressed if Ireland is to move forward socially, politically and economically.

UNION 'EFFECTIVENESS' AND ITS COSTS

The role of unions should be, in theory, to protect workers against oppressive employers who might use their extensive resources to exploit workers and ignore their statutory rights. In recent years, however, union membership has declined in Ireland,[1] as well as in the UK and much of the Anglo-Saxon world, because unions came to be seen as antiquated or not representative of an educated workforce that could exert its own rights. Paradoxically, declining membership seems to have caused the unions in Ireland to increase their power rather than diminish it. In fact, in certain key areas they have gained undeserved influence and power. In their defence one could say they have represented their memberships with great vigour and no doubt the employees who benefit in the short-term see their achievements as victories, but at what cost to the state? What seems to be the case is that unions have inflicted a long-term cost on the state that is only now becoming apparent.

Ireland, like many other countries, needs reform in the public sector. The unions will resist this, of course, because that is their *raison d'être*, a given that must be accepted. However, the government must in turn accept that real labour reform is difficult to achieve without industrial strife, that it is a natural corollary of radical change and must be endured. Those who have secure jobs in protected sectors—mostly the public service—and who are paid more than the open market rate will not give up these benefits without resistance, while the unions see their role as being to maintain the status quo. Simply appeasing the unions and engaging in various pacifying initiatives, like benchmarking, achieves nothing but the situation we have now, which requires even more aggressive cuts. This is the real weakness of union activities in Ireland: instead of anticipating and managing change, they have blocked change and this has simply let the problems inflate, leading to only one outcome—a draconian show-down with the government when the

---

1   *The Irish Times*/Ireland website, 10 April 2008.

public purse is finally drained of its last reserves. This does no service to the state, to the public servants or to the taxpayers.

Some examples will help to make the point. In October and November 2008 more than 16,000 people lost their jobs each month; the economy was slowly working its way back to pre-Celtic Tiger levels. These rises were significant for three reasons. First, they were the highest monthly increase on record. Secondly, for the previous ten years seasonally adjusted unemployment had fallen in October due to returning university students and the rehiring of temporary educational staff laid off over the summer. Thirdly, it was part of a continuing trend that had begun a year previously. Away from the real world, however, the number of public service workers actually increased, which meant an increase in the salaries and pensions bills.

This strange state of affairs is not unprecedented: over 100,000 public servants were hired between 2003 and 2006, a period during which manufacturing jobs were contracting. The annual pay bill for the public service is now approaching €19 billion, an increase of 47 per cent since 2002.[2] Plus, final-salary pensions are generous in the extreme; the future cost of pension liability to the government has been calculated at €75 billion,[3] a figure that is simply not fundable but everyone just ignores. To compound this, public service jobs appear sacrosanct and forced redundancies or dismissals of permanent staff are rare. One might think that such perks and job security would come with lower salaries, but in 2006, *per* CSO figures, public service workers were paid 48 per cent more per hour (€25.45 versus €17.11) than those working in the private sector.

If this wasn't enough, whilst the private sector is cutting its costs base, the public service unions always appear startlingly oblivious to the need for serious reform. In its 2008 report IMPACT, the largest public sector union, stated that 'Ireland remains a strong, prosperous country and, in the forthcoming pay talks, unions are determined that workers will get a fair share of the success they've helped to create.'[4] Meanwhile the general secretary of SIPTU argued

2   *Times* online, 19 October 2008.
3   *Times* online, 19 October 2008.
4   IMPACT Biennial Report, 2006–2008.

that 'The vast majority of public-service workers are not well paid'. If this is an opening gambit in national pay negotiations, it is a very brave one. Nonetheless the reality of the economic situation is evident when one considers that the government is now borrowing money to pay the salaries of public servants—a reality that does not seem to have struck the general secretary of the Civil and Public Services Union (CPSU), Blair Horan, who said that 'The Civil Service has been engaged in ongoing and successful reform over the past decade.'[5] If increasing the pay bill by 47 per cent over six years is reform, I would not like to see what a deterioration of the situation looks like.

This bull-headedness at the heart of the management of the public services is a recipe for fiscal disaster, exacerbated by the fact that taking something off people is politically more difficult than not giving it to them in the first place. Apart from the medical card fiasco, it is obvious the government does not have the nerve required to do the former. In one example of a system not in sync with the times, 8,599 staff were given performance appraisals, the outcome of which was that one person was denied his/her annual pay rise. Think of the effort and cost of appraising 8,599 people, and that was the sole result. No words are harsh enough to describe what the free market thinks of this and the effect of it. Jim Power, chief economist of Friends First, said: 'It is impossible for the unions to say they have more low-paid workers than the private sector because these statistics don't back it up. It's the sort of misinformed information thrown out by unions that resulted in the debacle that was benchmarking.'[6] In short, Power said the economy was being 'strangled' by the taxpayer having to pay the public service salaries and pensions. In spite of the view of economists, it takes an economic meltdown for the government to form a committee to investigate reforms.

To those working in the commercial world the attitudes and practices of public services unions are difficult to believe. Anyone with a basic grasp of business can tell you that paying people with borrowed money to do something that may not need to be done is

5 www.wrp.org.
6 *Times* online, 25 October 2008.

bad economics. It is no longer sufficient to freeze the public service pay bill, it has become necessary to cut it back drastically. It is too simplistic, of course, to suggest that all public servants are wandering around aimlessly doing crosswords, on the contrary many public servants are over-worked and contribute vital and essential services and in some areas more, not less, employees are needed. The problem lies in mismanagement of overall staffing and a tendency to let the unions dictate the agenda and 'reforms' rather than the government. For the government's part, it appears unwilling to have a major confrontation with the public service, but that conflict is necessary if the unions will not accept reality. There is little doubt that if the unions believe, as they appear to, that their mandate is to continually increase salaries and numbers of public service jobs, then a conflict is not only imminent, it is a vital necessity so that the government can control expenditure. If the government will not do this, then ultimately the IMF will have to do it for us two or three years hence.

The best time to reform the public service was during the boom, when the private sector labour market could have absorbed the extra workers and channelled them into productive uses whilst easing the public sector problem. It would have been a painless and natural process at that time, but unfortunately the public service unions convinced the government to engage in the bizarre 'benchmarking' process instead, which rapidly drove up the salaries of public servants and stopped the automatic process that would have seen people move into the private sector or at least made the public service less attractive. The funding for benchmarking came from borrowed money pumped into the economy and now that this has dried up, the chickens are coming home to roost. With unemployment soaring and jobs scarce, those in the public sector will cling to theirs even more, which in turn will make change even more difficult and divisive to achieve. The option of early retirement and voluntary redundancy has been mooted by the government, but only because this is the path of least resistance. It does not represent an amelioration of the underlying problems.

What is needed at this juncture is tough, decisive management by the government, and public sector unions that are really interested in social partnership and the long-term success of the economy. The reform won't be easy, but in the long run it will be beneficial. In an accurate foretelling of the situation an editorial in the *Kilkenny People* in 1999 stated that 'the public service unions are becoming the real rulers of Ireland'.[7]

QUASI PUBLIC COMPANIES AND UNIONS

There are two major 'Irish' airlines in operation: Aer Lingus and Ryanair. Aer Lingus came into existence in April 1936 as a semi-state company. It is now a quasi-privatised entity[8] and as of October 2008 had almost 4,000 employees[9] for the forty-two aircraft it operates. In 2008 one-third of its services did not operate 'on time'.[10] Ryanair has 166 aircraft, that's 400 per cent more than Aer Lingus, yet it has just over 50 per cent more employees, at 6,200.[11] Since taking to the skies about twenty years ago, Ryanair has become the world's largest international scheduled airline. By comparison, Aer Lingus' expansion within that timeframe amounted to opening a new base in Belfast and Gatwick—and it had to fight long and hard against its unions to achieve that.

The difference between the two companies is stark. Aer Lingus is currently losing money; Ryanair is making money. Ryanair is constantly berated in the Irish media for not giving free coffee or not having boarding passes, but it has proudly carried an Irish name

---

7   *The Kilkenny People,* 10 October 1999.
8   I say part 'quasi' because the government still owns a large enough stake that it was able to block a takeover bid from a real free market competitor, i.e. Ryanair. The price offered for the shares was good by the standards of the time and overvalued by today's share price. A real free market investor would have negotiated a higher price and then sold the shares, netting a good profit. Instead the government dodged the issue and effectively blocked the takeover. Thus it is clear the shareholding is political, not financial, and as such it cannot be said to be a truly independent, non-political business entity. This is compounded by the 15 per cent shareholding by the staff and other, non-business holdings, such as Denis O'Brien, who appears to have purchased his shareholding in order to frustrate the aims of Michael O'Leary. This is not a normal share-ownership structure.
9   Google Finance.
10 www.aerlingus.com.
11 Google Finance.

throughout Europe and continues to grow passenger levels at an impressive rate. Aer Lingus has been cosseted and protected by tightly controlled working practices that have limited its ability to expand. Its ownership structure is even stranger: the employees own approximately 17 per cent of the shares; the government owns just over 25 per cent; while Ryanair owns about 28 per cent. It isn't an Irish success story, although this is not for the want of trying by the management team. It has had, and lost, two superb CEOs, who moved on to very attractive posts.

In spite of all this, the unions have fought change in Aer Lingus tooth and nail. Even when the company faced losses in 2008 and 2009, the unions still resisted plans to reduce staff costs to normal international levels. They seem fixated on 'protecting' 4,000 jobs at the cost of the 4,000 jobs, rather than accepting that 2,000 jobs in a more viable airline makes better business sense. The unions are safe in the knowledge that the government will not allow the company to be taken over by anyone who will implement real change, so it is left in a no-man's-land of intransigent union workers, indifferent customers and a shrinking cash pile. It is insupportable that even in the face of a huge hole in the public finances, the government did not wish to sell its stake to Ryanair on its second attempt to purchase the airline. If Ryanair begins transatlantic flights, then the few natural advantages Aer Lingus has left will vanish. The Celtic Tiger essentially interrupted change that would have been forced by economic reality. More effort, more time and more energy has been spent on Aer Lingus by governments, the labour courts, the media and the public than many other issues that are more important simply because it is highly unionised and everyone is trapped in this situation from which there appears to be no escape.

There is little doubt that Aer Lingus does not pass the acid test of closeted business entities. This test asks the question: 'If it did not exist, would anyone create it?' Would any businessperson create a small airline with enormous staff overheads, intransigent unions, no clear strategy—is it a low-cost airline or a full service transatlantic airline?—and then disperse ownership over the government, the staff and its largest rival so that the only agreement that can be reached is an agreement to do nothing? The answer, obviously, is no.

Ireland is not the only country with such problems and issues, but that is no reason to tolerate them. Basic economics tells us that resources that are being wasted on such businesses would be better diverted to other, more profitable ones that will create a real competitive advantage, produce long-term, sustainable jobs and a tax base for the country and that will not need to be propped up by the government, for which read taxpayers. If you are an employee of Aer Lingus or a union representative, you don't want to read this, and that is perfectly understandable. But I'm afraid the bottom line is that the country cannot support such luxuries anymore.

THE ELECTORAL SYSTEM

The voting system used in Ireland, technically called Proportional Representation through Single Transferable Vote in a multi-candidate constituency (PRSTV, or PR), has had a significant impact on the governments elected to date. In theory the PR system is designed to ensure that no vote is 'wasted' and that an accurate representation of the people's wishes is formulated. This is achieved by nominating a first preference vote, second preference vote and so on, so that if your first candidate is not going to be elected, then your second preference vote comes into play. It sounds good in theory, in that it was designed to produce a more representative Dáil. However, the reality is that while it achieves this aim, it does so at the cost of creating unstable governments.

In recent years Ireland has produced a succession of coalition governments. Whilst coalition governments are not necessarily or inherently unstable, there are strong arguments that they are unable to take difficult decisions and can fracture easily under pressure— as evidenced by the medical card issue in 2008.[12] They tend to take the path of least resistance and not confront the difficult issues of the day. While this approach ensures their survival, it also ensures mediocrity in decision-making and lowest-common-denominator politics.

12 The announcement that automatic entitlement to medical cards for those aged over 70 years would be revoked and a means-testing scheme introduced provoked widespread public outrage and protests outside the Dáil. As a result the government was forced to do a U-turn on its policy.

In most developed democracies the major parties have usually shown their ability to run a country reasonably well. For example, in the UK both the Labour and Conservative parties have a proven track record of being able to take tough decisions when necessary because their voting system, which employs a first-past-the-post approach, produces stronger, more stable governments. Both the Conservatives and the Labour Party have been elected with popular voting percentages that would create coalition governments here in Ireland. A large parliamentary majority gives the electorate a chance to produce one government every four or five years, and that government is given enough room to implement enough of its decisions so that the voters can judge its performance. Ireland, on the other hand, with its PR system, simply does not produce enough stable majority governments that are capable of making tough decisions when needed. There is little doubt that if Fianna Fáil (FF) had a sufficiently strong majority in 2008, the party would not have backed down on the tough Budget decisions and would likely have taken an even tougher stance on some issues. With a strong majority the government can endure a few drop-outs and would not succumb to pressures from the constituencies so easily because each TD would know that he/she might be popular locally, but would lose the whip at the next election, and likely his/her job, once the current spat was forgotten about. The need to pander to special interest, to maintain knife-edge governments and to worry about marginal seats makes cowards of politicians who might otherwise be men and women of action.

Given the drawbacks inherent in PR, why does Ireland persist in using it? The system was put in place by de Valera, possibly because, as a maths teacher, he was drawn to its theory. Whatever the original attraction, de Valera himself realised its weaknesses, which is why he tried to change the Constitution and have PR removed before he left office. The referendum failed, however, as did a subsequent one on the same issue held by a later government. It is likely that at the time people feared—or perhaps de Valera wanted—a dominant FF government, but if that turned out to be the case, then so be it. If the voters vote for a dominant FF government, then a FF government should be elected, then the voters can judge it on its merits and either vote it in again or not. It is arguable that a first-past-the-post system would have created, and could create, a single opposition party from Fine Gael (FG)/Labour because otherwise those parties might never be elected.

It is time to address this issue and move Ireland's electoral system in line with that of other modern nations. The critics will say that opposition government gives greater representation to a wider range of viewpoints, but Irish history gives the lie to that aspiration.

CRONYISM

It is probably true to say that every country has some level of cronyism in government circles, but Ireland seems to be particularly badly afflicted by this problem. After several tribunals and many years of unanswered questions, most people now accept that some Irish politicians displayed a marked lack of ethical or moral conscience. This encompasses an unfortunate spectrum of wrongs, from questionable behaviour to corruption. Politicians are only human, of course, which makes them vulnerable to the excesses of power. The problem, at base, is that the Irish political system was not sufficiently regulated or controlled in order to keep its adherents on the right side of the line. The cost to Ireland of this lapse has not only been financial, it has also stunted the provision of real public services and, on a broader level, has slowly ground down the credibility of the political classes. Commentators have said time and time again that this rot must be stopped, and they are absolutely right. The ability to trust the holders of high office is essential for a nation to prosper.

The final months of 2008 threw up a series of revelations that were hotly debated across the country. As the economy began to slip, the public learned about the fantastic extravagances indulged in by public representatives on research trips to North America and other places. Chief among these in the newspaper columns was the director of FÁS, but he was certainly not alone in putting his own comfort before the public purse. This spendthrift attitude has been ingrained in the political system since the infamous days of Charles Haughey, who warned the country to tighten its belt whilst living the life of a wealthy man, thanks to the taxpayer. The stories are many and we are all familiar with them, but suffice to say that there is an attitude of entitlement that must be challenged, routed and regulated. Any person holding public office in Ireland should always be aware of his/her duties to the public and put the common good before his/her own gain. This is the basic requirement of ethical politics, and we should all strive to achieve it.

It would be wonderful to be able to say that, from now on, we shall elect only ethically sound people who have a finely tuned moral compass. Of course, it will never be that easy. Human beings are vulnerable to temptation, and that is a fact of life. The answer, therefore, is to put in place rules or guidelines that do the hard work on the humans' behalf. What needs to be established is a level of accountability that acts as an incentive and as a deterrent. This could be achieved by a very simple process of publishing the top thirty expense reports, in order of monetary value, of ministers and civil servants. The information could be made available on the government website so that voters could see exactly where their money is being spent. This sort of transparency would go a long way to solving both the problem of unethical behaviour and the problem of lack of trust in elected representatives, which can only benefit the public as well as the politicians.

ENCOURAGING PERSONAL RESPONSIBILITY

The term 'whistleblower' is often used pejoratively, but people who report immoral or illegal behaviour actually do a great service to their fellow citizens. The most common cases of whistleblowing have involved employees of large corporations who recognised that theft, embezzlement or gross mismanagement was taking place and resolved to do something about it, rather than avert their eyes. It takes much courage and tenacity to go up against a large company, and these qualities should be lauded, rewarded and encouraged.

Famous whistleblowers include Sherron Watkins, who helped expose the financial mismanagement at Enron, and Erin Brockovich, immortalised in film as the woman who refused to accept that polluted drinking water was a justifiable side-effect of industry. In Europe the most well-known whistleblower is Paul van Buitenen,[13] an auditor who in 1998/9 exposed corruption and cronyism within

13 BBC News.

the EU Commission. As a result, every member of the Commission resigned symbolically. Symbolism was as far as it went, however, and three years later van Buitenen claimed that little had changed. In 2007 he said: 'Things have got even worse. There is now a regulation which supposedly protects so-called whistleblowers which makes officials believe that they can uncover scandals. But in reality, if one does this, they are destroyed. So the regulation does not work.'[14]

Protection is the key concern here. If a person decides to blow the whistle on immoral or illegal behaviour, he/she faces being ostracised by colleagues, ignored for promotion or even being fired. This is where whistleblower legislation is needed—to protect employees who go to the police or to the media and present evidence of serious wrongdoing within organisations. It is in society's best interest that such people are given the forum in which to present their evidence and are protected from those who would seek to deter them from doing so.

Ireland is in urgent need of such legislation. Every now and then we are afforded a glimpse inside the world of government quangos and monolithic bureaucratic and state enterprises—leaked emails are circulated to the press, or a reporter hears from an anonymous source that something is going on—but few people ever come forward to give details. The Irish state bureaucracy is still a secretive place, where whistleblowers are often decried as informers, snitches or just vindictive people. The fact is that these people are often quite traumatised by the corruption or incompetence they have witnessed, especially in the medical arena, and are torn between doing what they believe is right versus what they know is good for their career. A hospital consultant may have sufficient confidence and professional independence to alert the public or the authorities to problems, but junior staff may not. Many potential whistleblowers simply do not wish to sacrifice their careers to the common good, and indeed they shouldn't have to. If there existed unequivocal legislation guarding the rights of the whistleblower, people wouldn't be forced into making such a difficult choice.

What legislation is needed, then? The required legislation needs to achieve a number of goals: to insulate the whistleblower from

---

14 www.dw-word.de, 2 April 2007.

civil suits for breach of employment contract or commercially sensitive information; to protect the whistleblower from retaliation by compensating them should their employers take action against them. In some countries, such as North America, substantial monetary rewards are offered to whistleblowers if they identify incompetence or embezzlement in contracts supplying the government. The reward can be as high as 15–25 per cent of the value saved by the government. In Ireland, where so many public contracts run over budget, such laws would have the potential to save the taxpayer significant sum of money.

CORRUPTION: THE TRUE COST OF PAST DECISIONS

Much has been written about corruption over the last decade, too much in many cases, and it is therefore easy to suffer from 'tribunal fatigue' and ignore the flow of information. It would be wrong, however, to let such weariness result in the real effect of corruption in Ireland not being scrutinised carefully because it is absolutely essential that a close study is carried out and recorded.

When Ben Dunne, then head of one of the country's largest retail chains, decided to take a holiday in Florida in 1992, it was a decision that would change Irish politics. To make a long story short, he was found in controversial circumstances, which in turn led to other members of his family questioning his ability to remain as head of the family business, Dunnes Stores. Out of the resulting corporate tussle rolled the fact that Mr Dunne had been paying substantial sums of money to the then Taoiseach, Charles Haughey. The McCracken Inquiry was established in 1997 to ascertain what exactly had occurred. This was accompanied by the Tribunal of Inquiry Into Certain Planning Matters and Payments, better known as the Flood Tribunal (and latterly as the Mahon Tribunal, after Justice Flood retired), and followed by the Tribunal of Inquiry into Payments to Politicians and Related Matters, known as the Moriarty Tribunal.

These tribunals were vast and complicated affairs, but from them came some simple facts. Three people were alleged to have received corrupt payments: Liam Lawlor, Ray Burke and Charles Haughey. The clear inference to be drawn from the evidence presented, and from common sense, is that if these three men did accept such payments, then so did many more people, but they evaded the scrutiny of the tribunals. The broader question, which is often missed in the whirlwind of 'donations', payments, bank accounts and Bertie Wooster-type financial scheming, is: *why* did they receive money? What did they exchange for that money? The answer is obvious: they sold their ability to decide between option A and option B or choice A and choice B. Whether it was planning permission, licences, contracts or even passports, when there was nothing left to sell, senior politicians made decisions based not on improving their constituents' welfare but on improving their personal financial well-being. The appalling notion of decisions sold to the highest bidder becomes, on the ground, a game of short-term financial gain for the politicians involved and long-term losses for the country. If the best decision was replaced by a paid-for decision, then the people suffered to some quantum and these added up, decision by decision and envelope by envelope.

Let's look at one example: the infrastructure in Irish cities. If, as has been alleged in the tribunals, money was the prime motivation in the planning decisions made for the cities, then the long-term needs of the citizens were never considered. Yes, there are houses, shopping centres and roads, but facilities such as schools, local shopping and transportation all took a backseat, presumably because there was nobody willing to pay 'political donations' to build such infrastructure. Accordingly, many of the infrastructural problems and traffic-jams that blight the modern Irish city were caused by the lack of a coherent plan over the decades. Cities cannot be planned with a brown envelope in one hand and a T-square in the other; the chaos people in Ireland experience today is due to the fact that the infrastructural landscape was scarred for a number of decades by corruption. Like building on top of weak foundations, it is very hard to correct the problem retrospectively.

If the public complain about the costs of the tribunals to date—and there are many reasons to complain—they should maybe be asking a more pertinent question instead: why were they necessary at all? Why do other European countries not have endless tribunals? What was their aim and what were they designed to achieve? It is my opinion that they were not designed to be efficient or ever to achieve anything of note. It is fair to say that the real, 'meaty' revelations occurred by accident rather than investigation. The tribunals were set up as exercises in the venting and exhausting of public anger, which function they have performed well: after ten years of tribunals and startling revelations, it appears that the people are irate at those conducting the tribunals rather than at those who caused them to be conducted and who have escaped with little or no punishment.

One of the lasting effects of the tribunals has been that they have damaged people's faith in politics. This has likely been the most serious impact and part of the reason why the first Lisbon Treaty referendum was lost. The leaders of all the main political parties, excluding Sinn Féin, told the people that the best course was to vote 'yes' for Lisbon, but that advice was ignored. The Irish people have acquired a deep distrust of the entire political class and their ability to control and punish their own behaviour; of course, as the country enters very difficult economic times, trust will be vital. When the politicians ask the people to 'tighten their belts' in the national interest, it will probably provoke widespread resentment because the people will no doubt feel that the belt-tightening is not being applied equally across the board. It is a case, people suspect, of do as I say, not as I do. The endless revelations in the media about the political class chip away at the foundations of democracy.

I believe the path to corruption begins with the lax attitude that the political classes are allowed to take taxpayers' money and do with it as they wish. Without real and effective controls, in recent times there was created the potential for certain people to believe they were entitled to much more, which seems to have led to corruption. The revelations in the media over the last year of wide-scale extravagances suggest that further tales of corruption are not far behind.

Tribunals—the solution to corruption?
There are two sides to the tribunals saga: the good they did and the weakness they exposed in the sphere of political control. The tribunals afforded citizens a glimpse inside the corrupt and seedy

world of politics in Ireland in the 1980s and 1990s. Brown envelopes, suitcases of cash, votes bought for rezoning and favours done for cash—it was all there in shameful abundance. In short, some elected representatives served the people who paid them rather than the people who elected them. The consequences of these decisions continue to impact the lives of people in Ireland. Put it this way, if shopping centres were public infrastructure, we would be living in a transportation Nirvana.

It requires a huge leap of faith to presume that at a juncture when an excess of money was in circulation in the economy, the politicians and businesspeople who were corrupt became honest simply because of the work of the tribunals. This is unlikely, indeed the recent banking and finance scandals are beginning to show that there was much activity going on below the radar that we knew nothing about and may not discover until it is too late to avert the consequences. This raises the second difficulty—other than exposing some dark secrets, what did the tribunals actually achieve? They have dragged on for over a decade, cost many millions of Euro, yet almost no one has been prosecuted as a result of their findings. In short, justice was both delayed and denied.

One could argue the case that the tribunals were set up to obstruct justice, being a form of special, privatised justice where the defendants turned up if they wished to, engaged in endless legal appeals and then complained in the media that the investigations were lasting too long and costing too much. The political classes appeared to believe that justice was for other people, that they should not be called to account for their actions nor accept responsibility for them. It brought to mind George Orwell's famous phrase—'all are equal, but some are more equal than others'. If the ordinary citizen commits a crime, the normal legal process is applied to him/her. Politicians, on the other hand, get tribunals. A justice system should be confident enough and capable enough to deal with any crime, committed by any person. For example, during the investigation into the sale of peerages for donations in Westminster, the police interviewed many politicians, including the then prime minister, Tony Blair. This is something one cannot imagine happening in Ireland. The Garda are simply too politically compliant, plus the reaction against such a move would likely be severe. There is a lesson to be learned here and learned well: if Ireland is to develop politically, every single citizen must be treated equally before the law. This would do away with the need for tribunals of inquiry because the Garda would be able to conduct inquiries per their legal parameters, with the full backing of the judicial system.

SCIENCE AND TECHNOLOGY

Compared with many Anglo-Saxon countries, Ireland has a generally good education system. It provides a broad education, avoiding the narrower curriculum, such as the A-level, and produces well-rounded students at the end. Maybe too rounded, though. In a world that is built on science and technology, the Irish educational system and government policy lack a focus on pure and applied sciences. Why should Ireland have a focus on the pure and applied sciences? Germany provides a good example of what can be achieved by supporting these growth areas. Germany is the largest exporting country in the world. It has a population of just over 80 million, which is just over 1 per cent of the world's population, and yet it exports 10 per cent of the total world exports. That is more than China, with a population of one billion, or the USA, with over 300 million people. Germany achieves this not only via the 'big names', like BMW, Audi, VW, Bosch, etc., but via what is known as the *mittlestand* companies. These companies, which have names few people would ever recognise, employ 22 million employees and apprentices. They are built around small towns and areas, which become specialists in certain technologies and processes. The economic success of these enterprises is built upon with intensive and continuous research and development of their products. It is an organic-based export success that is founded on converting scientific and engineering knowledge into long-term, sustainable jobs. It is no small feat to achieve this—even the Germans are having problems maintaining their lead. But it is a lucrative market and a sustainable one, which makes all the efforts in this direction worthwhile.

Ireland does have a government committee on this issue, called the Advisory Council for Science Technology and Information. Its latest report was titled *Towards a Framework for Research Careers*. With all due respect to the Council, experience tells me that any report title that begins with the word *Towards* suggests that whatever is being aimed at is a long way from being achieved. Furthermore, developing a competitive advantage is something that needs to be 'seeded' at a very basic level in an economy, its growth cannot be forced over a short period of time. The Council's report appears to be convinced that doubling PhD research posts over five years is the route to success. Yes, this may be helpful, but it is likely the route requires a much longer-term strategy: an investment of time to encourage indigenous companies that have realistic prospects of specialising and creating sustainable, long-term jobs in niche market industries. For example, Schwabach is a small town in southern Germany that I suspect few people have ever heard of, yet it is the centre for much of the world's goldleaf production. This is a highly skilled job that has changed little over the centuries, but it has created related small industries in the town and highly specialised high-tech jobs in metalwork, specialist lacquers, machinery and gold-related technology. Today, even with challenges from cheaper centres of production all around the world, Schwabach has kept its competitive advantage and expanded its skills-base in this area.

We cannot, of course, go back centuries and begin to seed industries, we are where we are now, but there are so many new technologies coming to the fore that we don't have to. The Irish government needs to bring in long-term strategies that identify and nourish such technological hubs and that run in tandem with current economic policy. However, if we are to look beyond our current difficulties, we must attempt to attract industries that can create local firms that generate knowledge and expertise, thereby tying the business to the local community because of local expertise, not because of national tax laws. On an even longer scale, we must fine-tune the educational system so that it produces students who are technologically oriented and well-versed in the kinds of needs these companies have and how employees can best fulfil them.

The road to economic success is very long and thus requires long-term planning, but it is critical that the country is now pointed in the right direction. Tax-avoidance schemes are of little long-term use. In fact, a more realistic tax base can be created when businesses are willing to stay and invest in the economy. Ireland's policy over the last century has vacillated between autarkism and provocatively flaunting its tax laws to seduce international companies. What is needed now is a hybrid of both approaches: an application of scientific and technological education to produce export-orientated firms that are Irish-centred.

THE IRISH LANGUAGE AND SCIENCE AND TECHNOLOGY

One might ask what the Irish language has to do with science and technology. The answer is, quite a lot. Anyone who examines the German education syllabus will immediately understand why it is a nation of precision engineers and scientists. From a young age those who are likely to attend university are streamed into schools called Gymnasiums. From the age of ten or eleven these students study science subjects that the average student in Ireland might not encounter for five years or more. Their young minds are stretched, pushed and challenged and those who cannot keep up are ejected. It may be a tad ruthless, but it obviously produces the right people. Compare this to the Irish education system, where the compulsory teaching of the Irish language saps resources, wastes valuable education time and, paradoxically, is, I believe, going to cause the demise of the language. This is a serious national educational issue in a high-tech world.

Approximately one-seventh of the average Irish student's time is spent learning Irish; this is much the same amount of time as is spent learning maths and more than is spent on physics, chemistry, French or German or, in fact, most other subjects. I sat recently with four Irish friends, all university graduates, and none of us knew what the Gaelic word for 'star' was. This says more about the education system than is apparent at first glance. While our German counterparts were learning applied sciences, we were spending study time learning things we would forget once out the door of secondary school. In a competitive, multi-lingual world where the focus is on science and technology, this is a luxury we simply cannot afford anymore. It is no longer a political issue or a nationalistic issue, it is an economic issue.

The problem is not just the time taken up with Irish in school but also the fact that the structures that have been built up around the language sap other valuable resources—mostly money. The Official Languages Act 2003[15] and the 1937 Constitution make Irish the first official language of the country and enforce its (mostly artificial) use. This state of affairs is maintained by a patriotic but very small minority of people, who continuously push this issue. It is not sufficient that they themselves speak Irish, they appear to want to force others to do so as well, something that might be described as either well-meant enthusiasm or blind zealotry. It is obvious to all that they are flying in the face of linguistic reality, yet the government is not willing to point this out to them. The first government ombudsman tasked with handling complaints regarding government departments' compliance with the 2003 Act admitted: 'While we are fortunate in currently having staff who have competency in the language, these staff are not available in all grades and areas of responsibility. One limitation we face is that we cannot readily recruit or replace staff with the requisite skills.'[16] In other words, one branch of the government is trying to compel other branches to use more Irish, but it potentially could not understand or deal with the complaints it might receive from the public if they were made in Irish. That is surely an extraordinary situation.

All of this is being fuelled by taxpayers' money, of course, even if the majority of taxpayers do not speak Irish. It becomes even more unreal when you consider that the government was pushed into having Irish made a working language of the European Union,[17] at a cost of €3.5 million. However, the EU was not as willing to close its eyes to the paradoxical situation and criticised the 'acute shortage of Irish interpreters' and pointed out that this was because there is 'no training course in the Republic in conference interpreting'.[18] And why is there no such training course? Because there was no real economic demand for it until the government created one artificially. Furthermore, the EU complained that upon requesting

15 www.oisin.ie/act.html: lists the outline legal requirements of the Act.
16 ombudsman.gov.ie/en/LanguagesAct/OfficialLanguagesAct2003Scheme/.
17 www.rte.ie/news/2005/0613/irishlanguage.html.
18 www.irishtimes.com/newspaper/frontpage/2007/1013/1192222978624.html.

an official grammar guide, it was discovered that the 'new edition of the official grammar has not been published for years and the current edition is out of print'. It took the EU to point out the folly of what the government was doing. This is all against a background of schools where classes are overcrowded and underfunded.[19] We are banging our heads with a mallet and then wondering why we have a headache.

There is an infinitely better scenario available for the vast majority of people in the country:

Step 1—scrap Irish as a compulsory subject and replace it with a less intense subject on our rich and diverse Irish culture, to which so many people seem oblivious, overshadowed, as it is, by the language.

Step 2—utilise the time freed up to teach a European language until children are ten years of age and then teach pure science subjects on a daily basis.

Step 3—take the money that is wasted on teaching and forcing people to learn, translate and transact in Irish and funnel it into the education system, where it can fund the learning of modern language, scientific subjects and capital programmes.

Step 4—harvest the results from the more honed group of students that will thus emerge. One way to do this would be to establish the future equivalent of a Google or a Microsoft, and from that begin to create a real Irish scientific industry.

Step 5—by removing the compulsory teaching of the Irish language and replacing it with a richer, deeper study of Irish culture and an optional Leaving Certificate language subject on Irish, it is likely the language will flourish again. This is not my opinion, but that of Manchán Magan,[20] an Irish writer and a very strong proponent of the language. Magan quotes Brian Stowell,

19 www.independent.ie/lifestyle/parenting/its-unheard-of-where-i-come-from-1475527.html.
20 *The Irish Times*, 18 March 2008.

who revived the Manx language on the Isle of Man and who said that 'the biggest problem with Irish now is that it is compulsory in schools'.

Ireland has the ability to pursue a win-win-win national strategy: to stimulate the scientific base of the economy and create more pure and applied scientific programmes, to bind us more into Europe by learning a second language and thereby attract European corporations and, finally, to teach a true understanding of Irish culture. All that is required to achieve this is one or two difficult decisions by the politicians and the people. The road to reform will not be smooth, that much is certain, but the benefits will be substantial.

THE QUESTION OF RESPONSIBILITY: NUREMBERG AND NEW ZEALAND

Before leaving these arguments, it is worth addressing one other issue that is of importance: responsibility.

When Ireland gained independence in 1921, the slate of economic history was wiped clean, in other words we should measure our politicians' performance since then. There has been a tendency in some quarters, however, to look back before 1921 and suggest that certain factors, such as the Great Famine of 1847, had such long-reaching effect that they can be used as quasi-excuses for the substandard performance of the country's political administrations. Here, I propose to look at two examples—Nuremberg and New Zealand—to provide a comparison and contrast to highlight the peculiarities and particularities of the Irish situation.

Nuremberg is a city in Northern Bavaria with a population of one million people; Dresden is a city in Eastern Saxony; both are important cities in reunified Germany. They share something in common: both cities were bombed extensively in the Second World War by incendiary bombing. This action caused huge loss of life and immense damage, leaving few buildings of any substance standing. It was also clear that some of these bombing raids verged on revenge for the *Luftwaffe* attacks in Britain, with no real effort being made to avoid civilian casualties. It was total war: Germany had started the war; British cities had been extensively damaged; the attitude of the

British was that they weren't going to risk total victory by observing the niceties of war, to which they felt Germany had not adhered.

After the war, Nuremberg and Dresden found themselves on either side of the Iron Curtain and subject to different political ideologies. Nuremberg was in the newly founded and democratic West Germany, while Dresden languished in the oppressive and communist East Germany, ruled by a Russian puppet government and its secret police force. Less than half-a-century later, communism failed and the 'wall' fell, revealing a Dresden that was dour and undeveloped. Much of the damage of wartime was still visible, for example the stunning Frauenkirche, in the city centre, was left in a pile of rubble for almost fifty years. What public infrastructure was completed was shoddy, and the quality of life for residents was low.

By comparison, Nuremberg was a modern, progressive city with a highly developed infrastructure, including an underground, a new airport, enviable public facilities and a generally prosperous and wealthy population. It was not Paris or Rome, but the residents were proud of it. They had even reassembled the magnificent stone cathedral in the city by finding all of the stones in the rubble, numbering them and putting the whole back together like a giant 3D jigsaw puzzle—as only the Germans could do. At this juncture, had a local politician in Nuremberg stood up and said that some failure to provide public services or the failure to improve some aspect of the city was due to the horrendous bombings by the Allies, he would have been ridiculed in the media and likely voted out of office.

One need only look to Dresden to see that the failings were political. Dresden was the way it was because of the failure of communism; Nuremberg was the way it was because of the success of German social-market capitalism. If Dresden had been part of West Germany, it too would have looked like Nuremberg or, more probably, like Berlin or Munich as it was a more spectacular city before the war. Now, in the twenty-first century, Dresden is slowly transforming itself into a modern city and in a number of decades will catch up with other European cities, if not surpass them. The Frauenkirche was rebuilt in 2005, exactly as it had been before, and reopened as a symbol of the renewal of the city.

   The point of this story is that the German government and the
local politicians of Nuremberg woke up the day after the Second
World War ended and began solving their problems, began dealing
with the contemporary realities of providing for their citizens and
they got on with that job. Problems were identified and those problems were solved. Europe has evolved in much the same way. Many
countries, in fact most, if one thought about it, could hold grievances
against the Germans for the atrocities of the war, but they don't. It
was a different time, with different people and different values;
Europeans of today look forwards, not backwards, and try to solve
their problems together. Ireland has been independent for almost a
century and its condition is the responsibility of the politicians and,
by inference, those who elected them. Compared to the condition
West Germany was in in 1945, we got the country in a reasonably good
state in 1921. In fact, more damage was done in the subsequent civil
war (1922–3) than in the preceding War of Independence (1919–21).

   New Zealand is similar to Ireland in many ways. It is an English-
speaking island country with a historically agrarian-based
economy and is located on the periphery of another, larger country
and trading region. At the time of the Great Famine in Ireland,
New Zealand was all but empty of European settlers—only 9,000
had arrived by then. By 1921—the date of Irish independence—it
had a total population of just over one million. By 1959, when Mr
de Valera had left office and Ireland's population had contracted,
the population of New Zealand had reached three million; it now
stands at 4.3 million, proving that a successful economy will
maintain its population and attract more people. Constant and
steady population is achievable from any population base, if a
country is governed competently.

   If a government does its job and creates a successful economy,
people will come—it is as simple as that. Whilst Mr de Valera was
fretting over the precise constitutional nature of the Irish state in the
1920s and 1930s, the New Zealand government worked to grow its
economy and population. Strangely, New Zealand is one of the few
countries in the world that has no codified constitution whatsoever.
It wasn't until 1986 that it was to rectify this and the Constitutional
Act was passed in parliament, outlining the legal parameters

pertaining in the country. Nonetheless, they currently rely on an unwritten constitutional system that is a blend of various statutes, decisions by the courts, unwritten conventions and prerogative powers. New Zealand does not have a constitution in the Irish sense of the word, yet I doubt few of its residents really care about this. Did anyone, or does anyone today, who is considering emigrating to New Zealand muse over this and say to themselves, 'does New Zealand have dominion status or is it a republic with a written constitution'? No, they do not. What they think about is a better life for themselves and their families plus other factors, like jobs, schooling, quality of life, etc. Even worse by republican standards, the Queen of England is the theoretical head of government in New Zealand. Yet this doesn't seem to concern the New Zealanders too much. They see it as a historical oddity, which is what it is, with a bit of pomp and circumstance thrown in for good measure.

The point of this story is that depopulation is a function of economic success or failure, as history has demonstrated in Ireland. Between 1921 and 1959 Ireland suffered depopulation, which is also probably going to occur over the next decade; using extrapolated figures, it is not too difficult to postulate that it is already contracting in 2009. The reality is that countries may draw lines in the water and along fields and define a country, as the Irish Free State did, but people often don't take much notice of such things. In the case of Ireland, after Independence we still had a *de facto* economic union with the UK because Irish citizens had freedom to travel to and from the UK, there was a common currency until 1979 and a common working language. The population therefore did what many people do in an economic union and simply moved within that area in pursuit of their own self-interest, as occurs in the USA every day of the week. De Valera was in a competition of competences as to who could run a country better—and he lost. If Ireland's population begins to contract again, it will be because of the failure of Ireland's politicians and nobody else. Responsibility cannot be shifted back in time or to another group or to the broader excuse of economic 'circumstances'. There comes a time when people must collectively decide to leave the past behind and move forward into a better future together.

CONCLUSION

So, it is clear from this overview of the problems besetting Ireland that there are a number of stumbling blocks that stand between us and change, and that these must be tackled and removed. This is not simply a matter for the politicians, however. We are all guilty of thinking by rote at times, of slipping into comfortable attitudes instead of challenging ourselves and deciding for ourselves. If the attitude of entitlement is visible at political level, one can be sure it is found throughout society. Indeed, the Celtic Tiger brought out the worst in many Irish people, leading to a grasping avarice that has left its mark on the country. The best way forward now is to acknowledge the mistakes of the past and to learn from them, to recognise our own weaknesses and be vigilant against them. There is an onus on every citizen to behave for the common good, it's something we should ideally teach our children in school, so that the next generation will not be condemned to repeat the mistakes this one has made.

Chapter 8
Solving the Key Problems

What we are examining primarily is how and why the Irish state failed. The economy, in my opinion and in the opinion of others, went wrong in 1999. Instead of working to rectify what had gone wrong, the government drove us recklessly into a narrow cul-de-sac, and now the very shape of the economy has been altered. The credit-driven growth went on so long that many people don't seem to understand the wrong turn we took; there seems to be a genuine inability to see or comprehend the full extent of the problem that has been created by mismanagement of the economic system. Instead of building hospitals, undergrounds, airports railways, etc., we built spas, shopping centres, hotels, expensive restaurants and golf courses. Many of the businesses in Ireland are simply not viable because they are based on spending driven by borrowing, not earning. In effect, the money Ireland spent over the last decade must now be repaid, but the banks who lent this money are insolvent. The businesses built on the loans are insolvent. The country shifted away from production to consumption and servicing that consumption, which was a tragic mistake.

Some of the media coverage in Ireland of the boom and bust has been excellent, but there is also appearing a self-censorship that runs along the lines of, 'oh well, there is too much doom and gloom, we have to be positive'. There is an instinct in everyone, it seems, to be positive and optimistic, and anything that goes against this, that points out the reality of the situation, is criticised as being negative or 'doom-laden'. The impression is given in some quarters of the media, and particularly by the government, that this is simply a setback, a temporary halt in the progress of the economy, and that we just have to get over this hump and all will be grand once the world economy recovers.

This approach is entirely unhelpful. The words 'optimism', 'pessimism' and 'positivity' must be replaced by a new word: realism. The worse the situation becomes, the more critical commentary is generated about the Irish economy. Yet such commentary, even if it is constructive, is batted away as if it is malevolent or even part of the problem. There is even a pattern developing: commentary from London is deflected by suggestions that they don't like the Euro or that they were jealous of Ireland's success and are now gleeful; criticisms from entities such as the IMF are explained away by the fact that such bodies don't understand the Irish economy. One would imagine that criticisms from a Nobel Prize-winner such as Paul Krugman would be difficult to deflect, but it is still the response. On *Prime Time*[1] (21 April 2009) the gist of the reaction was that Ireland simply had 'image problems'. One guest said that criticism by Paul Krugman had 'a distinct whiff of paddywackery' and the usual phrases, such as 'talking down Ireland', made their appearance, along with suggestions that some commentators were 'bringing their own prejudice'. The inference was that Paul Krugman, writing in the *New York Times*, didn't understand the Irish economy and was looking at the figures superficially. Well, I don't think Mr Krugman received a Noble Prize in economics by being superficial. The shocking fact was that those appearing on *Prime Time* were not even government representatives.

Of course, when government ministers do get involved, the results can be just as shocking. Early on in the crisis the Minister for Finance, Brian Lenihan, contacted RTÉ to complain about a Liveline[2] programme that broadcast comments by some people who were taking their money out of the banks—those would be the same

---

1   The national broadcaster's flagship current affairs programme.
2   'Liveline' is a discussion programme aired on RTÉ Radio 1. As it is a public discussion forum, it often reflects the most pressing issues for the ordinary people of Ireland.

banks he had to guarantee subsequently, to the tune of €400 billion. One has to wonder how the Minister views the world when he can take time at the height of an economic crisis to ring RTÉ to try to censor it. Only recently, Mr Lenihan said there was going to be a roadshow of sorts to dispel the 'misinformation' being peddled around the financial centres. Mr Lenihan, who is a barrister by profession, had no economic training or experience whatsoever prior to taking over at the Department of Finance, yet it appears he is going to explain to people like Mr Krugman what they don't understand about economics. Among those of us who are trained economists, there is a general consensus that the Irish economy is like the *Titanic*—it is fatally holed below the waterline and nothing can now save it. The banking system is failing and will need to be nationalised, but even when that happens it will merely shift the problem to the government, which will simply not be able to issue enough debt and service it. The banking system would have failed in 2008 but the government stepped in and saved it. In doing so, the government shackled itself to the banking system and it will, as a consequence, default on its sovereign debt one or two years hence. This leaves aside the issues that the IFSC will raise. The result will be that the IMF or the ECB/EU, or some combination of both, will be brought in to run the country. The solutions those bodies will propose will make the last efforts of Mr Lenihan look very mild by comparison. The government is literally issuing bonds, payable over five years and beyond, to pay a portion of current public service salaries and social welfare. Within one year, the Irish government's debt will go from about 20 per cent of GDP to potentially approaching 100 per cent.

Some of Ireland's media commentators are like the 'happy clappy' brigade, seeming to believe that if you say nice things and are optimistic, then everything will be fine. To extend the *Titanic* metaphor, my point is that you could have stood on the deck of the *Titanic* and been as optimistic or as pessimistic as you liked—the ship was still going to sink; there is nothing you could have done other than to get to the lifeboats and pray to God that you got a seat. So, if the economic ship is sinking, what does the future hold for the country? In order for Ireland to recover and reshape itself for the future, there needs to be a strategy incorporating short-, medium- and long-term solutions. While the most pressing problems must be addressed quickly and decisively, there must also be a cohesive vision of where the country wants to be in twenty, thirty and fifty years time. For this reason I have divided the discussion on solutions across two chapters: here we will examine a number of practical strategies that will help to resolve the key, day-to-day issues; in the next chapter we will examine larger structural changes that could be made to the system of government and how the country functions. These practices and strategies may or may not be implemented, but the issues raised here need to be discussed and understood by the people. That is the aim of this book: to spark a debate on these critical issues. I think everyone reading this realises now that what we are facing is not a cyclical recession but a potential depression caused by decades of mismanagement. It is time to act.

SOLUTIONS FOR THE PUBLIC TRANSPORTATION SYSTEM

The Dublin Underground

Ireland's capital city is a busy hub of people and industry, but getting around is difficult. The problem is clear: Dublin lacks an integrated public transport system that is efficient and reliable. The solution is an underground rail system, which would make city travel easy and would also reduce the number of cars on the city's streets. The financial outlay to achieve this would be considerable, so are the arguments in favour of an underground convincing enough? Here are the advantages that would be accrued:

- an underground does not take up any surface space on the streets, does not require street-level tracks or stations. The only requirements are surface access zones. This approach fits well with Dublin's needs and current infrastructure.
- Underground trains speed up transport times because they can accelerate faster and travel faster than surface trains. An average underground speed is 50–80km, which would mean a trip from O'Connell Street to Dundrum could be completed in five minutes. Underground train stations also allow large numbers of

people to embark and disembark quickly, which keeps the flow of people moving smoothly and efficiently.

- It is an environmentally friendly transport mechanism in numerous ways, including low carbon emissions, very low surface architectural impact and very low noise impact on the surface once completed.
- Dublin's traffic problems have compelled many people to live near the city-centre, even though many of the houses are unsuitable for family living. An underground removes the time cost associated with travelling out from the city-centre, which releases the vast, untapped green-field sites around the city for development. There is a considerable amount of land available around Dublin, which is amazing when one considers how many people live outside the county and commute back into the city.

Any discussion of an integrated transport system—which would be a huge undertaking requiring meticulous project management—throws up an associated problem that must also be addressed. First, the problem, for which we will take the example of the Luas. The budget for the Luas more than doubled between planning and construction. Assuming this budget runs over by 'only' 50 per cent, then the final bill for the Irish public will be €7.5 billion for a system that might not be operational for another five years (projected end date is 2013). According to calculations made by one newspaper, in order to recoup even the projected capital sum an operator would have to charge €22 from Swords to St Stephen's Green. The problem, then, is that the government is inefficient when it comes to planning and managing large infrastructural projects. If that is the case, the underground could become a millstone around the neck of the Irish public. A project on that scale needs the right managers or else it will end up costing far more than it ever delivers in benefits.

Planning and Development
In order to improve its efficiency in planning and development, there are three simple lessons the government should learn.

1. *Efficiency of design*

Often when governments set out to build a national project, they start from the premise of wanting something unique, something different, something impressive that will stand as a legacy to their tenure in power. This is the wrong place from which to start. The only consideration should be: what is the best way to do this in terms of time, money and requirements? By taking this view, it would soon become apparent that the simplest way to design large-scale projects, such as an underground system, would be to take designs from other cities, designs that have been proven to work, and implement them in Ireland using the same design and/or engineering firm and altering the detail to suit local conditions. Architects might throw up their hands in horror at this 'simplistic' approach, but really, if it comes in on time, on budget and it works, will anyone care if it looks like something in a different city?

2. *Limited public and inter-agency consultation*

While a certain level of consultation is welcome and can be critical to success, too much consultation can stall a project without any gain. Consider the stages the Railway Procurement Agency (RPA) must go through before it can lay a length of track:

> **Step 1 *Pre-Application Consultation Process*:** The applicant (RPA) is now required to engage in pre-application consultations with An Bord Pleanála (ABP) before lodging a railway order application. At this stage the prospective applicant must provide ABP with 'sufficient information' to enable them to assess the proposed railway works. It is usual for there to be at least two pre-application consultation meetings held.
>
> **Step 2 *Application Process*:** When ready to make the railway order application, the applicant must publish a newspaper notice in accordance with the terms of the legislation.
>
> All documents required to accompany the railway order application must be placed on display for public inspection at various locations for a period of at least six weeks. The application documents include a draft railway order, a book of reference, a plan of the proposed railway works and an Environmental Impact Statement.

All documents must also be served on the relevant planning authority (or Local Authorities) and any other bodies prescribed by ABP.

A notice must be served on all owners and occupiers shown on the Plan of the proposed works along with a copy of the newspaper notice and all relevant extracts of the application documents.

The purpose of this display period is to allow all interested parties to view the plans of the proposed scheme. All interested parties have the opportunity to make written submissions in relation to the project to An Bord Pleanála during the six-week display period.

Step 3 *An Bord Pleanála*: On receiving the railway order application An Bord Pleanála may, at its discretion, hold an oral hearing in relation to the railway order application. This procedure replaces the previously mandatory 'public inquiry', which was required to be held by an appointee of the Minister of Transport upon receipt of a railway order application. An Bord Pleanála appoints an inspector who will chair the oral hearing and submit a report setting out the findings of the oral hearing and any recommendations considered appropriate in relation to the application. An Bord Pleanála will then decide whether to grant a railway order and what conditions to attach thereto. The railway order comes into effect eight weeks after the decision is issued unless judicial review proceedings are brought within that period.

This is a considerable investment of time in pre-planning consultation. What is needed is for the process to be streamlined, with the Department of Transport assuming full control. A core group of planners should be hired on a permanent basis from the most successful public transport agencies in the world. The only consultation meetings that should take place are between this group, the planning authorities and the Minister for Transport, whose job it should be to ensure works are completed on time and on budget, per the recommendations of the planning group. Public consultation should be limited to allowing the public to object to the planning applications in the same way as to any other planning applications. The premise for this approach is that the public good is better served by providing public services when needed. Compensation, if any is needed, can be quantified retrospectively while the building goes on.

3. Quick and efficient land acquisition

The final lesson will be the most difficult to put into practice. When a state begins large public projects, it needs one resource above all else: land. Land is the key because roads, railways and canals all run in straight lines and will cross over many privately held lands. This is provided for in the Constitution, Article 43 of which states that private property is guaranteed subject to 'social justice' and 'the common good'. Thus the government has at its disposal the instrument of land acquisition through compulsory purchase order (CPO). However, in Ireland the CPO process is slow and expensive, and the state can be reluctant to employ it.

In theory the land for public projects should be identified, a market price plus adequate compensation calculated and the land acquired. In practice, in Ireland at least, legal problems often give rise to huge costs, both in money and time. The compulsory purchase of land is a vital issue to public projects and needs to be executed swiftly and with only one consideration in mind: acquiring the land. Fair compensation should be paid and that should be an end to the matter.

The solution is clear: what is needed are aggressive, comprehensive laws regarding the compulsory purchase of lands for projects that benefit society as a whole. If necessary, a land court should be established to deal quickly with any disputes that arise. This will create a situation where landowners do not regard a CPO as a winning lottery ticket, but rather understand that the lands are required for public works that will benefit the whole community. Once the government is seen to be acting efficiently, it will encourage landowners to accept a fair price and not take legal steps to secure a larger pay-out. The Constitution is the primary legal authority and it permits land to be taken for the social good, therefore the government should not shirk from doing so. It is not the role of the government to please all of the people all of the time; its role is to run our cities as efficiently as possible.

The privatised transport solution

Look at a map of Irish railways 100 years ago and you will see names such as Great Southern and Western Railways. Most railways in Ireland and England at that time were operated by private companies. Railways began as private enterprises and flourished as private enterprises, but were all but eliminated by state control. There is a valid argument that cars impacted on train services, but there is an equally valid argument that a bad train service allowed the car to gain a foothold, which led to the demise of the train. A good train service and a good road network co-exist in most European countries; it does not have to be a battle because each serves a different function.

Governments know that private enterprises have their place in a broader transport system. The difficulty in introducing private services is that the state services are not docile creatures; they have become fiefdoms and when their monopolies are threatened, they can turn aggressive as they seek to protect what they see as their 'patch'. The state monopolist airline tried, successfully, to snuff out competition when it was first introduced on the North Atlantic in the form of Sky Train. British Airways later tried, unsuccessfully, to eliminate Virgin Atlantic. The tactics used were quite staggering,[3] including trying to hack into the Virgin computer, impersonating Virgin staff, trying to lure Virgin Business Class passengers to change their reservations whilst they were arriving at the airport[4] and planting negative stories about the company in the press. State monopolists don't take 'upstart' competition lightly.

Something of the same sort of behaviour has been seen in Ireland. For example, not only does the state provide an inefficient bus service that never conforms to a timetable, that service allegedly 'crowds out' private competitors trying to serve the public on similar routes. The Circle Line Bus Company, which ceased trading in June 2008 with the loss of twenty-seven jobs, has made such assertions.[5]

3   http://books.google.de/books?id=e_1-0C96uxEC&pg=PA235&dq=dirty+tricks+
    campaign+against+Virgin.&lr=&hl=en&sig=ACfU3U0NojzJytmUAH5CvgyckqX
    qMaC8ZQ.
4   http://books.google.de/books?id=4pmUjowqAzoC&pg=PA163&dq=dirty+tricks+
    campaign+against+Virgin.&hl=en&sig=ACfU3U2xZPD5E1Zb8vMAxe63b5B780AXZg.
5   RTÉ Business News, 8.53am, 20 June 2008.

The company claims that Dublin Bus effectively put them out of
business by the continued saturation of its route by a large number
of Government-funded buses, the operation of which was being
subsidised by the taxpayer.[6] The owner of Circle Line said that it was
a small company, one that 'cannot fight a state company', describing
the state company's activities as 'a slaughter with tax-payers'
money'. Dublin Bus has denied the allegations and the minister
responsible has said the government is in the process of introducing
legislation to protect such companies. It was later revealed that the
claims of Circle Line were not only true but, even more serious,
Dublin Bus had in fact been running unauthorised buses on the
same routes as Circle Line,[7] which behaviour was described as
'predatory' by the Minister for Transport. Furthermore, the
Department of Transport had been monitoring the situation and
pointed out its concerns to Dublin Bus, which said it was doing
nothing wrong *per* its interpretation of the law. Circle Line has
begun legal action against the state, as has another bus company,
Swords Express, alleging similar 'predatory' behaviour.

The issue is not whether there is or is not a state monopoly on
bus services in Dublin; if the government believed a monopoly
system was the best policy, it should implement one. The situation
is that the government has stated that it wants competition, as
evidenced by its own policy and by the actions of the Department
of Transport in this particular case. As a result, private operators
were drawn into the transport market and invested money. Then
Dublin Bus, apparently working in contravention of this government
policy, attempted to eliminate the competition. Any private operator
hearing of these allegations will 'get the message' and think long
and hard about entering a market where the biggest 'state' operator
might try to put a private entrepreneur out of business. In other
words, one section of the government is promoting private buses,
while the other is opposing it. The government is either hypocritical
or it cannot control all of its networks. The net result is that a state-
run service is allegedly spending taxpayers' money on eliminating
private competition, which was arguably providing an improved

6   RTÉ Business News, 8.53am, 20 June 2008.
7   www.rte.ie/news/2008/0725/dublinbus.html.

service. The Department of Transport spent more taxpayers' money trying, unsuccessfully, to prevent them from doing this and twenty-seven people lost their jobs, along with private individuals losing investment money. The owners of Circle Line no doubt have a strong case—provided in part by the Department of Transport—for substantial compensation if these allegations are proven to be correct. If that happens, it will be the taxpayers who have to pay the compensation bill. It is not only an issue of public or private transportation policy, it is an issue of management and control and waste of the taxpayers' money.

Private transportation may offer a solution for Dublin. The difficulty with private transport is that such companies can cherry-pick the best routes, which would leave Dublin Bus with the uneconomic routes. They would also interfere with an integrated ticketing process, which would allow people to move around more efficiently. The advantages they offer, however, are that they could stimulate real competition, like Ryanair did for Aer Lingus, and improve the level of services offered by Dublin Bus. The Air Coach service has shown the added value that privatised services bring to the capital and as such the advantages outweigh the disadvantages. What needs to be put first in any such proposed solution is the primary requirements of the populace—the government would do well to remember that.

SOLUTIONS FOR THE HEALTH SERVICE

Ireland's beleaguered health service is proving to be one of the biggest obstacles to quality of life. There are many problems, much disillusion and few good ideas about how to make it better. The best way to find the solutions is to detail the problems very clearly. There are two major problems: the inefficient administering of the current system and the type of system that is in operation. The two are linked, of course, because the type of system in use is one that gives rise to inefficiencies at all levels. Therefore a root-and-branch reform of the health service is necessary.

Inefficient administration

Professor Crown, a consultant in St Vincent's Hospital, Dublin, views the Department of Health as a centralised *politburo* of bureaucrats and describes the HSE as their 'military wing'.[8] From this it is safe to infer that he feels the system would be better with less management and more healthcare. The problem for the HSE is not a lack of critics and ideas, but rather a tendency to ignore the voices of dissent that try to talk about the problems and the possible solutions. Professor Crown identified one key thread running through much of the scandals in the health service over the last ten years: whenever medical staff spoke out, they were ignored or silenced. As a result, many medical professionals have been forced to go to the media surreptitiously, to try to raise the issues they have encountered in a public forum. Although they are motivated by a desire for change and improvement that would benefit all health service users, they are usually seen as troublemakers. This is a crucial issue: if the HSE will not listen to its staff, it will lose all the relevant experience and knowledge it needs to deliver a working service. The divide that currently separates the staff from the administrators and the Minister for Health must be bridged. As long as that divide exists, there will be tension and friction between all sides. The question, then, is how do we bridge that divide? The answer is by rethinking how the system is set up and run.

The wrong system of healthcare
What kind of health system should Ireland have? The health service should provide medical care based on each individual's needs, not on their ability to pay, and should also motivate its staff by rewarding ability and excellence. This can be achieved by operating a policy where the money follows the patient. In the current system, there is a disconnection between use of the service and payment for that service, which does not motivate staff to excel. What must be created instead is a free-market system. At the moment, much of what the Department of Health and the HSE are doing is trying to duplicate what the free market does and anticipate the needs of sick people. In other words, bureaucracy follows the patient. That is not an efficient system.

On the other hand, a 'money follows the patient' policy is far more efficient. It means that whoever treats a patient gets paid

8 *Sunday Independent,* 6 April 2008.

directly from the fund of taxpayers' money set aside for this purpose. Thus the medical services that are in demand will receive more resources—not because they are in the right constituency or because a large bureaucracy decides to deliver those particular resources, but because they are actually needed and used. The patient needs to become the compass for resource allocation. In the current system taxes are given to the Department of Health, which passes most of the funds on to the HSE, which then tries to figure out where to put the money to best serve the population. There is much guesswork and political interference in this unwieldy process. What is needed instead is a situation where the patient effectively has unlimited money in his pocket for healthcare recommended by his GP. Then, and only then, will patients' needs be met.

If money followed the patient, it would alter how medical care is delivered. The most important change would be that medical care would be delivered closer to the point of use, through primary care centres. Primary care centres, a reasonably new innovation, deliver care in the community and are linked to a GP's practice and other health professionals, all clustered in one building. The evidence proves that if such centres are available, the waiting times in hospitals are reduced drastically. Furthermore, by keeping people out of hospitals, it helps to keep the whole population healthy, given that hospitals are breeding grounds for contagious infections.

Everyone in the system knows that primary care is an excellent solution for the problems crippling healthcare provision in Ireland: the GPs want it, the HSE has promised it and the patients have demanded it. In spite of this, however, delays have prevented progress as the infighting rages. The HSE declares that primary care centres are being 'rolled out', but the medical professionals have accused the Executive of spin and argue that provision is not being made, as is claimed. This debate exposes the weakness inherent in the whole system: lack of motivation. If we had a system where money follows the patients, primary care centres would have been provided already. What is agreed is that the current system does not work and must be changed. Now we need a new blueprint that we can all agree on. I would like to suggest that the model provided by the Netherlands could fit the bill.

Healthcare in the Netherlands

The Dutch system is very effective. It operates as follows. There is mandatory private insurance for all adults over the age of eighteen. Every person must be insured and the premiums are deducted from salary, in the same way as income tax. Health insurance is offered by private companies that must offer a fixed standard package to everyone who applies: no one can be refused and premiums must not be dependent on age. The insurance companies can charge what they wish, as long as they offer the standard package; obviously this means there is very little price variation as they compete with one another. Long-term care and insurance premiums for those under eighteen and those unable to pay are paid by the state. The government also compensates the insurance companies if a claim is made that falls outside the statistical norm, i.e. people with long-term health issues, such as diabetes, who might transfer between one insurer and another. This ensures that people who have conditions that might otherwise lead to higher premiums get insurance at the same rate as everyone else. The cost of the premiums is split between employers (50 per cent), the individual (45 per cent) and the government (5 per cent). Some employers choose to make insurance a perk by paying for it; others subsidise it. No matter what, every individual has medical insurance.

The health insurance companies can also offer top-up insurance for extra, 'premium' services outside of what are considered core medical services as defined by the state. These extras are optional and give the market variety and encourage competition. Any insured person is free to leave one insurance company and join another. Most of the hospitals that provide healthcare are private, for-profit ventures, and they claim off the insurance companies for the medical care in the normal way. Although there can be government hospitals and hospitals run by charities, all operate the same way and claim from the patient's health insurance company. This leaves people free to choose which hospital they want to attend or to rely on their GP to make that choice for them. The performance and the waiting times of hospitals are published on the internet, which helps GPs and patients make the right choice for them.

The Dutch appear to have overcome the conundrum facing the HSE, in that everyone has coverage but most services are provided by private companies that are remunerated adequately. The government sets the rules and funds on the periphery, but services are delivered mostly by private entities and are insured by private entities. This removes political interference and empowers the patients and, most importantly, delivers an excellent and efficient healthcare system. The advantages are that being private ensures the insurance companies are run efficiently. Use and payment are directly connected, which stimulates performance and value for money, but at the same time the core social element of healthcare for all is maintained.

Could it work in Ireland?

The best solutions are usually the simplest ones and this system sweeps away much of the bureaucracy and politicking bogging down the system. There are concerns about the applicability of this model in the Irish context. The first is that 'forcing' a person to buy private health insurance is a draconian measure. If that is the case, we are already accepting draconian measures without demur: the government forces people to pay Pay Related Social Insurance (PRSI) and to buy car insurance from private companies. Furthermore, a majority of people already voluntarily buy their own health insurance, so it is a matter of facilitating a minority that need to buy it.

The other major fear is that if one falls ill, the private insurance company will point to clause number 4,447, in the fine print, and claim there is no coverage. The way to guard against this is to copy the Netherlands model, whereby the core insurance package is defined by the government and fixed at the centre of the health insurance policy. It is locked in place, no ifs, ands or buts. The 'big leap' for the Irish government would be giving up political control of the allocation of healthcare. It might be difficult to wrest this from the government because control equals power and power means you can influence voters, such as by handing out medical cards. Once that change has been made, however, the government will soon accept that the new system works better, which means happier voters all round.

The final concern will be that raised by the nay-sayers: it simply could not be implemented in Ireland, it would not work. This is not true. It would work in Ireland and could be implemented without too much struggle because the basic elements are present already, we just have to join the dots. Let's look at exactly how it would work. In the new system the Department of Health would define the standard health insurance contract, which would include normal illnesses, procedures, treatments, A&E care and whatever else the government believes the citizen should be entitled to. This is the government's policy input: it will define the level of coverage and expand it when and if it wishes. The price of individual premiums would be set by the free market, but normal competition will ensure fair prices. It is unlikely to be anywhere near what the average person currently pays in taxes for healthcare.

There are already a number of private insurers operating in Ireland and competing with one another and they would continue to do so, the only difference being they will be providing all care under a core contract. Nonetheless, they can still distinguish and sell their products by adding on attractive extras. The likely outcome is that more companies would enter the market, confident that the rules were consistent and fair.[9] Premiums would obviously rise, but taxes could be reduced to compensate this. In 2008, under the category of 'health and children', €13.7 billion was spent by the government and in the same period €13.17 billion was collected in income tax—that expenditure was already up by €1 billion on 2007 spending.[10] I am not saying income tax could be abolished, because a portion of it would be needed for state payments for healthcare for minors and long-term invalids, but it should be reduced substantially to provide the extra needed to pay the premium. One key advantage to this system is that people would immediately see the benefit of any improvements in the healthcare system by a reduction in premiums.

The hospitals, primary care centres and private health professionals are all in place, so none of this would change in the short

9 The whole issue of 'community rating' would need to be ironed out, but that needs to be done anyway—it is not a hurdle to an overhaul of the system. The likely solution would be premium adjustments paid by the state to the insurance company, which could be changed to encourage new insurance companies to pursue older clients. As the companies cannot alter insurance rates based on age, the problems affecting the old system should not arise.

10 www.finance.gov.ie.

term. In the longer term, however, each hospital will become a private entity, funded by its patients. It could be bought out by management or doctors, or run independently by charities, or publicly owned by the government. It does not matter who owns the hospitals, the fact is that all claims for health payments will be made via the private health insurance companies and paid directly to the hospitals. The owners of each hospital would have a definite incentive to treat patients, while patients could take their 'business' elsewhere if they felt service was below par. The advantages of this system are numerous: vastly reduced administration costs, fewer waiting lists and a reactive service that can respond to 'demand' by the market.

While we have shown that the Netherlands model could be adopted and implemented in Ireland, it is necessary to point out that the Irish context presents some unique problems that would have to be addressed, namely the Leitrim effect, staff training and the effect of the EU on healthcare in Ireland.

The Leitrim effect

If you come from one of the smaller counties in Ireland, your first reaction to the Dutch model is likely to be: what private business would build a hospital in my area, with such a small population?

This is a potential problem, so how can it be solved? Private business will set up hospitals in remote areas if they can charge the insurance company more because of the higher costs involved. In the same way that the government subsidises Ryanair or Aer Arann for running certain public service routes to remoter parts of the country, the government could inject a variable into the equation to compensate the private medical insurers for paying above the average in certain counties. It could be called a rural weighting, for want of a better phrase. This would have to be capped to some degree so that hospitals did not begin to sprout up like holiday homes. We have learned the lesson from tax incentives that filled rural Ireland with unnecessary houses that now lie vacant; if used correctly, government subsidies can supply the same areas with much-needed medical facilities. Furthermore, many rural hospitals are already losing vital services, which means the current system is already failing the rural communities.

Staff training

Professor Crown makes a very good point about the drawback of smaller hospitals. He notes that the key to the training of any doctor is dealing with a very wide range of cases, so as to gather as much experience as possible. His criticism is that Ireland already has too many small hospitals, which can never reach the critical mass necessary to train highly qualified specialists and therefore will always 'be too small to ever be truly excellent'.[11]

The professor is absolutely right. This is exactly why so many doctors go abroad for specialised training. In spite of knowing this, however, we must accept that with a population of only over 4 million people, we cannot escape having small hospitals. There is no real solution to the problem and no point pretending there is. Irish hospitals will never be able to offer the level of experience that can be gained in the large teaching hospitals in London, New York or Berlin. Many of our doctors will continue to go abroad to be trained because there is simply no way around this. What the private insurance system will do is to centralise services as much as is feasible, based on real demand from the people paying for the medical service. It will give those living in rural communities the best service possible, which the new model will ensure is better than the service they currently have. Specialist hospitals will naturally gravitate towards large population centres, while smaller hospitals and primary care centres will provide basic care in more remote areas.

The impact of the EU on the Irish healthcare system

For a country that is moving towards European integration, Ireland takes a very insular approach to healthcare. However, there is one piece of EU law that is coming down the tracks that will expose this very problem.

Thanks to an impending EU directive,[12] it may soon be possible to obtain non-emergency healthcare outside of Ireland, in other Member States, without prior approval. The treating country would simply bill the Department of Health in the patient's country. If we

11   *Sunday Independent,* 6 April 2008.
12   *The Irish Times,* 3 February 2009.

assume that many other EU countries have more efficient services because of their size and that 'practice makes perfect', then it is inevitable that Irish people will opt to get healthcare elsewhere. The obvious destination is the UK. This will mean that even less experience and economies of scale will be obtained within Ireland in these areas. If the government does not solve the problems of the health service, it will face a critical situation if its citizens shun the services on offer here. This gives the government even greater impetus to find the right solutions and start delivering a proper level of healthcare for all its citizens.

In the final analysis, Ireland's healthcare system will always be small by comparison to other countries, therefore trying to compete against true centres of excellence in London or Paris is pointless. This does not mean we have to settle for a second-rate system, however. It means we have to concentrate on the 95 per cent of services that people most want and deliver those in excellent facilities situated as close as possible to the people who demand them. The key word is 'reform', that must be the guiding light for the government and the HSE.

SOLUTIONS FOR LAW AND ORDER

The problem of rising crime rates

Ireland, like many countries, faces rising crime rates and repeated demands for the government and the Police Commissioner to do something about it. Looking to other jurisdictions for guidance, the zero-tolerance strategy in place in New York City provides a very workable model for Irish cities and towns.

Zero tolerance is often misunderstood as a general crackdown on crime, but it is a more sophisticated concept than that. The strategy is based on the 'broken window' theory of crime and is practised— consciously or not—by many police forces worldwide. First discussed by James Q. Wilson and George L. Kelling in an article in the *The Atlantic Monthly*,[13] the theory is that if a broken window in a house goes unrepaired, more windows will be broken and vandalism against the property will escalate. Eventually the house will be

13   March 1982.

broken into and become a centre of crime in the area. On the other hand, if the broken window is repaired quickly, further decay will not occur.

In practice, this takes the form of prosecuting 'smaller' crimes and infringements of the law, with the aim of preventing serious crime before it happens rather than reacting to it after it has happened. The underlying rationale is that those who commit larger crimes start by committing smaller crimes earlier in the day and progress only if they are not interrupted or apprehended. If small crimes proliferate because of a consensus that they are not worth pursuing or prosecuting, the crimes being committed in the community will get progressively larger, fear of crime will drive away the 'respectable' people and the problem will become much more difficult to tackle and eradicate.

Irish policing is mostly responsive in that people call the Garda when they perceive there to be criminal activity. The gardaí who patrol the streets and roads on foot and in cars are there to enforce the law and arrest troublemakers, yet there is an undercurrent of anti-social behaviour that goes untargeted because it is seen as not important enough. There are frequent surges of enforcement in one particular area or another as public or political pressure is applied. Control is centralised along the command structure, and I have not been able to locate any instance of a member of An Garda being fired for not doing his/her job efficiently.[14] It is a public servant's job, where one's job is rarely on the line for results. Contrast this to the USA, where a police captain is responsible for his/her precinct and has wide discretion on the techniques and tactics employed. If he/she doesn't perform, he/she will lose his/her command. There is a much higher correlation between control and responsibility.

Does this approach actually work? An instructive case in point is that of New York City in the early 1990s. Following the implementation of a zero-tolerance approach and a linking of control and responsibility, there was a fall of 39 per cent in general crime levels and a 49 per cent[15] fall in the murder rate over a short period of time. This was no mean feat. At that time, New York had graced the

14 For corruption or negligence, yes.
15 BBC News.

cover of *Time* as the 'rotten apple'—the trains were littered with graffiti, the stations were full of down-and-outs, crime was high and the quality of life was low. In some areas roads were strewn with rubbish and burned-out cars. The murder rate had increased dramatically, as had most other violent and property-related crimes, such as burglary, as well as smaller anti-social crimes. No doubt it all sounds terribly familiar if you live in certain parts of Dublin.

The standard solution of hiring more police officers had been tried, but had made no significant impression on the crime rates. The police were young and inexperienced and lacked the ability to tackle the core problems. Then, in 1994, Rudolph Giuliani was elected mayor and he hired William J. Bratton to implement a more radical approach to crime and policing. Equal credit must go to Jack Maple, a transit cop working the late-night shift in a tough area, who worked out a very simple system for mapping and identifying where crime was occurring. He and Bratton finally got together as a team and their efforts have become known as Zero Tolerance.[16]

The phrase, Zero Tolerance,[17] is a slight misnomer, however, and really just a front-line phrase for what was a more complex strategy. The aim, in essence, was to improve the quality of life of New Yorkers by targeting petty crimes with as much effort as serious crimes. In the normal course of affairs a city that is experiencing crime problems tends to focus on the big crimes, with publicly announced 'crackdowns', longer sentences and one-off programmes. The zero-tolerance approach, on the other hand, knew that targeting smaller crimes would increase the quality of life, improve the neighbourhoods and send signals to petty criminals that there were consequences to their actions.

Jack Maple said that they started at the most basic level: 250,000 people were dodging fares on the New York transit system. They began by policing this and stopping those who were jumping the turnstiles to avoid fares. What they found was quite revealing— some of the people jumping fares were also carrying guns, or were the subjects of outstanding arrest warrants, or were carrying

16 Drawn from interview in http://sunday.ninemsn.com.yu/sunday/cover_stories/ transcript_309.asp.
17 www.adamsmith.org/80ideas/idea/14.htm.

contraband on their person. It became apparent that those who committed more serious crimes later on in the day were committing the less serious crime of not paying fares earlier in the day. By stopping people for smaller crimes, the result was that more serious crimes were prevented. Slowly, the spiral began to work in reverse and the quality of life began to improve—and fare-dodging was down 90 per cent.

Zero Tolerance was also about giving senior police officers powers and responsibilities for crime in their areas. The first step that Bratton took was to flatten the command structure and give autonomy to every precinct commander and make each one individually responsible for his/her precinct. The obsession with crime detection figures—something that has led UK police forces astray—was replaced by a focus on quality of life indicators and reductions in actual crime. Bratton computerised Maple's crime statistic system, creating COMPSTAT, which gave real-time crime statistics to commanders. COMPSTAT on its own is a very powerful system that can affect crime: even if crime is falling, it will accelerate the fall; and if it is rising, it will limit the rise. There were twice-weekly meetings in precincts to see if targeted crimes were falling.

In reality, then, it was a combination of the pure zero-tolerance policy mixed with a 'try and buy' approach that saw individual precinct commanders decide what worked on their patch and apply it. The result was dramatic and within three years crime was down substantially. By the end of that decade there were impressive reductions in overall crime and an increase in the quality of life. Maple gave a very good description of why the system worked:

One of the big problems in policing is, for example, you call up the police department and say there are two guys on the corner dealing drugs. They send a radio car. The guys see the radio car and what do they do? They step back into the doorway. The radio car keeps going. In police work, nobody memorializes that complaint. It drops right off the screen. What should happen is that those complaints should go to narcotics in the local district or precinct to be worked on, to see if it's a chronic condition.

That is why you hear people say that they keep calling and calling and calling, and the cops never do anything. It is because that simple complaint is never memorialized and the cops, from one day to the next, don't see that it is a chronic condition.[18]

The zero-tolerance strategy was controversial because it sometimes resulted in police excesses, but mostly the criticism was theoretical or in the form of arguments that other factors had brought down the crime rates in New York. But it is difficult to argue with the results, and anyone who visits New York now will notice immediately that the city has changed substantially. All it took was three years, just thirty-six months to start seeing real results and the difference has had a real effect—tourism has soared and the city has prospered. Now compare this to Dublin, where it took more than five years for the government to go from deciding that it wanted a digital radio system to signing the contract. Pause for a moment and think about that: three years to turn around the city of New York; five years to sign contracts for a new radio system. It is, at base, a simple issue of management and proper control of resources.

Saying this ought to be applied to Ireland is, of course, an easy thing; doing it presents a different challenge. It would require a relinquishing of control within the police force and the government. It would require that the command structure of the Garda be flattened out so that each area has its own head officer who is called to account, on a monthly basis, for crime in his/her area and also for his/her budget. This head officer would be free, within obvious legal limits, to utilise tactics and methods that he/she feels best suit his/her particular area. If he/she doesn't perform, then he/she loses his/her position and is replaced by someone who does perform. This process would allow the best and most efficient to rise up quickly, while each area can learn from successful tactics tried and proven in the other areas. It would be an efficient and cohesive way to police the streets of Ireland.

The problem of drugs
Some people would immediately state that drug use is the problem, but any police expert is likely to retort that it is trafficking and its related industries that are the problem with drugs. This is certainly

18 www.govtech.com/gt/articles/94865.

true in Ireland, where 'drug wars' are being fought on a daily basis by gangs in Dublin and Limerick, with the levels of money involved pushing the criminals to ever greater heights of violence. The drug business is lucrative because profits are commensurate with the danger and risk involved. As a result, Garda resources are diverted away from other activities so that they can merely scrape at the surface of the drug problem. If Ireland can implement a solution that undermines the illegal drugs trade, it would deliver a death blow to the criminals involved in the trade.

There is such a solution, but it is a very controversial one: legalise drugs. This is not as far from current policy as one might think: the Irish government has a large methadone programme in place, which is a tacit admission of the need to supply opiates to addicts. The government even supplies the needles the addicts use to inject the drugs they buy on the streets. What the government doesn't do is get involved in supplying what goes into those needles, they leave that to the criminals. It is a pointless exercise because the government is facilitating at one end of the supply chain what it is attempting to stop at the other end. According to the Dublin-based support group Merchants Quay Ireland (MQI), which provides services to the homeless and drug users, there are approximately 14,500 heroin users in Ireland, of which half are outside the main methadone programme.[19] This means thousands of people forced to commit crimes to feed their habit, which wastes a huge amount of the resources of the judicial system. The government has become trapped in an illogical position, and the only ones benefiting are the criminals.

To call for legalisation of illegal drugs is not to suggest there are no consequences to the use of those drugs, there most certainly are, but they pale into insignificance when one considers the effects of legal drugs. In the EU more than 600,000 people die every year as a result of tobacco use. According to a report by the European Commission: 'Over 650,000 Europeans are killed every year because they smoke, one in seven of all deaths across the EU, and over 13 million more are suffering from a serious, chronic disease as a

---

19 http://www.mgi.ie/page.php?id=15.

result of their smoking'.[20] In Ireland it is 6,000 deaths per year. Nonetheless all governments allow tobacco to be sold in every corner shop, taxing it sufficiently to ensure a steady tax income but not enough that it would halt the trade completely.

It might seem radical to suggest that drugs should be legalised, yet this 'radical' solution is advocated by people across the political spectrum, from police officers and senior politicians to reputable medical journals and conservative magazines. A few examples will illustrate the point. In Wales former Police Chief Constable Francis Wilkinson suggested that, following the Swiss and Australian models, drugs should be available on prescription[21] for supervised use. Police Chief Constable Richard Brunstrom echoed these sentiments, stating that the war on drugs was 'unwinnable' and that during his time in office, 'Drug crime has soared and profits from illegal trading have supported a massive rise in organised criminality.'[22] Julian Critchley, former director of the Cabinet Office's anti-drugs unit in Britain, called for legalisation and claimed that his views were shared by the 'overwhelming majority of professionals in the field'.[23] He rejected the argument that drug use would increase if drugs were legalised, pointing out that tobacco use was decreasing precisely because it was controlled by the government, and went on to say: 'Yet publicly, all those intelligent, knowledgeable people were forced to repeat the nonsensical mantra that the government would be 'tough on drugs', even though they all knew that the government's policy was actually causing harm.'

The argument in favour of legalisation can be viewed in the light of the prohibition on alcohol in the USA in the 1920s and 1930s. This is a classic example of what happens when a desirable substance is prohibited and made illicit: it is forced underground and the criminals take over, at the expense of the whole of society. Look, for example, at this graph illustrating the murder rate during the period of prohibition.

20 http://ec.europa.eu/health/ph_determinants/life_style/Tobacco/Documents/ tobacco_exs_en.pdf.
21 BBC News, 17 October 2001.
22 *Daily Mail* online, 11 October 2007.
23 *Daily Telegraph*, Julian Critchley, 13 August 2008.

During prohibition the murder rate peaked in America,[24] as did the levels of other types of crime. Instead of regulating and controlling the alcohol industry as envisaged, by banning alcohol the government handed it over to criminals. Banning something sounds very invigorating because it appears that a government is in charge. In reality, it had the opposite effect and the criminals got a strong foothold, leaving the government less in charge than ever before. The US authorities realised this after thirteen years and legalised alcohol again because it was easier to manage and regulate a legal industry and it disenfranchised the criminals. The noble motives behind prohibition were well founded, but they simply didn't work. Many other countries have also tried prohibitions on alcohol without any major success. John D. Rockefeller, a noted teetotaller, summed it up well: 'When Prohibition was introduced, I hoped that it would be widely supported by public opinion and the day would soon come when the evil effects of alcohol would be recognized. I have slowly and reluctantly come to believe that this has not been the result. Instead, drinking has generally increased; the speakeasy has replaced the saloon; a vast army of lawbreakers has appeared; many of our best citizens have openly ignored Prohibition; respect for the law has been greatly lessened; and crime has increased to a level never seen before.' This, surely, is a blueprint for what has happened with other drugs.

Even if, as a non-drug-user, you oppose the usage of drugs and therefore legalisation, it is still worth it as a means of unseating the criminals involved in the drug trade. The impact of legalisation on the gangs would be quick and devastating. Demand would be diverted to the controlled centres of distribution, crippling the illegal trade. If drug-users purchased from the government, the criminals would have far less cash in hand, which would mean far less weapons being brought onto the streets. Drug-dealers would be removed from the equation, which should result in a reduction in new users. Established users would now be monitored and given help to manage or break their addiction. The benefits are enormous: a reduction in drug-related crime, a reduction in addiction and a

24 www.csdp.org/edcs/page24.htm.

freeing up of resources for the police service, the judiciary and the prison service.

There is no doubt that there would be issues and problems stemming from the legalisation of certain drugs, not least a backlash from America. But as has been done in other European countries, it could be started quietly and discreetly, proving its worth in order to silence the critics. Ireland has an opportunity to seize the initiative on this issue. We could 'write the book', so to speak, and instead of always following other legal developments could lead the way and contribute to the defeat of the drug gangs. The Criminal Assets Bureau was an innovation when it was introduced and has since been copied around the world. With a coherent, comprehensive, well-thought-out drug strategy and legislation, Ireland could set the standard once again.

Using technology in the fight against crime

There is a basic problem facing policing work in Ireland: the Garda are behind the curve in terms of technology and are trying to staunch a flood of crime with old-fashioned methods and tools. There is absolutely no reason for this because the solutions are there and indeed are being added to all the time. We shall examine just one new technology that could bolster detection rates and save lives.

Shot location technology can pinpoint the exact location of a gun shot in a city within two seconds of a shot being fired. This information is sent instantly to GPS-style units in police cars or helicopters and can direct the cars to the location. This greatly increases the chances of intercepting gunmen.

The system works as follows:[25] wireless sensors are placed on buildings, about eight to twelve sensors per square mile. These are essentially sophisticated microphones, which can detect gunshots. When a gunshot is registered, the sensors triangulate and produce a precise location for the sound, down to approximately 25m. This information is then passed instantly to the police and ambulance service. The technology is so sophisticated, it can tell if the source of the gunfire is moving, i.e. a drive-by shooting, how many cars were involved, their speed and direction of travel.

25 ShotSpotter Inc.

This system has been in use for almost a decade in the USA and the results are impressive. It would be of enormous benefit to Irish cities and is available now. Why no one has implemented this technology, at least in Dublin and Limerick, is beyond comprehension. If it saved one life or put one shooter in prison, it would be worth the investment. This links back directly to the flattening-out of the command and control of the Garda. If a police captain[26] in Limerick needed to reduce crime and increase convictions in that area, he/she would likely be willing to test it out without having to go through the bureaucracy associated with it.

Maintaining military might

As already noted, neutral Ireland has Defence Forces that are relatively well-equipped for engagement, but strong arguments can be made in favour of abolishing some or all of those Forces. With all due respect to the service men and women, they constitute a misuse of resources and are completely mismatched to the needs of a modern, progressive country. The arguments in support of dissolution of the Defence Forces are reasonably straightforward, and we shall examine them service by service.

The Irish Army

First, a number of countries do not maintain armies; it is not compulsory. Iceland, for example, has no army even though, as a member of NATO, it is not considered neutral. Ireland, on the other hand, is a neutral country, with no known adversaries and no recent history of defensive or offensive military action. It is not even clear from whom we need to be defended. And even if the country was threatened by another power, it is highly likely that other power would be a much bigger geographic entity, with far superior resources, so our army could offer only token resistance. This is not a good enough reason to have an army in the first place.

Secondly, while the Irish Army does carry out a number of important roles, these have very little connection with what a national army is supposed to do. The only military role undertaken

---

26 This rank does not exist in the Garda, but is the illustrative title I have given to the potential office of someone with similar power.

by the Army is in UN peacekeeping operations. Irish soldiers take part in these missions to gain experience, but what are they gaining experience to do—serve in more UN arenas? If Ireland did not have an army, we wouldn't create one in order to send soldiers to far-flung corners of the world just to gain experience to repeat the same cycle. This in no way detracts from the work the Forces do as UN representatives, it is simply to state the fact that gaining military experience is pointless if that experience will never be called upon in the defence of the homeland.

Over the years service personnel have been engaged in other, non-military roles here in Ireland, such as escorting cash delivery vans and acting as emergency back-up for the civil authorities. It is clear that roles such as this do not need to be carried out by trained, equipped soldiers. It could be equally well met by a professional civil defence force that would cost far less to maintain. The Army has long been drafted in to perform *ad hoc* roles for which they are neither fully equipped nor fully trained. This is a waste of resources given that the taxpayer pays for military hardware, barracks, foreign peacekeeping missions and all the attendant requirements of a defence force. The money spent in this way could be far better used.

The Air Corps and the Navy

Much of what can be said of the Air Corps can also be said of the Navy. The Air Corps' roles, according to its own website,[27] are to support the Army, to support the Navy and to 'support the civil powers'. Taking support of the Army first, it stands to reason that if the Army is dissolved, the support role of the Air Corps will also be defunct. With regard to the civil powers, this mostly entails providing the Garda with helicopters and pilots. In other countries, this role is performed by the police force and incorporated within its structures. Strangely, the aircraft the Air Corps has at its disposal have zero military use—one is a gulf stream Mark IV jet, the other a Lear Jet Model 45. These are used to ferry senior politicians around Europe and America. If the government needs a private jet, it should buy one and operate it like individuals in the private sector do; there

---

27 www.military.ie/aircorps.

is no real need for a private jet to be kept and operated by the military. In fact, there is probably little need for a private jet to be kept at all. If the Queen of England can travel on commercial airlines, it does not seem too much to ask the average Irish politician to do the same.

The same points apply to the role of the Navy, which is less military than civil defence. It is primarily engaged in fisheries protection, with occasional drug intercepts. This work could be carried out very successfully by a properly funded and equipped professional coast guard service.

Those are the arguments, but if the Defence Forces were dissolved, what would Ireland need in their place? There are three things needed. Number one, a coast guard service that can handle fisheries protection, sea rescue, drug enforcement,[28] etc. Number two, a professional Civil Defence Force comprising a permanent core of professionals who are well resourced and well trained in all civil emergencies. They would need to specialise and train in dealing with floods, medical emergencies, mountain rescues, etc. This body could be supplemented with volunteers drawn from the local community and having local knowledge and expertise, which would in turn bind the service to the community. Number three, a better resourced, better funded and better supported police force. Abolishing the military might seem unusual, but there are precedents: Panama did it in 1990 with a constitutional referendum, and a number of smaller European countries have opted for very limited or no military forces, such as Andorra, Liechtenstein and Monaco.

THE ENERGY QUESTION

Energy is a hot political topic at the moment, with wide implications across a spectrum of socio-economic issues. Although not addressed previously, it is important to bring energy into the discussion of recommendations because it is a pressing issue that requires urgent attention. Energy is not only a critical aspect of the infrastructure; it also presents enormous opportunities for the future. The problem facing Ireland is that it needs a constant, renewable and reasonably

---

28 Which will of course be reduced if previous suggestions are applied.

priced source of energy. An EU report highlights the difficulties we face in meeting this need:

> Ireland depends to a great extent on energy imports. The majority of imports concern oil—mainly from the UK and Norway. The UK is also the only source of imported natural gas for Ireland. Colombia and Australia are the main suppliers of hard coal. Increasing demand and decreasing domestic production have led to a total growth of energy imports by 93% over period 1990–2004.[29]

If Ireland intends to assume its place as a hi-tech, developed, wealthy industrial country, then it must have a source of energy under its control. Currently almost 80 per cent of the country's electricity is generated from coal, oil or gas, but this cannot continue as those sources are potentially unstable and energy generation for peak-load use is not stable even in the short-term; each winter EirGrid publishes a statement on the security of supply.[30] In previous winters massive generators had to be imported in case there were problems.

Oil and gas are commodities that will eventually run out and whose price is volatile; we have seen the effect price spikes can have on energy costs. The challenge now is to shift to a policy that produces energy that is sustainable, renewable and constant. The solution is twofold and controversial: wind energy and nuclear power. It may seem radical to opt for nuclear, but that is exactly what many other countries are already doing. Ireland has an enormous opportunity to become energy independent, carbon neutral and attractive to industry, all within a decade. A low tax environment can be effective, but it is not unique; cheap and stable energy, however, would give a real competitive advantage to the Irish economy.

Nuclear power
Nuclear power has a bad reputation, but it is undeserved, often the result of hyped-up inaccuracies. The common perception is that nuclear is dangerous, generally because it makes people think of

29 Ireland Energy Fact Sheet, European Commission.
30 www.eirgrid.ie.

nuclear bombs and Chernobyl. It is true that Chernobyl was a catastrophe, but it has since been proven that the accident at the plant was the result of bad design, bad construction and bad management and could have been avoided. Hundreds of nuclear power stations operate safely around the world every day and it is statistically a safe source of power, even more so since technological advances have improved it. If Ireland embraced nuclear power, it would be entering the industry at its safest period.

The environmentalist lobby finds itself in a difficult position: nuclear power produces no greenhouse gases and is an 'on demand' energy, i.e. can react to demand surges, but traditionally it has campaigned against it. Greenpeace and other environmentalists rallied against nuclear power for decades, which contributed to the decline, but it is now on the rise again.[31] Environmentalists don't offer any real alternatives, however. They were against nuclear, which meant governments found it easier to build fossil fuel stations. France was the only country that aggressively pursued the nuclear option for electricity generation and it currently produces 78 per cent of its electricity from nuclear and is still building more stations. Now the environmentalists are anti-fossil fuels because of global warming, but we are fast running out of options. The fact is that nuclear energy ticks many of the boxes and many governments now realise that it must form part of an overall long-term energy strategy.

In Ireland, the government needs to demonstrate the difference between the statistically insignificant fears concerning nuclear and the enormous personal benefits it would accrue to every citizen. Most nations have already done this and countries such as America, Brazil, France and India are building new plants, while Australia has such a plan under consideration. The Massachusetts Institute of Technology assembled one of the most prestigious groups of experts on the matter and in its report, *The future of Nuclear Power*, concluded: 'The authors of the study emphasized that nuclear power is not the only non-carbon option and stated that they believe it should be pursued as a long term option along with other options such as the use of renewable energy sources, increased

31 Department of Nuclear Engineering, University of California, Berkeley.

efficiency, and carbon sequestration'.[32] Let's be realistic, if oil-rich Saudi Arabia is considering building a nuclear power plant, then option-poor Ireland should do so too. Even those countries that decommissioned their plants after Chernobyl are now considering moving back to nuclear. As a result, Ireland has the opportunity to enter the industry at the most opportune time: the early technology has been improved and many countries are building power plants so we can learn from their experiences and build the safest and most efficient systems.

The latest technology is impressive. The European Pressurized Reactor is a highly efficient new type of nuclear plant reactor, developed by the French and Germans.[33] There are new units being built in Finland and France, with others proposed in China, America and the UK. The capacity of each unit varies, but they can produce up to 1500 MW;[34] the cost of construction is approximately €5 billion.[35]

Ireland currently produces around 4000 MW of power from its various peat, oil, gas and coal stations.[36] Many of these are not only inefficient but produce small amounts of energy. They could all be replaced by three or four nuclear plants, complemented by a renewable source such as wind. The potential is huge: not only could Ireland become self-sufficient in energy, it could become a net exporter to the UK, which is likely to have its own energy supply problems in the future. Instead of being an importer of oil and gas, Ireland could be a net exporter of energy, delivering long-term benefits to the state's finances. This is an opportunity to turn around the energy welfare of the country in less than a decade. We can move from being a country that needs to lower its taxes to attract industry, to a country where energy security becomes a

32 web.mit.edu/nuclearpower.
33 Areva is a French-German consortium, although the French are in the process of acquiring majority control.
34 www.areva-np.com.
35 There was an original price of €3.2 billion fixed, but overruns suggest this could rise to €5 billion by completion.
36 **West Offaly Power** 150 Peat **Lough Ree Power** 100 Peat **Turlough Hill** 292 Hydro (Pump Storage) **Liffey** 38 Hydro **Ardnacrusha** 86 Hydro **Erne** 65 Hydro **Clady** 4 hydro **Lee** 27 Hydro **Moneypoint** 915 Coal **Tarbert** 620 Oil **Great Island** 240 Oil **Aghada** 525 Gas **Poolbeg** 1,020 Oil and Gas **North Wall** 266 Oil and Gas **Marina** 115 Gas. (All figures are Megawatt Capacity.)

positive attraction. We need industries that are knocking on our door to come in and set up in Ireland, irrespective of the tax base. Taxes and death are certain, as Mark Twain warned us, and our tax advantage will eventually be eliminated by the actions of other countries, such as the USA. However, nothing can remove permanent, tangible benefits like an abundant and secure power supply.

Wind-powered Generation (WPG)

Ireland has the second greatest potential for wind power in Europe after Scotland. While we are beginning to exploit this source aggressively, there is more potential that is as yet untapped.

By 2008 Ireland had a capacity of 1,244 MW and 'showed a dynamic growth far above the average'[37] and this is expected to continue to grow dramatically. The potential is enormous, but there are some limiting factors to wind energy that are very complex but revolve around some core issues: the energy requirements to start each wind turbine; the complexity added to the electric distribution system by having numerous smaller generation sites,[38] the issue of energy being produced not when it is needed but when the wind is blowing and the security of supply issues. A report by EIRGRID stated: 'Therefore as WPG increases additional or 'surplus' generation capacity is required if security of supply is to be maintained. There are significant costs associated with having 'excess' capacity on the system. Therefore the capacity surplus that results from WPG adds to the total generation costs.'[39] This will effectively put a cap on wind generation, but nonetheless we should go to this maximum. Both wind and nuclear complement each other and maximise the amount of energy we could export. The nuclear option gives a stable background in centralised locations and the export option allows us to export excess supply, which means the excess necessary for renewable could be used productively, thus overcoming the problem identified by Eirgrid.

---

37 World Wind Energy Report 2008.
38 Smaller and more diverse sites are required to statistically ensure the highest level of availability, but the more production sites there are, the more expensive it is to build a distribution system.
39 www.eirgrid.com.

Nuclear power is not cheap, and the debate continues over exactly how costs can even be measured beyond the initial capital costs, but the industry is beginning to gain credence once again because it is a good solution—not a perfect solution, but a good solution nonetheless. The basic costing analysis is that the capital cost initially is high but the running costs are low, which means it is the ideal long-term investment. There are other costs, such as storing spent nuclear fuel, that need to be included in the equation, but again many other countries have calculated these costs and are pushing ahead aggressively with nuclear plants. Those who are opposed to nuclear fuel use figures to compare the cost of each megawatt and this can make nuclear look expensive. But it isn't as simple as that. First, these costs often include huge figures for reprocessing or storing waste when such costs have not been quantified. Furthermore, the one cost that is difficult to quantify is sustainable *energy security*. How do you calculate the risk of oil at $300 a barrel in a decade or no oil in three decades or the oil supply from the Middle East being cut off due to war there or Russia ceasing gas exports? We cannot calculate these factors, but it is not too difficult to calculate the costs of being unable to generate the electricity we need in a decade.

The ESB is currently planning to spend €22 billion in an attempt to obtain 30 per cent of our energy needs from sustainable sources. For roughly the same price we could build four nuclear plants that would generate the other 70 per cent of the electricity that Ireland needs and potentially become a net exporter as well. Ireland could become the first zero-emissions country that is energy independent and can supply sustainable constant energy to its industries. This would be a enormous attraction for FDI and help maintain the plants we already have in Ireland. Ireland's politicians must stop thinking in five-year increments; what is needed is long-term strategic planning for the next fifty years. In that framework, nuclear power is a viable option that must be seriously considered.

Now that we have looked at the practical strategies that could be implemented by the Irish government in response to the current economic situation, we shall turn to the larger structural changes that could be made to the system of government and how the country functions.

Chapter 9

The Broader Political and Social Solutions

I n 2004 Fergus Finlay remarked that 'If Ireland were in Africa, we'd send in observers to help build democracy.'[1] Funny as it was, it is a comment that should be taken seriously. Whilst practical changes are the ideal and can be implemented more easily than broader political solutions, one cannot ignore the fact that many of Ireland's problems are also manifestations of deeper problems, some of those being of a constitutional nature. The magnitude of the economic turmoil we are facing will lead to serious questions being asked about how the country is run. We should be willing to ask some difficult questions.

Without wishing to start a philosophical debate, I doubt anyone would disagree with the assertion that a society could be defined as a collection of people who live by rules. Some of these rules are social conventions or mores, while other activities are considered so detrimental to the efficient operation of society that there are civil sanctions to penalise them. The most detrimental activities attract criminal sanctions and can likely lead to removal from society and incarceration. In other words, a society is concerned with shaping behaviour in certain ways for the betterment of the collective. A constitution is simply an overarching framework of fundamental rules that must be respected at all times. In Ireland the Constitution

1   *Irish Examiner*, 17 April 2004.

is over sixty years old—it belongs to another, lost era. Although it has been tweaked, it has never been changed substantially in all that time. One of the problems it propagates is that it gives politicians many rights but not much responsibility; now might be a good time to alter this.

We are facing not an economic recession but a depression that threatens the very foundations of the state. There is now the possibility that we will see the failure of all private banks and the bankruptcy of the state[2] as a result of the guarantees provided by the state to the banks and/or because of the chasm between government spending and government income.[3] This would require the IMF, or a similar body, to effectively move in and run the finances of the country. This is not fiction anymore: it is occurring in countries such as Iceland, where the rise and crashing fall of the economy is a frightening mirror image of our own. The cost of debt to both the Irish banks and the Irish government has risen and this signals the market's concern. The government's deficit has been widening at a faster pace than it can cut spending or raise taxes. If a sovereign default occurs, it will be time for serious constitutional change. Unfortunately, it always takes cataclysmic events for real change to occur because up until then politicians just patch over problems, never able to fully dissolve one system so as to establish a new one. This is what the inertia built into every complex state system demands in normal times. If you believe Ireland needs such changes, such a time may now have arrived for the Irish Republic. These are not normal times.

There is nothing unprecedented about this and it would likely be beneficial in the long term. France is currently on its fifth republic; the republican system has been replaced four times since 1789, not counting restorations of the monarchy and the two empires under Napoleon and his nephew. The last time was in 1958 when a

2 There is historical precedent for this, but not in Europe since the war. Coincidentally, the Bank of England wrote a paper on this in 2006, outlining the costs to an economy: www.bankofengland.co.uk/publications/fsr/fs_paper01.pdf.

3 By bankruptcy, I mean the government defaulting on sovereign debt, i.e. government bonds or the guarantees made to the banks. Alan Ahern, an economist at NUIG, also commented on this possibility: *Prime Time*, 1 December 2008. Ahern was subsequently hired as a consultant by the Department of Finance.

constitutional convention drew up a new Constitution. In fact, in the time since Ireland adopted its Constitution, most of the major European countries have drawn up new constitutions. It makes no sense to adhere rigidly to a document drawn up by Church and state in 1937, a time that was very, very different from our own, and that was passed by only 56 per cent to 44 per cent. The problem is that the current system allows only the Dáil to present the people with referenda: the people have no power of constitutional initiative. The points outlined here present a continuum of constitutional changes for Ireland, ranging from mild to radical reform.

MEASURES TO IMPROVE THE DEMOCRATIC PROCESS

1. Term Limits

Power is too concentrated in Dáil Éireann: all power radiates out from the Dáil and the Executive it elects. Once they placate a majority of their constituents, TDs can be elected continually, which can breed a sense of complacency. 'Term limits' is a phrase that refers to a legal limit being put on the length of time a person may serve in public office. If term limits were applied to Irish TDs, it would achieve a number of very important objectives:

- It would break any cycle of incompetence, corruption or simply disconnection with the people. Ireland is so small that politicians often mix with the most influential people; friendships are formed and favours requested. This casual situation can lead to 'irregularities'.
- Politics in Ireland, as elsewhere, has become a long-term career. We have moved from a concept of serving the people to a highly paid career choice. The longer the politician spends in office, the less chance he/she has of obtaining employment outside of that office and so the more likely he/she is to cling to power because his/her professional abilities have atrophied. If there are term limits or automatic rotations, that would allow politicians to work in the broader economy, which would reconnect them with the real world and broaden their skill set and experience.
- It would attract a broader group of people into politics because there would be a higher turnover of politicians. This could

encourage talented individuals to enter if they saw politics as a 'cleaner' option. Few people in Ireland ever leave stellar business careers to enter politics, but if they saw it as an eight-year stint, then it would bring increased competencies to governance.

The main argument against the application of term limits is that long tenure in the Dáil allows politicians to build up experience over decades, which would be lost to the people if they had to quit the house after eight years. This might be true, but it is some of this 'experience' that is in fact the problem. Government is mostly about management—managing a massive system with a huge budget and millions of people. It is clear that management is not a skill our politicians have. Why not? Because the 'experience' they gain is politics and politicking, not in any form of management. Senior politicians shift around their ministries between each other: one year minister for education, the next transport and the next year finance … and yet the minister in question might be a doctor by trade. If politics were based on achieving some form of practical experience, then the repetitious moving of ministers would defeat that. It would be far preferable to have an experienced hand that has just spent ten years working in the transport industry to run the Department of Transport for eight years than some minister who is simply ascending the ladder towards higher office.

Another oft-cited argument against term limits is that it is anti-democratic, that the people should be allowed to vote for whomsoever they want to put in office. This is true; there is also another argument, however, that ensconced politicians become dangerous. Companies, for example, are obliged to change their auditors regularly for fear they might become too 'involved' with the business they are auditing. If the people democratically express their desire that it is better for politics that there are term limits, then this is a valid democratic statement. Furthermore, a rotation system would allow any politician to return to office if he/she wished, once the rotation criteria were met.

2. Re-call elections

Term limits are not the only process by which the democratic process could be improved. Re-call elections have also become a popular method for targeting corrupt or incompetent politicians. A re-call election allows voters to demand that an elected representative be subject to a new election to determine whether he/she keeps his/her job. It is triggered by 25 per cent (or whatever number chosen) of the number of voters who elected the representative signing their names to a petition calling for a re-call election. Once this is done a special ballot, just like a by-election, is carried out, asking if Representative X should be re-called, yes or no. If the yes vote is greater than 50 per cent, Representative X loses office. It is a control mechanism that would not be employed often (only two governors in the history of the US have been re-called), but it provides the people with an important tool by which to check unacceptable behaviour.

3. Initiatives and referenda

The current constitutional system in Ireland stipulates that the Dáil alone can sponsor a referendum. Under the initiative system used in Switzerland and other countries, the people can also trigger a constitutional referendum by collecting a sufficient number of signatures on a particular question. Once this occurs, an election commission shapes the question and it is put to the people in a referendum. The function of the initiative process is to ensure that the people as a whole can dictate to the politicians what referenda they want, rather than allowing them be driven solely by political concerns. In Ireland we have had twenty-five referenda to date, but many more might be held if the people had the power to demand them. There are, of course, important referenda that might never be demanded by the public, which is why the power of initiative should also stay with the government. This should never be interfered with, but neither should the people be permanently denied a chance to shape the most important legal document in the country. There would naturally have to be a very high hurdle set so that time is not wasted on spurious referenda. The argument against such powers is that people express their will at election time. But that is putting too much focus on one election. It is too blunt a democratic process to require people to juggle party allegiances, personal preferences and a myriad of other demands in one single voting process. The people need the power to be able to alter the Constitution.

4. Responsibility and Accountability
One of the arguments against the sort of democratic 'enhancements' outlined here is that elected politicians should be left to do their job, for which they will be held responsible come election time. This is correct, in theory, except that Irish politicians seem intent on divesting themselves of much of their responsibility.

QUANGO stands for **qu**asi-autonomous **n**on-**go**vernment **o**rganisation. It describes an organisation or entity to which certain powers are devolved from the government. In theory such organisations are semi-autonomous from the state and pursue a specific function, utilising the expertise of their appointees. In reality they can be a case of 'jobs for the boys', or a way of shifting responsibility away from the government. Ireland has approximately 500 national level quangos[4] and more at regional level, with over 5,000 members spending a budget of over €13 billion. A study completed by the think-tank Tasc suggests quangos are becoming less and less accountable.[5] The director of Tasc has said that 'The unplanned and ad hoc mushrooming of public bodies, combined with the lack of good information about them, is bad for democracy.'

Two examples of Quango types will demonstrate the democratic and financial issues they raise. The first is the smaller, innocuous but well-meaning type of quango, of which there are two forms: the long established dinosaur, such as FÁS, and the new organisation with a 'trendy' remit, such as Diversity Ireland. The former type, epitomised by FÁS, is a quango that has become so firmly entrenched in people's minds that few ever wonder what it does or whether it does it effectively. These quangos were created in a time of high unemployment, yet in a time of full unemployment their budget grew, which proves the maxim that 'old quangos never die they just find something else to spend the money on'. They consume resources, although squander might be a more accurate description in the case of FÁS, which has been blasted by recent allegations of

4   www.tascnet.ie.
5   www.tascnet.ie.

misuse of expenses. Furthermore, an internal audit report by FÁS described its own monitoring of one programme for €19 million as 'out of control financially'.[6] According to the *Irish Times*, 'It is understood there are a series of ten or more internal audit reports that are critical of aspects of the organisation's operation over recent years.'[7] Subsequent revelations have exposed a pattern of spending by some senior staff that was reminiscent of the last days of the Weimar Republic. There is, however, nothing surprising about the excesses at FÁS; the truth is that many quangos are blackholes for money, which is misspent and squandered.

The newer quango is smaller (at least to begin with) and is established to address niche 'trendy' issues. An example is Diversity Ireland—National Action Plan Against Racism, the logo for which is 'Ireland Embracing Cultural Diversity'. Its function, according to its website, is to provide 'the strategic direction to develop a more inclusive, intercultural society in Ireland through reasonable and common sense strategies that have the potential to receive broad support across Irish society.'[8] These are noble motives, but the problem is that diversity within a nation grows organically, it cannot be engineered by a quango. The real racists are unlikely to either read or be affected by any policies put forward by the National Action Plan Against Racism. One can only conclude that this is simply feel-good political correctness, the costs of which are borne by the taxpayer.

Every quango has a budget, and this must be monitored, the organisation staffed, its accounts audited, etc. Even worse, eliminating such quangos is difficult because what politician wants to be seen shutting down something designed to counteract racism? This is how they solidify and ossify into an entrenched position, draining money year on year from the Exchequer. There is no doubt that all of the people working in Diversity Ireland are decent, well-meaning people, but they are costing money that could be used elsewhere. Yet it is only when the government's financial situation is dire that it decides to address the situation of the myriad quangos.

6   *The Irish Times*, 2 September 2008.
7   *The Irish Times*, 5 September 2008.
8   www.diversityireland.ie.

This is not the best approach; rather, there needs be constant careful management.

The second type of quango carries out what should be core functions of government, such as the HSE. The government divested itself of the day-to-day running of the health service to the HSE and appointed an unelected head. It is not too difficult to see that it was attempting to distance itself from the problems of running the health service, retaining only responsibility for long-term strategy. The people elect a government that in turn appoints a Minister for Health, who carries ministerial responsibility for her department. Ministerial responsibility used to be a key method for holding individual ministers responsible to the Dáil and hence to the people. Quangos such as the HSE help push this responsibility further and further away from the voters, so that we often end up with a situation where no one is responsible. Harry Truman, president of the USA from 1945 to 1953, had a sign on his desk that read: The buck stops here. Irish politicians are more likely to have one that reads: It's not my responsibility. Power comes with responsibility, without this there is no accountability, which will lead to sub-standard performance. In 1927 there were three quangos, in 1979 there were ninety, now there are 500 and rising. Each one costs the taxpayer money and erodes democratic accountability.

During one of Bertie Ahern's appearances at the Mahon Tribunal there were allegations that he might have appointed members to the boards of public bodies because of a benefit he had received from them. This was flatly denied. Mr Ahern said he had only done so because they were his friends. Whilst attempting to dodge one bullet, Mr Ahern had inadvertently revealed the true nature of the quangos in Ireland. He later backed away from this statement, having realised what he said, but it had attracted media attention to the issue. When the media examined an assortment of state bodies and agencies to which the government can appoint members, significant links were found to the governing party, Fianna Fáil, and to the now-defunct Progressive Democrats.[9] While many members of quangos are ably qualified, many are just friends and acquain-

9   *Sunday Independent,* 7 January 2007.

tances of ministers. It appears statistically extraordinary that the most qualified people should *all* have links to the governing parties. It is more likely that it is just as Mr Ahern testified, that the government doles out the jobs like a medieval pope doled out bishoprics. There is nothing corrupt here. It is just that quangos are stuffed with friends and acquaintances for whom the government is doing a good turn. In return they have people on these organisations with whom they feel comfortable, who they know will be 'on message'. Fine Gael may criticise this, but no doubt if that party were in government, the pendulum would swing the other way and they would do likewise. They have done in the past.

There is no doubt that specialist agencies are required to run a modern democracy, but it is unlikely that we need 500 considering that the UK has 900. Government is there to govern, not to delegate, and governments should be accountable directly to the people. We are a nation of only 4 million people and we have a large civil service, so we should not need layers of quangos. We should either privatise the areas concerned or let accountable ministers run them with civil servants. What, for example, is the point of having a public health service if it is run by people who are not directly accountable to the people?

The Bonfire of the Quangos[10]

The solution to quangos is two-fold. First, the function and role of every single quango should be examined and an analysis done to ascertain cost benefit. If the benefit cannot be identified *in monetary terms*, the quango should be terminated. One policy that could hasten this is that no payment whatsoever, including any expenses, should be made to those on the boards of quangos. Private citizens give their time everyday, without a cent of payment, for the Boy Scouts, soccer practice, hurling, choir and hundreds of other beneficial clubs and societies. Those who serve on quangos should be willing to donate their time for the public good, that should be part of the selection criteria.

The second solution is that Ireland needs to introduce a piece of legislation that sets an overall time limit on quangos. This 'twilight'

---

10 Phrase first used on CNBC.

provision could be one of the easiest pieces of legislations to draft and yet save substantial amounts of money. A twilight provision, once passed, establishes a law that automatically dissolves a quango after a fixed period of time, unless the Dáil votes to allow it to continue. In parts of the USA this has been set at five years, which seems a reasonable time limit. It would prevent quangos going on and on and taking root, never to be moved. Irish politicians have a terrible record when it comes to being able to end what they once created. If a quango is necessary, then a vote would have to take place and the matter debated in the Dail. This measure would ensure that quangos could be extinguished without anything actually having to be done.

A NEW CONSTITUTION

The Irish Constitution, Bunreacht na hÉireann, allows for little voter-driven democratic control of politicians, it is largely a one-way system. It was written in 1937 and still reflects a 1937 Ireland, with a few amendments thrown in; it is desperately in need of some attention and alteration. The Irish state is founded on the tripartite separation of powers theory, which dictates that power in the state is divided between the Legislative (i.e. Dáil and Seanad), the Executive and the Judicial. In theory this separation is designed to balance the powers to ensure no one branch becomes too strong. However, as Ireland copied the UK system of government, the Executive and the Legislative have effectively been fused because the Legislative is divided along party lines and it elects the government. The party whipping systems ensure the Executive controls the Legislative and each needs the other to survive. This is especially so in parties like Fianna Fáil, where loyalty to the party is critical and while a member may leave the party, few ever vote against it.

This leaves the Judiciary as the main constitutional method to control the Executive, but this has not worked sufficiently because the Judiciary appear unwilling to be sufficiently assertive, as has occurred in other jurisdictions. If this wasn't the case, tribunals of investigations would not be needed because politicians would have been dealt with through the normal judicial channels, i.e. arrest, questioning and prosecution in the courts, where necessary.[11] The UK judiciary has become more assertive in recent decades, using Judicial Review to tame the powers of the Executive and the Legislature and whilst it would argue that it is not being political, it is clear that it is.

The bottom line is that in Ireland power is unbalanced and centred on the Dáil, without any real control extended over its members. The obvious riposte to this is that the people elect the TDs and they should express our will, but they do not do this with sufficient precision or accuracy. We are given a choice of FF, FG, Labour and Green at every election, and we make our choices based on personal political persuasion and from this one vote flows everything. In other countries, such as the USA, voters can vote for the head of the Executive, the president, independent of voting for the Legislative. There are a myriad of permutations and combinations of constitutional systems and it is unlikely we stumbled upon the correct one in 1937. It is not within the scope of this book to outline a new constitution for Ireland, merely to suggest that as a people we should be considering remodelling the 1937 Constitution or creating a constitutional convention to allow us to draft a new constitution. It is not radical, merely responsible.

SOCIAL REFORMS

The main issue worth looking at here in terms of social reform is the question of the degree of social control in Europe, how it operates and its advantages and disadvantages.

Most governments in Europe require that all people register where they are living. When a person first arrives in any European country, whether by birth or by travel, he or his parents is legally required to attend at his local town hall to register his personal details. These details include educational qualifications, profession, even religion. The town hall then gives him a form confirming the registration, which is used for most other public services. Nationals are given a National ID card once they attain the age of sixteen years. If a person is moving to a new area, he must de-register his old address and register the new one.

11 The word 'judiciary' is used in its broadest sense to include the whole judicial system, including the police.

This is second nature to all Europeans and they think little of it, but it is an alien concept to Irish and British people. It is not the same as a social security number or electoral roll, this is real-time knowledge of where everybody is and what they are doing. If you move apartment on Tuesday, for example, you must de-register your old address on Tuesday and re-register at your new address. It is mandatory and strictly enforced. You can and will be heavily fined if you are discovered not to have registered a change of address. I have seen police go from door to door in apartment blocks checking that everybody is registered as living there. Furthermore, if you are stopped by the police, the first thing they want is your ID card and they can fine you up to €500 if you fail to produce it. Whilst such laws may seem onerous and oppressive, they are designed to ensure that at all times the state knows where all its citizens are and there are very comprehensive data protection laws to ensure the information is controlled and only used for the purposes for which it was designed. To many Irish people this might seem oppressive and overly intrusive, but we are the exception rather than the rule in Europe. Ireland and the UK are the only EU countries that do not have national identity cards or a registration system.

The advantages of this system are numerous, although there are some enormous disadvantages as well.[12] The first advantage is that it reduces crime and increases the efficiency of the enforcement of law. When Irish friends visit my local city in Germany, they are often amazed to see the shops with their merchandise lining the streets and people leaving wallets and cameras on tables outside cafés when they go inside. They often comment that the Germans must be very honest. The Germans are no more and no less honest than the Irish, but they are more afraid of breaking the law in Germany. They know that if they steal, they will likely be caught and punished because their identification will most certainly be found out due to the need to always carry an ID card, and with an ID card their

---

12 If you ever wondered how the Germans rounded up all the Jews for deportation so efficiently, it was facilitated by such a system; they only needed to examine the records at the town hall to find out who was Jewish and exactly where they lived. This is how they were removed from society without too much difficulty. The police would turn up with lists in the middle of the night and they knew exactly where to go and who was living there.

address can be located and consequences will follow, be it through the civil or criminal system. They are not anonymous, so there will be little chance to wriggle out of the consequences of their actions.

Identity cards also reduce fraud because each person can accurately identify themselves in commercial transactions. Mobile phones cannot be bought anonymously in Germany, each mobile phone is 'attached' to an identity card. The cards also reduce underage consumption of alcohol and tobacco and negate the need for passports when travelling within Europe. In general, a national ID makes society more controllable. Those French or Italians may look relaxed and easygoing sipping their wine, but I can guarantee you few of them left home without their national ID cards. I have seen anarchists with 'smash authority' tattooed on their arms compliantly produce ID cards when buying beer in Germany, and they don't seem to see the irony.

The system also has numerous advantages directly related to the quality of life, which are the real long-term benefits for the citizens. As it is the local town hall that collects all this information, local authorities know precisely how many people are living in any town, city, county or region at any given time. Ireland suffers from one significant difficulty in planning: we do not know how many people are living in any particular location nor do we know their demographic make-up, the number of children they have, etc., so as to be able to gauge accurately the viscosity of the population. A census is taken every ten years, but it often takes two years for all the details to be collated and released. The CSO also conducts quarterly household surveys, but these cannot compensate for a lack of accurate real-time data. Technology allows us to instantly see how much money is in our bank accounts or to get satellite pictures of anywhere on Earth, yet our public services cannot tell even the most basic details about the people to whom they are providing services. This is a huge drawback because accurate, responsive and pre-emptive planning requires basic information that precisely describes the profile of the people and the areas for which the plans are being made. Without this information, there is a 'stab-in-the-dark' quality to planning that benefits no one.

The real stumbling block to introducing any such system in Ireland would, I suspect, be psychological. Irish people would be naturally resistant to this idea; Europeans, on the other hand, would be puzzled by this and wonder how people expect their local or national governments to provide public services if they do not know where they are or their democratic make-up. Much has been made of Ireland's position as a Member State, of the fact that the Irish are now Europeans. If we are truly committed to Europe, we must do more than give lip-service. Bringing Irish society in line with European norms would be beneficial all round. If we are truly European and want European levels of social services and facilities, then we would have to implement a national identity card system and a registration system like the rest of Europe. It is not so much about control as about provision of services. I believe the Irish would be more amenable to a higher level of social control if they could be shown the benefits, such as lower crime, more political responsibility and better public services. The provision of timely and attenuated public services requires a higher level of social control—everything is give and take.

Chapter 10
The Three Choices

I reland is at a crossroads—our politicians have created the perfect economic storm due to their incompetence and it is the average citizen who will now have to pay the price. The government may like to explain it with reference to external shocks to the economy, but it was the politicians who created the fragile economic landscape in the first place. Ireland is not so much impacted by what is now called the Credit Crunch, rather it is part of the problem. We have been focusing on possible solutions, now we shall attempt to map out the three paths we can choose to take. Our choices boil down to: no substantial change, a worst-case scenario (the Easter Island scenario) and the choice to take our destiny in our own hands and make real, quantifiable changes.

In all of the scenarios presented the key factors are debt and population and how we handle them. These have already been covered in some detail, so suffice to say here that the government's choices regarding how much it borrows and what it uses the borrowed money for will have a huge impact on the future health of the economy. Every step taken now must be assessed carefully to ensure it leads in the right direction. Similarly, the country faces a significant drop in population, which would exacerbate the financial and social problems we are struggling to contain and overcome. What is needed now, more than ever, is decisive, creative and consistent leadership—that is the only hope for the future.

CHOICE 1: NOTHING CHANGES SUBSTANTIALLY

The first option could be described as 'the usual, please': the government will wring its hands and tell us that world events caused our problems and that things will get better again at some undefined point in the future. And in part this is true, in that world events have triggered many of our problems. Nonetheless, the politicians must take responsibility for the current situation. The 'Credit Crunch' was the economic storm that exposed the weakness of Ireland's position and not the underlying cause of the current economic problems. The Irish economy was allowed to turn away from real productive growth almost a decade ago, and it became addicted to property and debt. The property bubble was fuelled and tended, but all the while it was displacing what had been the real drivers of our economic success. It took the 'Credit Crunch' to expose this false economy. The government was warned by many people over the years about the effects of what was occurring, but chose to ignore that advice. World financial crises come along on a regular basis—in the last ten years there has been the Asian Debt Crisis, the Russian Crisis, the collapse of Long Term Capital Management and the bursting of the Dot Com bubble. It is a predictable facet of the global economy. Yes, the Credit Crunch is probably the most significant economic crisis in fifty years, but the stark truth is that Celtic Tiger Ireland was a house built without a roof during a long, hot summer; that it eventually rained should have come as a surprise to no one.

In this scenario the country will hope for the best and assume that somehow the international financial system will right itself and the world experience a recession from which it recovers in a few years. With outside factors improving, the key factor for individuals in terms of riding out the recession will be debt: how much personal debt you have and whether your income stream is secure enough to service it. The contraction of credit will push unemployment towards 15 per cent and likely exceed it. The government is caught on the horns of an economic dilemma: it realises that spending must be cut and/or taxes must be raised, but the effect of either measure will be to dampen economic growth further and exacerbate the problem. Yet, it has little choice. The economic path of the last ten years showed that instead of controlling its expenditure, the government expanded spending aggressively, adding to the economic growth bubble. The obverse of this economic coin is that now the government must extract money from the economy at the worst possible time. The economic highs were higher, so the economic lows will be lower.

To date, the government, in its search for funding, has raided the National Pension Reserve Fund, even though it was designed to address problems decades ahead, has raised income taxes and will likely cut the National Development Plan. However, none of these extra taxes or cuts was sufficient to balance the Budget and the government has now taken the well-worn path of least resistance and begun to borrow heavily again.

The absolute level of national debt in Ireland at the end of 2008 was €50.4 billion.[1] If we add on the expected €25 billion borrowing requirement for 2009 and €50–€60 billion of debt issues to fund the National Asset Management Agency (NAMA), then debt levels will easily rise to in excess of €100 billion by 2010/11. If we assume there are two million adults in Ireland, that is close to €60,000 per person in debt that is growing, with interest, and that must be paid off at some point. And this does not include the further borrowing that may be required beyond this period. The standard international comparator for measuring debt is the debt to GDP ratio. This helps reveal the ability of the underlying economy to service and repay the debt. In Ireland, the debt to GDP ratio peaked in 1991 at 96 per cent and then subsequently declined over fifteen years to 25 per cent in 2006. However, in just four short years we risk reversing this entire decline. It is a starkly depressing thought that we are back to 1991 so quickly. One advantage, however, is that currently the cost of servicing this debt is substantially below what it was in 1991 because the ECB is effectively willing to subsidise us and provide us with substantial credit to keep the government going. The key word here is 'currently'. We do not know the underlying politics and the intentions of the ECB, especially after the second Lisbon vote is passed, nor do we know the future interest rate environment in which we would have to raise money. This debt will have to be

1   National Treasury Management Agency.

repaid by Irish taxpayers; we are currently paying a very low level because interest rates are low internationally and we still benefit from the aura surrounding the Euro, but the debt will never be written off—it must be repaid.

Thus this 'usual, please' cycle foresees an 1980s-style, decade-long recession in order to 'pay for' the Celtic Tiger decade. The government will have to eventually balance the Budget as it will not be able to borrow any more money and this will require draconian measures. The mathematics are quite simple: taxes go up, or spending goes down, or both. No matter how difficult it is politically, items such as the universal children's allowance will be targeted, along with any other benefit that is not means-tested. The government will also need to introduce a new property-based tax, such as exists in America. It will be sold as a more stable tax and a fair tax, but for someone who borrowed substantial amounts of money to buy a house and paid stamp duty on top of this, only to see the asset value fall by 40 per cent, it will be a very bitter pill to be taxed on this depreciating 'asset'.

With less disposable income, living standards will fall. Public services will also disimprove: if the government could not get it right when spending was expanding rapidly, it is unlikely to do so when it has to slash spending. In all likelihood the government will also have to reduce the minimum wage in order to stimulate growth; with double-digit unemployment, Ireland simply cannot afford to have one of the highest minimum wages in Europe. Otherwise, it will drive people to work illegally in order to avoid taxes, thereby compounding the problem.

On the other hand, those employed in industries immune from the property market, transitory consumption and banking are likely to do better. As we have discussed previously, Ireland is an economy of two halves: if you took on a large amount of debt in order to purchase property, you will struggle in the coming years; if you are employed in the newer industries unaffected by property, then as the world recovers you will be able to endure much of what happens in the economy because your income will not be dependent upon it. There will even be a significant group of people who are not too indebted and have liquid assets and will benefit from the recession. This enviable group includes the generation who did not need to buy a house because their kids had flown the nest and who were net sellers of property. So, as in the 1980s, there will be a group who will have resources salted away and will benefit from prices being substantially cheaper across the economy. The government will not reform the public service and social welfare bill, however. Public servants perform essential tasks, but their pay, and numbers, has been allowed to balloon out of control.

If this scenario plays out, then as the recession deepens the world economy will begin to recover, allowing emigration to rise and facilitating the normal Irish safety valve to open again. The belief that if the world economy recovers then Ireland will follow is too simplistic, but that recovery will ease matters in Ireland by reducing the social and economic costs of unemployment as people flood out of the country. However, the budgetary and debt problems will not vanish with a recovering world economy. In fact, any serious recovery could risk exposing the Irish to severe economic pain. To date, we have been fortunate that world interest rates have fallen dramatically. If there is any recovery or serious inflation due to 'quantitative easing', then rates will begin to rise again. The absolutely last thing the Irish economy needs is rising interest rates. That would expose the weakness of being part of the economic bloc with which we have been economically out of phase for the last decade. When we needed higher rates, we got lower rates and vice versa. Should the Eurozone recover or suffer inflation, then rates would begin to rise again. If people are having difficulty repaying their mortgages with ECB rates at just over 1 per cent, then what would happen if they rose 2–3 per cent from here?

The banks will suffer huge losses, but they will be saved by cheap loans from the ECB via the NAMA[2] and will likely have to be nationalised or will fall into government ownership by virtue of the fact that the government becomes a majority shareholder due to the need to fund the banks with so much new capital. Some smaller financial institutions will follow Anglo Irish Bank and fail and will be merged with larger institutions. In general, it will be a very

---

2   The NAMA is simply a procedure to save the Irish banks with ECB money. The government does not have any other options because it could not raise the money it needs on the open market.

painful recession, like the 1980s, but it is necessary in order to wean ourselves off house-building and pay for the excesses of the last decade. Ultimately, it presents an opportunity for real and lasting change, but then, like before, it is unlikely this will be seized upon by the government.

The government might even engineer a mini-boom again, or slow the economic decline in 2010/11 by forcing the banks to lend out the money they obtained from the ECB. This money could then be forced into the economy, via loans, to try to kickstart it. With the government in charge of the banks, it could engage in some serious meddling with 'job creation' projects—the temptation would be enormous if it had such a pot of cash available. This would be a terrible mistake, of course, as it would temporarily prop up businesses that should fail. Instead of weaning people off debt, the government would use the easily obtainable ECB money to keep the country hooked on it. It would be hailed as a recovery, but it would be nothing of the sort. The ECB's willingness to lend more and more money is an unknown, as would be the reaction of the ECB if the government could not maintain interest payments on the debt it has already issued. This, however, is by far not the worst scenario.

SCENARIO 2: THE EASTER ISLAND SCENARIO

The sad history of Easter Island has many parallels with the Irish economy. Initially it was a self-sufficient island community that, for reasons unknown, decided to build large stone statues. It did this with increasing frequency and fervour. They built so many, in fact, that most of the workforce became involved in the construction work. They consumed all the forests on the island for firewood and for rollers, and with them went the eco-system. Crop-rotation was abandoned to maximise food for the builders and the land was eventually exhausted. They then consumed the seabirds and any wildlife on the island and fought each other for what was left and even, finally, resorted to cannibalism. In other words, a perfectly workable society made some bad decisions that proved to be its undoing.

This is the worst-case scenario, and unfortunately it now seems the most likely scenario, although it may itself lead to the third

scenario, eventually, which in the long term would be good. It will
occur in three conditional phases. The first is the government does
not attempt to make any structural adjustment to the economy and
tries to borrow its way out of the current situation. This it began
doing aggressively in 2009, with absolute debt levels and the GDP
ratio rocketing at unprecedented rates. The Budgets, if we can call
them that, of 2008 and 2009, whilst tough, were not sufficient to
control the discrepancy between what the government was spending
and what it was collecting in taxes.

One of the biggest reasons for this is that spending tends to be
what economists call 'sticky' and there is always resistance to taking
something off someone who has it already. For example, the
benchmarking process drove up salaries to unrealistic levels and
these must be reduced by a least one-third to bring them in line
with what the country can now afford. Currently, the government
lacks the political will or ability to inflict this level of pain because
to do so would inflict penury on people who have structured their
spending around a certain level of income. The irresistible force
meets the immovable object. Yet with debt levels already predicted
to approach €100 billion by the end of 2009, there is little reason to
expect that this will not continue to increase, so eventually spending
will have to be cut. The government is clearly caught in an
impossible situation. It knows that if spending is cut, the economy
will contract more than the record-breaking level at which it is
already contracting, which in turn would drive down government
income even more. Hence, it chose the least worst of two options
and borrowed. But this, too, will have serious consequences.

The longer the borrowing goes on without any reform, the more
dangerous it becomes. With the private sector maxed out on debt,
the government would start down the same road. Hence we could
end up, in a short number of years, with unsustainable private debt
and unsustainable national debt as well. In 2008 the politicians and
commentators were waving around 'low national debt' as a
percentage of GDP as if it were a new credit card obtained by a
spendaholic. Yet less than two years later we had already breached
the Maastricht Treaty requirement of 60 per cent debt to GDP ratio
and the national debt was growing at the staggering amount of over

€450 million a week. To put it in more accessible terms, in 2009 the government will borrow €500 per week, per average family in the country.[3] This money will have to be paid back eventually, with interest. This payback will require higher taxes or lower services; either way, people will emigrate.

When Ireland joined the EMU it accepted two simple limits: that Budget deficits be no more than 3 per cent of GDP and that overall national debt be no more than 60 per cent of GDP—these limits were included in what was known as the Stability and Growth Pact. These conditions were sacrosanct to joining EMU and the government all but genuflected to them, promising it would never break the rules once it had been let into the club. Then, at the beginning of 2008, the ESRI and other bodies began suggesting that the limits could be ignored without too many consequences and in tough times could be stretched and bent. The government initially played 'hard to get' and stated that it would not breach the criteria, but eventually the temptation to ignore the 3 per cent limit proved too much and it was abandoned flagrantly. The overspend by the government annually exceeded 10 per cent of GDP by 2009; on the other limit, it is predicted that by the end of 2010 the total debt to GDP ratio will be approaching 100 per cent.

The reason these particular numbers have been set is simple: the aim is to try to ensure that countries don't become like Ireland in the 1980s. Let's be honest, nothing Ireland does or does not do could ever really affect the stability, exchange rate or policy of the ECB, save a massive failure by all of our banks suggesting that other countries might do likewise. The reality is that when the currency was being established, Germany wanted a strong currency like the Deutsche Mark, so it set 'growth and stability' criteria in the same way Disneyland sets height limits for its rides. It wanted fiscally prudent countries (what it ended up with is another story for another book). By breaching limits it agreed not to breach, Ireland is sending a clear signal to the rest of the financial world that the country could be heading back to its bad old ways, which is why we began losing our AAA rating with the debt-rating agencies in 2009. We can lather

3   Figure based on €24 billion in borrowing, four million people and a family of 2+2.

whatever excuses we want over the breaching of these criteria, but what we are doing will be noted and there will be consequences in the form of higher borrowing costs for our debt and a loss of financial credibility. It will play into the hands of the hardliners who said that Ireland should never have been allowed into the currency in the first place. Action could be taken against us at a European level, but this seems unlikely—in other cases when breaches occurred there have been no real sanctions, just deadlines and empty talk. The real punishment is loss of credibility and a deeper hole to dig ourselves out of. On a broader note, we gain stability from the Euro but without contributing anything to the project as a whole. We have been consuming a long line of supposedly free lunches, but it now seems we are about to get a tap on the shoulder and be asked to foot the bill.

The country could probably ride out this crisis, like many before, if it wasn't for one key factor: the banks. Recessions come and go in the economic cycle, but Ireland's was amplified by huge lending injected into the economy by the banks. It is clear that the government never knew how serious the situation was from 2007 onwards; at each juncture it appeared genuinely shocked that matters were getting worse. Like a slow-motion car accident, the finances of the government and the banks collided and imploded together. At each stage, the government tried to avoid any more damage rather than realising that its main focus should be damage limitation. By the time it did realise this, events were moving too fast to alter the outcome. It was hurried into, first, guaranteeing deposits up to €100,000 in the main banks, at the time all deposits, and then all the borrowings of the banks. Consequent upon this, it had to nationalise Anglo Irish Bank because the bank was losing its deposit base and that guarantee may have been called upon.

The fundamental weakness of that massive government bank guarantee was that it could, of course, never actually meet it. The government was at this stage borrowing money to meet day-to-day expenses, so it was a cheap fiction to even believe it could afford €400 billion or any fraction of it. Thus the fatal mistake was not so much nationalising Anglo Irish Bank but issuing the broad guarantee in the first place. The government was simply reacting to events and was trapped by circumstances that had been built up over the previous decade. Furthermore, these decisions appeared to have occurred in very rushed circumstances and under extreme pressure—never a good environment in which to make such dramatic decisions. The hope was that once the famous words, 'I guarantee', were uttered by the Minister for Finance, that stability would return. But in effect the Minister was doubling down his bet. It is clear that, as a highly qualified barrister, Mr Lenihan would have been an excellent Minister for Justice, but he had only recently been appointed Minister for Finance and had little understanding of economics or finance.

At that stage, the fatal weakness in the Irish banking system was very simple. A bank is a very straightforward creature: it takes in deposits and money from various sources and lends this out to borrowers. It charges them more than it pays the depositors and makes a profit on this differential, as well as charging for maintaining accounts. But during a decade-long boom it had lent out tens of billions recklessly, foolishly and sometimes negligently, a hotch-potch of bad investments by developers, squandering and people living beyond their means. The initial loans actually created demand for more loans and made them look rational in the first place. Put bluntly, all of the money was now gone, with questionable hope of recovery, yet the depositors and international investors still had claims on the banks.

The essential skill of a banker is in making careful lending decisions because a banker is lending out other people's money. Both small depositors and large lenders to the Irish banks realised this in 2008 and what was left of the deposit base began to be slowly withdrawn and the share prices tumbled as the hopes of the banks' financial viability were undermined. Like a game of financial musical chairs, there were fewer seats than people to sit on them and depositors instinctively knew this. The government tried to change the tune by guaranteeing the banks, but in effect it just shackled itself to the bad lending decisions made by the banks and put off the day of reckoning. It is quite astounding what the government did, if you think about it. It not only guaranteed all the borrowing by the banks without knowing the quality of the assets behind them but effectively allowed the banks to write government bonds for two years by backing any debt issue it made. The banks' and the government's interests were being slowly merged together. Once the Anglo Irish debacle exploded and its deposit base began haemorrhaging, the government had no option but to nationalise it. This was the crossing of the Rubicon; at this stage efforts should have been made to let Anglo fail, but the government was trapped into worse decisions by the bad decisions it had previously made in a panic.

At this point the government could, in theory, have reversed its bank guarantee and cut Anglo Irish loose. It was a miniature bank of no systemic significance to the banking system, except for the fact that the government had guaranteed it in the first place. Had it reversed its guarantee, then those who funded AIB and BOI would have fled along with ordinary depositors on the assumption that their guarantee was also worthless. In reality, the basic financial infrastructure could have been maintained by rescuing AIB and BOI, but it would, of course, have been an economic earthquake and the government would have had to admit the country was bankrupt, but so be it. It would at least have gotten ahead of the problem rather than stepping out onto the slippery slope on which it is currently teetering. As it was, the government was making matters worse, but it likely didn't realise that until later.

By early 2009 the loan the government had guaranteed was beginning to smell from its decay. Billions of depositors' money lent to developers was producing no return and the properties securing the monies were plummeting in value. The banks would soon be insolvent because they could not stick with the minuscule amounts they were setting aside for bad debts in the face of economic reality. Thus if the banks were forced to declare their true anticipated bad debts in their audited accounts, the government's guarantee would no doubt have been called upon. Thus the government was prodded further down the slippery slope. Its next move was to set up NAMA. The expressed purpose of this 'bad bank' was to save the main banks and free them up to 'begin lending again',[4] but underlying

4   The business and government representatives appear to be obsessed with lending more money into the economy, yet the fundamental problem is lending. In order for any real economy to be developed, lending must contract and suffocate those

this was the real purpose of the Agency, which was to try to save the banks by tapping money from the ECB. At this point the ECB was already partially funding the government by giving cheap credit to the banks to buy their bonds when others might not have bought them.

Putting aside the legal and financial complications that surround NAMA, it was an extremely shrewd and arguably cynical move by the government and revealed how it intended to 'rescue' the banks and, by inference, the country. The government itself has no money left to buy distressed loans from the banks, but it could issue new bonds as a sovereign state. However, as it could not use these bonds to borrow from the ECB—national governments are precluded from doing so—and the market would never absorb this level of borrowing from Ireland, the government cleverly decided to buy the loans from the banks directly, using the bonds. Obviously the banks could not sell these bonds for the same reason; they would have to be sold at an extreme discount, which would cause panic among those holding government debt or about to buy other bonds being issued by the government to fund its daily expenditure. Hence a cash-rich patsy had to be found to take the bonds—that patsy was the ECB.

Critical to the success of NAMA, the ECB could, in theory, be obliged into taking the government bonds and at face value, instead of applying a heavy discount to them as the market would. The response of the ECB to this situation will be revealing. The ECB is unlikely to refuse to take the bonds or to apply a cut as that would question the underlying assumptions of monetary union. The ECB will probably have to embrace such a scheme with a smile, otherwise it risks a serious threat to its creditability and possibly even to the survival of the Euro as a currency.

How the ECB deals with this situation in the medium term is going to present a complex political problem. If successful, however, the government will effectively have found someone to get stuck holding the proverbial crying baby and will have converted the

businesses that need a constant supply of credit to survive, i.e. that are not viable. It is true that there are businesses that truly need working and expansion capital, but I suspect these are in the minority.

junk loans it guaranteed from the Irish banks to the ECB. This is why the government is pushing for such a low discount on the loans. The lower the discount, the more money the banks get from the ECB. The government/ banks would have to pay interest on the ECB money, of course, but it would be very low compared to the open market, and the ECB would be in a very awkward position *vis-à-vis* enforcing the debt. This is why the ECB was precluded from lending to national governments, but the establishment of NAMA has deftly sidestepped this. The government's logic, from a nationalistic viewpoint, is simple and brilliant. The plan for NAMA is to effectively box the ECB into assuming bad Irish property loans laundered into Irish government bonds. The ECB is too diplomatic to ever question a government's motive and will always utter, on the record at least, reassuring messages to the media, even though it might not like what it is being forced into doing.

Projecting forward, this scenario, beyond any short-term boost provided by the ECB money, is reasonably straightforward. With unemployment rising to a predicted 17 per cent in 2010, bad debts would grow across the full spectrum of the banks' portfolio, not just the property portfolios, e.g. car loans, credit cards, mortgages, released equity products, etc. It is unrealistic to assume that the banks were just lending recklessly to property developers and not to everyone else. Inevitably, those without jobs will be unable to repay their loans. The bad debt situation would grow until it would eventually overcome the ability of the banks/government to rectify it. This scenario envisages the ECB and open market eventually refusing to lend any more on Irish government debt or giving debt based on preconditions.

This is what faces the Irish economy. When the government and the banks eventually fail in their plate-spinning exercises of trying to keep the banks going, the IMF or the ECB will have to become involved. The problem is simple: Ireland Inc. is living beyond its means and if we cannot sort out the problem internally, we will run out of cash and outside agencies will come in to sort out our problems for us. Either way, this will drive down our standard of living far below what it is now. In 2009 the hope was that the world economy would recover and thus allow Ireland to begin growing again. This hope does not demonstrate an understanding of the core problem. Even if this recovery were to come about, we would still have our national debt and the inefficiencies in the economy, with low competitiveness. Companies like Dell and SR Technics are leaving not because of any downturn in the Irish economy but because the costs have become too expensive. The biggest advantage to the Irish economy of a world recovery would be escape for three groups of people: those economic migrants who came for the good times; the diaspora lured home over the last decade; and the new generation of Irish who have not known bad times and are not willing to wait around to get a taste of them. In a world of extensive geographic mobility, the danger is that those experiencing the evil twin of the Celtic Tiger would simply leave the country, taking their money and their experience with them. This would be the real long-term damage envisaged in this scenario.

As a result, the population would contract severely, possibly by 250,000–500,000,[5] and the country would enter a severe recession from which it would be difficult to recover for generations. I realise that such an emigration figure seems very high, but once a trend begins it is difficult to reverse it and, as discussed elsewhere in the book, the viscosity of any inward migration was always questionable. Viewed positively, emigration would be good in one respect because it would cap unemployment at 1980s levels.

This economic failure would be significant and would be different from earlier recessions because any resurgence in five or ten years would be treated with suspicion and many potential immigrants would be unwilling to risk it and return again because there would be that memory of the last Celtic Tiger, which ended in disaster. It is a case of three strikes and you're out. There have been three periods when the Irish economy has done well: the 1920s, just after independence; the 1960; and the 1990s. Two have ended with

---

5 This figure is based on the increase over the last decade; half would be foreign nationals who are economic migrants and would simply go elsewhere in search of work. The other half would be Irish nationals lured home over the last decade and new Irish emigrants; the latter have bought houses and are engaged in raising families and therefore would be more resistant to leaving. But left without work and with previous experience and job contacts abroad, they too would leave.

prolonged recessions; if this one goes the same way, then the country will be tarnished permanently, or at least in living memory. This scenario of a Celtic Crash is more possible, I think, than anyone cares to imagine.

Ironically, the complete economic failure of the Irish state would finally suggest that the Eurozone had achieved real economic and monetary union. The phrase that Irish politicians thought meant another free lunch might in fact mean no more free lunches. All real economic areas have huge disparities of wealth and living standards because people and money follow success, without any national borders to inhibit them. In the UK, for example, Scotland and Northern England are poorer and have a lower standard of living than the south; in America, the state of West Virginia has grinding poverty while two hours' flight away there is gleaming success. The proverb that you should be careful what you wish for just in case you get it might apply to Ireland: we may get economic and monetary union, but become the West Virginia of the Eurozone.

SCENARIO 3: REAL CHANGE

The final path, the best-case scenario, is real structural change in how the country is governed. The Irish population has shown its abilities and attracted world-class companies to Ireland, yet those who governed them have failed them decade after decade. Ireland has the potential to become a Switzerland or a Singapore, but that can only happen if we can bring our governance up to the quality of what is expected of, and provided by, the average Irish person.

The positive view of deflating the property bubble is that it will engender consequences so serious, it will prove to be a wake-up call to the electorate. Change occurs only when events are serious enough to provoke significant demand for change. The demographics of the electorate are now changing and a new generation is coming to the fore that is more educated, more travelled and less susceptible to simplistic 'patriotic' political arguments in the place of quantifiable performance. The political classes have shown that while they may be incompetent and corrupt at times, they are also highly responsive. Following the tragic death of crime journalist Veronica Guerin, for example, the Dáil established the Criminal Assets Bureau within a very short period of time. It was a novel and innovative solution for the time and was copied by many other jurisdictions, including the UK. The tragedy is that it took shocking events to jolt the politicians into action, but it did provoke positive action nonetheless.

The economic earthquake that will now be experienced could also act as a powerful catalyst for Irish society, if it prompts outside intervention by the IMF or EU. It might just be enough to shatter the political system that has ruled Ireland since Independence. The IMF/EU would be willing to slash and burn the sacred cows of Irish politics like no Irish politician has ever done. Hence, those bodies could undo what should have been undone over decades, and any subsequent Irish government would have to work from a brand new base. Many of the changes needed in Irish society simply require that we make a break with the past, but unfortunately the Irish political classes have been unable to do this. Once drastic changes have been completed, the IMF/EU would hand fiscal control back to an Irish government and the political topography might be changed forever. There are competent and honest politicians in all the political parties who know what needs to be done and are capable of doing it. Too many people have invested too much in Ireland to stand by while it implodes. Ireland has enormous potential and the opportunity presented by the recession means that over the next ten years we can remould our laws, increase our levels of democratic accountability and renew our Constitution, if need be. We can set ourselves to be the society the majority wants to be.

- Crime can be reduced substantially, if we are willing to introduce simple social measures and fund the police force adequately.
- We could free ourselves from dependence on fossil fuels within a decade by developing a combination of renewable resources and nuclear power stations. This would save the country billions of Euro every year and guarantee energy security for the next century. Guaranteed energy would attract industry in greater numbers than tax-avoidance schemes.
- We could modernise public transport in Dublin by building an underground system. This would provide modern and efficient travel for a significant portion of the population, would reduce

the traffic volumes on the city's streets, would reduce commuter stress and allow more surface areas to be devoted to people rather than cars. It would also allow more people to live outside of the city, where there is more space for families.

- Our health service will never become cutting edge because we simply do not have the population to generate the necessary expertise. But this does not mean it cannot be world-class at providing 95 per cent of the care the people need with competent local services that are free at the point of use for those who cannot pay.

Real change may be difficult, but essentially it is the next step in the process and there are many politicians who are willing and eager to achieve it. We have to stop saying 'no' and 'that's not possible' and 'that's too radical'. The real statement we need to make is: 'what do we need and how can we achieve it?' Ireland has a great future if we can leave the past where it belongs and look forward.